Grammar
Form and Function 1

Teacher's Manual
Second Edition

Milada Broukal
Kristin Sherman

Form and Function Teacher's Manual 1, Second Edition

Published by McGraw-Hill ESL/ELT, a business unit of The McGraw-Hill Companies, Inc., 1221 Avenue of the Americas, New York, NY 10020. Copyright © 2010 by The McGraw-Hill Companies, Inc. All rights reserved. No part of this publication may be reproduced or distributed in any form or by any means, or stored in a database or retrieval system, without the prior written consent of The McGraw-Hill Companies, Inc., including, but not limited to, any network or other electronic storage or transmission, or broadcast for distance learning.

1 2 3 4 5 6 7 8 9 10 QPD 13 12 11 10 09 08

ISBN: 0-07-719226-5

Developmental Editor: Kathleen Schultz
Project Manager: Jenny Hopkins
Publishing Management: Hyphen – Engineering Education
Cover Designer: Page2, LLC
Interior Designer: Hyphen – Engineering Education
Cover photo: Sailing boat, British Columbia (Canada): © iStockphoto.com/laughingmango. Back cover (top to bottom): © The McGraw-Hill Companies Inc. /Ken Cavanagh, Photographer, © Andrew Ward/Life File/Getty Images, © Library of Congress Prints and Photographs Division (LC-USZ662-117580), © Getty Images, © Comstock/JupiterImages.

www.esl.mcgraw-hill.com

Contents

Introduction	Page
To the Teacher	iv
Teaching Guide for the Student Book	v
Teaching Guide for the e-Workbook	x
Teaching Guide for the Teacher's Manual	x

Student Book Answer Key and Teaching Notes	Page
Unit 1 – The Present of *Be*	1
Unit 2 – *Be*: *It*, *There*, and the Simple Past of *Be*	20
Unit 3 – The Simple Present	38
Unit 4 – The Present Progressive	54
Unit 5 – Nouns and Pronouns	69
Unit 6 – The Simple Past	84
Unit 7 – The Past Progressive	104
Unit 8 – The Future	112
Unit 9 – Quantity and Degree Words	128
Unit 10 – Objects and Pronouns	139
Unit 11 – Modals	151
Unit 12 – Special Expressions	168
Unit 13 – Adjectives and Adverbs	177
Unit 14 – The Present Perfect	197

Unit Tests	208
Unit Test Answer Key	245
Internet Activity Procedures and Worksheets	247

To the Teacher

Grammar Form and Function, Second Edition is a three-level, communicative grammar series. Students successfully learn the rules of essential English grammar (form) and when to apply them and what they mean (function). This new full-color edition ensures academic success and a greater ability to comprehend and communicate with ease through the addition of a robust listening program, new academic readings, new communicative activities, and more opportunities for practice with the new interactive e-Workbook.

Mastery of grammar relies on students knowing the rules of English (form) and correctly understanding how to apply them (function).

> **Form** is the structure of a grammar point and what it looks like. Practice of the form builds students' accuracy and helps them recognize the grammar point in authentic situations, so they are better prepared to understand what they are reading or what other people are saying.

> **Function** is when and how we use a grammar point. Practice of the function builds students' fluency and helps them apply the grammar point in their real lives.

Providing abundant practice in both form and function is the key to student success. *Grammar Form and Function, Second Edition* offers new and exciting ways for students to get the practice they need in both the form and the function of English grammar.

Each of the three levels of *Grammar Form and Function, Second Edition* (Basic, Intermediate, and High Intermediate to Advanced) has five components: Student Book, e-Workbook, Teacher's Manual with Unit Tests and reproducible Internet Activity Worksheets, Complete Audio CD Program available on CD or MP3, and EZ Test® CD-ROM Test Generator. Used in conjunction, these tools provide students with ample opportunity for practice and teachers with multiple occasions for assessment.

> The **Student Books** feature engaging full-color photos to ensure comprehension of both the form and the function of grammar points. Each level contains 14 units of varying length that proceed from basic to complex grammar. Book 1, the basic level, starts with the present of *be* and ends with the present perfect. Book 2, the intermediate level, begins with a review of the present and ends with reported speech and conditional clauses. Book 3, the high intermediate to advanced level, starts with a review of the present and ends with conditional sentences. The Self-Test in every unit encourages student independence and increases competence in following standardized test formats.

> The new **e-Workbooks** follow the scope and sequence of the Student Books and contain additional practice of both form and function for every grammar point. The e-Workbooks also feature Self-Tests in every unit to provide additional assessment opportunities and the chance for learners to monitor their own progress. Color photos, audio segments, and video clips further enhance the e-Workbook activities. The e-Workbooks can be found at **http://books.quia.com/books**.

The **Teacher's Manuals** provide unit overviews, Notes on the Photos, Warm-Up Activities, teaching tips and techniques, Notes on Usage, Notes on Pronunciation, Notes on Vocabulary, answer key for the Student Book, answers to Frequently Asked Questions about the grammar structures, and new reproducible Internet Activity Worksheets and corresponding Internet Activity Procedure sheets. The Teacher's Manuals also include Unit Tests with both multiple choice and open-ended questions, along with Unit Test Answer Keys.

The new **Complete Audio Program** includes all of the listening activities from the Student Book. Instructors can use the Audio CDs, and students can access and download the MP3 files at the McGraw-Hill Audio Download Center. Go to www.esl.mcgraw-hill.com/audio. Select *Grammar Form and Function, 2nd Edition*, choose the correct level, and download the audio files.

The new **EZ Test® CD-ROM Test Generator** enables instructors to access a wealth of grammar items that they can use and customize to create tests for each unit.

Teaching Guide for the Student Book

Format

For each grammar point, the *Grammar Form and Function, Second Edition* Student Book follows a consistent format:

- **Presentation of Form.** The Student Book presents the complete form, or formal rule, along with several examples for students to clearly see the model. There are also memorable full-color photos to help illustrate the grammar point.
- **Presentation of Function.** The text explains the function of the grammar point, or how it is used, along with additional examples for reinforcement.
- **Practice.** Diverse exercises practice the form and function together.
- **Application.** Students apply the grammar point in open-ended, communicative activities that integrate all language skills.

     All-new **Listening** and **Listening Puzzle** activities provide students with numerous opportunities to develop their oral/aural and discrimination skills.

     Pair Up and Talk encourages students to practice conversation and structures with a partner.

     Your Turn invites students to personalize the grammar and language.
    Read and **Reading Challenge** activities develop reading and thinking skills.
    Writing tasks develop writing and composition skills.

- **Self-Test.** Students take a quiz to see what they have learned and what they still need to work on and practice.

Using Photos

The high-interest color photos in the presentations and activities capture students' attention. When they see a photo aligned with a grammar point, the photo helps them remember and contextualize the grammar. The photos reinforce the learning and the grammar point, and students are more likely to recall the grammar point because they have formed a mental picture. Photos can be used in a variety of ways:

Pre-teaching: to establish a context
- Call on students to describe photos.
- Ask students to name the characters, perhaps using names of classmates.

Teaching: to make a connection between image and form/function
- Instruct students to complete the tasks associated with the photos according to the directions.
- Have students work on the expansion activities connected to the photos in the Teacher's Manual.

Post-teaching: to reinforce the grammar point
- Review the photos at the end of the unit, eliciting the grammar points.
- Have students write a few sentences about the photos on their own or with a partner.

Using Grammar Charts

At the beginning of each section, the form of the grammar point is clearly illustrated in a clear, traditional grammar chart. The comprehensive charts include affirmative and negative forms, contractions, and question and answer forms. A photo or illustration and example accompany the chart to provide meaningful context. Various functions, or uses, of the grammar point are then simply and clearly explained. Another photo may accompany the explanation of the function. The grammar charts can be used in different ways, and it is a good idea to vary the use of the charts throughout the unit. Some students may need the explicit nature of the chart to feel comfortable at the beginning of a lesson. Others may want to start the exercises without spending too much time on the chart, so balancing the needs of everyone in the class is an important consideration when planning a lesson. Here are a few ideas on how to use the charts:

Pre-teaching: to preview the lesson
- Tell students to look over the chart for homework and then present it in class the next day.
- Give students a diagnostic test to see how much they know and then introduce the chart, concentrating on the areas they might not have understood.

Teaching: to introduce a lesson
- Elicit oral examples of the structure before students see the chart.
- Put samples of the form on the board before using the chart.
- Explain the grammar point and then go over the examples on the chart.
- Go over the examples and points in the chart one by one before explaining the grammar point.

Post-teaching: to reinforce grammar points
- Using the photos, elicit key sentences to illustrate form and function when you finish a unit.
- Before the Self-Test or Unit Test, review the charts in each section.
- Ask students to write the form and function of each structure on the board as a review at higher levels.

Using Audio

The new listening activities are an important addition to *Grammar Form and Function, Second Edition* and increase students' ability to understand spoken English. Each unit includes five to six listening activities, a Listening Puzzle for students to integrate new grammar concepts, and numerous opportunities for students to practice their listening skills with their classmates. Here are a few ideas for using the listening activities:

Pre-teaching: to prepare students for listening
- Have students locate the audio download icon with the tracking information.
- Many of the activities have students complete a written exercise and then check it by listening to the audio. Have students review the grammar and complete the activity.
- Put students in pairs to compare answers and discuss any differences.
- For the Listening Puzzle, have students look at the photos before listening and make predictions about the topic of the listening passage.

Teaching: to listen for meaning and clarity
- Have students listen carefully one or more times.
- Focus on the pronunciation of the words and structures in context.
- Check answers.

Post-teaching: to reinforce comprehension and pronunciation and to promote production
- Encourage students to repeat each answer out loud.
- Have students practice saying the answers with a partner.
- Have students use the information to personalize the words and grammar.

Each listening activity includes an audio download icon with the audio download track number, as well as the CD and track number for the audio CDs. Instructors can use the CDs from the Complete Audio Program, and students can access the MP3 files at the McGraw-Hill Audio Download Center. Go to **www.esl.mcgraw-hill.com/audio**. Select *Grammar Form and Function, 2nd edition*, choose the correct level, and download the audio files.

Using Readings

Grammar Form and Function, Second Edition includes new story-based readings and longer academic Reading Challenges to promote competence and fluency in reading. These readings recycle key vocabulary and grammar in longer contexts, prompting students to integrate their language and critical thinking skill development. The activities and reading skill tips provide a framework for students to develop their reading skills. Here are some ideas for using the readings in class:

Pre-teaching: to activate prior knowledge
- Ask students to review the picture, the title, subheadings, captions, or anything else that might get them thinking about the topic.
- Many of the readings are fables that might have a similar version in students' native culture. Encourage students to think about what they already know about the topic.
- Review the reading before presenting it in class and pre-teach any new vocabulary.
- Discuss the reading skill before reading. Have them practice the skill before and while they are reading.

Teaching: to practice reading and comprehension
- Readings can be done for homework, in a group, silently, or aloud in class.
- Encourage fluent reading by asking students to read whole sentences, not just individual words.
- Reread the passage several times, focusing on grammar, understanding, reading practice, and skill practice.

Post-teaching: to reinforce comprehension
- Ask comprehension questions to gauge understanding of the reading.
- Invite students to locate answers to questions in the text.
- Encourage students to comment and ask questions about the text and the story.

Using the Activities in Class
General activity types
The exercises fall into several types that range from tightly to loosely controlled. At the beginning of a section, there are fill-in-the-blanks, substitution, transposing, matching, labeling, choosing items from a list, sorting items into a list, and writing statements or questions. The answer keys in the Teacher's Manual list the answers for these activities. At the end of some sections, there are *Your Turn* and *Pair Up and Talk* exercises that are more open-ended and allow for personal opinions, predictions, or other sorts of creative communication. The answer key gives suggestions as to what these answers might be, but they will vary with each student.

Oral exercises, written exercises, and exercises that can be either
Most of the exercises are designed to include writing practice so that students not only see and hear the structures, but write them as well. Instructors can also use these exercises as oral practice in several ways; if the exercises are easy tasks, students can take turns saying them aloud while writing in a small or large group setting. If they are more difficult, allow students to complete the exercise before checking the answers. If students are working in small groups, they can easily check among themselves and ask questions if they are not sure of the answers. If time is a constraint, instructors can simply give the answers after students complete the exercise, stopping every now and then to see if everyone agrees.

Using *Your Turn* and *Pair Up and Talk*

The purpose of these exercises is to encourage students to express opinions, make predictions, and solve problems, using the grammar point recently learned. Students' answers will vary greatly in these open-ended activities. They can discuss the topics in pairs or small groups as you circulate around the classroom, listening and answering questions. The activities often ask students to then respond in writing. Instructors can go over some of the answers with the entire class if time allows or if a large-group discussion is warranted. Sample answers are given as models in the Teacher's Manual.

Using the Writing Section

In this section, students are given a model in the first few units, such as a simple postcard or letter. In later units, models are not given, as students should be familiar with the format, and they are asked to write a more complex piece, such as a description, comparison, narration, or process. In pairs, they do pre-writing activities, asking each other questions about the topic and jotting down the answers. Then they rewrite their answers following the format suggested. Finally, they edit the paragraph according to a checklist, monitoring spelling, punctuation, vocabulary, and grammar, and make a final copy to hand in. This approach to guided writing specifies topic and format so students are not at a loss for words; at the same time, it allows them to activate their background knowledge and experience and to communicate personally and creatively with a reader (their partner or teacher). While the entire writing assignment can be completed in class, other options include doing the question-answer pair work in class and the writing and editing at home, or doing the writing at home and the editing in class the next day. The flexibility of this section allows the instructor to determine the method that best fits the class schedule and needs.

Using the Tests

Every opportunity for student self-assessment is valuable! *Grammar Form and Function, Second Edition* provides three tests for each unit – one at the end of each Student Book unit, another at the end of each e-Workbook unit, and a Unit Test in the Teacher's Manual. Instructors may use the tests in the way that best meets student, teacher, and institutional needs. For example, instructors may first assign the Self-Test from the e-Workbook as an untimed practice test to be taken at home. Then in the classroom, instructors may administer the Self-Test in the Student Book for a more realistic, but still informal, test-taking experience. Finally, instructors may administer the Unit Test from the Teacher's Manual as a more standardized timed test and/or create a custom test using the new EZ Test® CD-ROM Test Generator.

The Self-Tests build student confidence, encourage student independence as learners, and increase student competence in following standardized test formats. In addition, the Self-Tests serve as important tools for the instructor in measuring student mastery of grammar structures.

Each Self-Test contains two parts. The first section has ten multiple-choice items in which students have to identify the correct answer and darken one of four ovals (A, B, C, or D). The second section has ten multiple-choice items in which students have to identify the incorrect answer.

Teaching Guide for the e-Workbook

Each unit of the Student Book has a corresponding unit in the new e-Workbook. Students have the opportunity to practice the forms and functions of the grammar structures outside the classroom. Many activities are enhanced with color photos, audio segments, and video clips, expanding the input for the student. Ideally, students can finish most of the material in the Student Book during class time and complete sections of the e-Workbook at home. The e-Workbook gives students the opportunity to work independently to perfect their understanding of English grammar.

At the end of each e-Workbook unit, there is a Self-Test modeled on those in the Student Book. These Self-Tests provide an additional opportunity for students to assess what they have learned and review what they have not.

For every new grammar point in the Student Book, corresponding e-Workbook activities are indicated at the bottom of the page so that students can go to the e-Workbook for extra practice. Students can access the e-Workbook at **http://books.quia.com/books**.

Teaching Guide for the Teacher's Manual

Units
Each unit of this Teacher's Manual includes:
- an overview of each unit to summarize the contents
- **Notes on the Photos** to describe the photos in the Form and Function sections and give background and cultural information
- **Warm-Up Activities** to engage students in the topic and activate the target grammar
- Useful teaching tips and techniques for both new and experienced instructors to provide students with the information they need
- multiple expansion ideas, games, and writing activities to extend and personalize learning
- **Notes on Culture**, **Notes on Usage**, and **Notes on Vocabulary** to help instructors clarify, explain, and present the information with ease
- answers to **Frequently Asked Questions (FAQs)** to provide the instructor and students with a deeper understanding of the structure
- answer key for the exercises and **Self-Tests**
- **Unit Tests** in a standardized test format and test answer key to assess understanding and mastery of the unit
- reproducible **Internet Activity Worksheets** with **Internet Activity Procedures** to encourage students to expand their online learning and research skills

Instructors are encouraged to read through all of the activities and notes and to select what might be appropriate for the class and/or individual students.

Unit Tests

The 14 Unit Tests are found in the back of the Teacher's Manual. Each Unit Test is two to three pages long and printed on reproducible pages so that instructors can make photocopies for their class. These tests are more challenging than the Student Book and e-Workbook Self-Tests, because they contain both a standardized test section and one or more writing sections, where students must apply the grammar structures. The writing sections are similar to exercises in the Student Book, so it is easy to determine if students have mastered the material. The tests give students a chance, not only to show that they can recognize grammar forms, but also to show that they can produce the grammar forms and functions of each unit. After each section, there is a space to tally the number of correct items, so these tests are easy to score.

Unit Test Answer Key

Complete answer keys for the Unit Tests are provided in the Teacher's Manual in the section immediately following the Unit Tests.

Internet Activity Worksheets

Instructors will also find all-**NEW** reproducible **Internet Activity Worksheets** that prompt students to use the Internet to find answers and information about a variety of topics. The activities encourage students to develop their research, reading, critical thinking, analysis, and writing skills in an interesting and motivating format, while practicing the target grammar. Students are also asked to use the information they find to create small projects, such as a poster or a flyer.

Internet Activity Procedure pages offer instructors step-by-step teaching suggestions and lesson planning ideas for the Internet Activity Worksheets, making lesson preparation fast and effective. Each one-page Internet Activity Procedure sheet includes:
- *Objectives and Overview* to focus the lesson
- one or more specific *websites* to visit
- *Prepare* suggestions that get students thinking about the subject
- *Research and Writing* instructions that send students online to find specific information
- *Wrap-Up* suggestions to summarize and discuss students' findings

The Internet Activity Worksheets can be used at any point during a lesson, but each one corresponds with a particular section of the unit and is clearly marked underneath the section head with an Internet icon. To maximize comprehension, it is helpful if the *Prepare* and *Wrap-Up* sections are done in class. The *Research and Writing* activities can be completed individually or in pairs or small groups, either at home or in a computer lab environment.

Additional Components

The **Complete Audio Program** includes all of the listening activities from the Student Book. Instructors can use the Audio CDs, and students can access and download the **MP3 files** for *Grammar Form and Function, 2nd edition* at the **McGraw-Hill Audio Download Center**. Go to **www.esl.mcgraw-hill.com/audio**. Select *Grammar Form and Function, 2nd edition*, choose the correct level, and download the audio files.

The *EZ Test® CD-ROM Test Generator* enables instructors to access a wealth of grammar items that they can use and customize to create tests for each unit. Instructors will enjoy the ready-made tests for each unit, can choose the specific questions they want to include or create their own questions, and can print multiple versions of the same test.

Unit 1
The Present of *Be*

Unit Sections		Notes/Activities*	SB page	TM page
1A	Nouns: Singular	Notes on Pronunciation: the alphabet	2	2
1B	Nouns: Plural	Notes on Usage: words ending in *o*; Notes on Pronunciation: plurals; Dictation Activity	3	3
1C	Subject Pronouns	Notes on Usage: gender in animals; Number Activity	5	5
1D	Subject Pronoun + Present of *Be*	Notes on Usage: titles; Frequently Asked Questions	8	8
1E	Negative of *Be*	Introductions Activity	10	9
1F	*Be* + Adjective	Notes on Vocabulary: countries and nationalities	12	11
1G	Possessive Adjectives	Category Sort Activity; "Favorites" Activity	17	13
1H	Demonstratives: *This*, *That*, *These*, and *Those*	Realia Activity	19	14
1I	*Yes/No* Questions with *Be*	Notes on Usage: long answers; Photo Activity	21	15
1J	Questions with *What*, *Where*, and *Who*	Internet Activity; Notes on Pronunciation: *wh-* words; Notes on Usage: asking about professions	24	16
1K	Prepositions of Place		26	17
✦	Listening Puzzle: Countries		29	18
✦	Reading Challenge: Uluru		30	19
✦	Writing: Describe Yourself	Writing Expansion	32	19
✦	Self-Test	Answer Key	33	19

*Each unit section begins with **Notes on the Photo(s)**, which describe the photos in the Form and Function sections of the Student Book and give background and cultural information. Following these notes are one or more optional **Warm-up Activities** that engage students in the topic and practice the target grammar. In addition, a variety of notes on usage, pronunciation, and grammar; answers to "frequently asked questions"; and extension activities are provided. These are listed in the chart that opens each unit in this Teacher's Manual.

Unit 1 introduces the present tense of *be* by presenting singular and plural nouns, both regular and irregular, to increase and reinforce students' vocabulary. Then the students learn subject pronouns with *be* in affirmative and negative statements. Adjectives, including nationality, are introduced so that students learn language to describe themselves, their classmates, and their surroundings in a more meaningful way. This gradual transition allows them to ask questions, give answers, and get to know each other.

Question words, possessives, demonstratives, and prepositions of place further expand this ability to communicate on a very basic level. If students are true beginners, they may work through all the exercises in the Student Book and the e-Workbook and all the activities in the Teacher's Manual. If students have already studied English, they may be able to skip some exercises or do them on their own.

While teaching, try to vary the exercises and activities so that types of input and output change. Rotating work (individual/pair/group/class and at the desk/at the board) maximizes student practice time, maintains student interest, and alleviates the pressure on the teacher to continuously instruct. While students work together, you can give individual attention to those who need it or prepare for the next activity.

1A Nouns: Singular

STUDENT BOOK P. 2

Notes on the Photos and Warm-up Activities

- This **dog** is a *Golden Retriever*. Because they are easy to train and have a gentle nature, Golden Retrievers are popular as family pets. In some countries, people like to have dogs as pets. In other countries, however, people don't keep dogs as pets.
- **Apples** are an ancient fruit that are popular around the world. China leads the world in growing apples, followed by the United States. Apple pie is a traditional dessert in the United States. The saying, "as American as apple pie," is used to describe things that are typically American.
- We don't know what the **boy** in the photo is doing, but he looks happy. He's wearing a T-shirt, so he is probably playing outside on a nice day. Maybe he's playing "fetch" with his dog!

List Animals

- Have students work in small groups or pairs and ask them to list on a piece of paper as many types of pets (or animals) as they can (*a dog, an elephant, an ostrich*). Instruct them to write the singular form of each noun with the article *a* or *an* before it.
- To do this activity as a contest, give one point for each correct use of *a* or *an* before a noun. The team with the most nouns and correctly used articles wins.

Talk about Pets

- Tell students that Golden Retrievers usually love to play "fetch." Then have students discuss these questions in small groups or as a class: *Have you ever played fetch with a dog? Would you like to? Do you*

have a dog or another kind of pet? Which animals are good to have as pets? Why? What can you do with them?
- Next, have small groups work together to make a list of items that a dog might have or use (*a bone, a leash, a whistle*). Remind them to use the singular form of the noun with the article *a* or *an* before it.

Brainstorm with the Expression "As American as Apple Pie"
Brainstorm with the class about other things they think of as typically American. Write the words *as American as …* on the board and list the students' ideas. When possible, they should use the singular form of a noun with the article *a* or *an* before it (*a hamburger, an American football game*).

1 Practice

A.
1. a	4. a	7. a	10. a	13. a	16. an
2. an	5. an	8. an	11. a	14. an	
3. an	6. an	9. a	12. an	15. an	

CD1/2, 3 **B.** Play tracks 2 and 3 so students can check their answers. Then play track 3 again so they can listen and repeat the phrases.

Notes on Pronunciation: the alphabet

- To review the alphabet, elicit the letters from students and write them on the board in order. Then rewrite them in the following groups: A H J K – B C D E G P T V Z (zee) – O – Q U W – R – F L M N S X Z (zed) – I Y
- Point out the similarity in pronunciation of each group of letters and ask the whole class to repeat them. Then call on individuals to repeat them.
- After practicing each group of letters several times, ask the class to recite the alphabet that you first wrote on the board, and then call on individuals to say letters as you point to them at random. If students make mistakes in pronunciation, point to the groups of letters to remind them of the correct pronunciation.

1B Nouns: Plural

Student Book p. 3

Notes on the Photos and Warm-up Activities

- The two **boys** wearing sunglasses may be brothers, cousins, or friends. They may be at the beach or an outdoor swimming pool. They stopped what they were doing and are posing for the picture.
- The **men** in the two photos on the right are practicing karate, a martial art. *Karate* is a Japanese word

The Present of *Be*   3

that means "empty hand." They are each wearing a *gi*, the typical white karate uniform, with a black belt, which indicates that they have reached a very high level in this martial art. Some people practice karate to learn self-defense skills. Others practice martial arts for physical fitness or for spiritual reasons. Martial arts originated in Asian countries, but they are popular throughout the world.

Discuss Boys and Girls

Have students work in small groups to list things that boys often like, things that girls often like, and things that both boys and girls like. They must use the plural form and list objects, not activities. Here are some examples:

Things that boys often like: *cars, trucks, action figures*

Things that girls often like: *dolls, dress-up clothes, jewelry*

Things that both girls and boys like: *books, balls, crayons, stuffed animals*

Personalize

✦ Ask students these questions:

Do you participate in a sport or a physical activity of any kind? What is it? What do you need for this sport? Do you watch sports? What do athletes need for this sport?

✦ Have each student write a list of what they need for their sport or activity, using plural nouns or singular nouns with articles. Then put students in pairs and tell them to share their lists with each other and to listen for and write down plural nouns.

Notes on Usage: words ending in *o*

✦ Point out that when a word ends in *o* preceded by a consonant, you add an *-es* to make the plural (*potato – potatoes, tornado – tornadoes*). An interesting exception to this rule are nouns that relate to music (*piano – pianos, alto – altos*).

✦ When a word ends in *o* preceded by a vowel, you add an *-s* to make the plural (*radio – radios, video – videos*).

2 Practice

1. keys
2. children
3. cities
4. wives
5. women
6. pens
7. leaves
8. mice
9. fish
10. stories
11. feet
12. lemons
13. houses
14. sandwiches
15. brushes
16. matches

3 Practice

-s	-es	-ies	-ves	irregular
chairs	classes	ladies	wolves	children
pens	glasses	libraries	shelves	women
streets	beaches	parties	wives	fish

Notes on Pronunciation: plurals

- Point out that when we add *-s* to voiceless consonants (*f, k, p, t*), the ending is pronounced as an *s*, but when *-s* is added to a voiced consonant (*b, d, g, l, m, n, r, v*) or vowel sound, the *s* sounds like a *z*.
- Point out that *-es* always sounds like *ez*.

Dictation Activity

- Divide the class into two. While one half of the class goes to the board, the other half looks at their books and dictates words to the students at the board.
- The students at the board write both the singular and plural form. For example, the first student dictates the word *child* to the first student at the board, who writes *child – children*. Then the second student dictates the word *class* to the second student at the board, who writes *class – classes*, and so on.
- After a few rounds, the two groups change places.

1c Subject Pronouns

STUDENT BOOK P. 5

Notes on the Photos and Warm-up Activities

- This **man** looks happy and relaxed. The setting appears to be a park or a backyard.
- This **little boy** is celebrating his first birthday. In many countries, a birthday cake is a regular part of a birthday celebration. A child's first birthday is an important celebration for the family.
- This **woman** is probably middle-aged. She is wearing a headscarf with a decorative pattern and long earrings. Women have worn hats, earrings, and other accessories for centuries.
- This **girl** is probably somewhere between nine and eleven years old. She is wearing a bead necklace.
- Many people like to have **a kitten** as a pet. This kitten's eyes are wide open. Kittens do not open their eyes until they are several weeks old.

The Present of *Be*

- This type of **chair** is usually found in a dining room. In some cultures, people do not sit on chairs in a dining room; they sit at low tables on floor cushions.
- There is a strong family resemblance between the **father** and **daughter** in this photo.
- Sometimes people give away **books** they do not want anymore. Bookstores that specialize in used books often buy books from people. Libraries usually accept donations of used books.

Tell about Yourself, Tell about Each Other

- Tell students that the man in the photo is relaxing on his day off work. Say, "He meets his friends on the weekend."
- Have students take turns saying what they do on the weekends, for example, *I go to the movies.*
- When all the students have had a turn, call on volunteers to restate what some of their classmates like to do. Here are some examples: *She visits her mother. He plays the guitar. You watch soccer. I go to parties.*

Discuss Favorite Clothing

Tell students that the woman in the photo is wearing her favorite scarf. Ask students to discuss the following questions in groups: *Do you have a favorite piece of clothing? What is it? What does it look like? Why do you like to wear it?*

Describe the Girl

- Ask students to discuss the following questions in groups: *Who is this girl? Why is she smiling? What is she looking at? How does she feel?* Encourage them to be creative.
- Invite them to share their ideas with the class. Then have the class vote on which description of the girl is the funniest and which is the most realistic.

Talk about Cats

Ask students to discuss these questions in groups or as a class:

Do you like cats? Do they make good pets? Why or why not?

Do you have a cat or a pet? Do you know someone who does?

Describe the cat or pet. What does it look like? Is it friendly?

Describe Something or Someone in the Classroom

- Put students in groups to describe something or someone in the classroom.
- Instruct the students to discuss first and then write down at least five sentences that describe this item or person (appearance, location, use, personality, feel, color, etc.). Make sure they use subject pronouns but do not directly state what the item or who the person is.
- Have groups present their clues and have the class guess what the item or who the person is.

Talk about Family Resemblances

Have students work in pairs or small groups to discuss family resemblances. Ask them to tell which family member they look like and in what ways.

Notes on Usage: gender in animals

Point out that when we know the gender of an animal, we often use *he* or *she* rather than *it*.

4 Practice

1. they
2. they
3. he
4. it
5. it
6. they
7. they
8. they
9. she

5 Practice

1. he
2. she
3. they
4. they
5. it
6. they
7. it
8. they
9. it
10. we
11. you
12. she

Number Activity

This activity can be done with almost any section of Unit 1.

+ Put the numbers on the board in rows, like this:
  1, 2, 3, 4, 5, 6, 7, 8, 9, 10
  11, 12, 13, 14, 15, 16, 17, 18, 19, 20
  21, 22, 23, 24, 25, 26, 27, 28, 29, 30
  40, 50, 60, 70, 80, 90, 100
+ Say the numbers as you point to them, encouraging students to join you if they know them. You will soon establish a rhythmical chant that students find enjoyable. Point out the difference in stress between numbers like *thir*<u>teen</u> and <u>thir</u>*ty*, *four*<u>teen</u> and <u>for</u>*ty*, *fif*<u>teen</u> and <u>fif</u>*ty*, etc.
+ After you practice with the class, point to certain numbers and call on individual students to say them.
+ Ask how many students, desks, chairs, lights, books, etc., are in the classroom.
+ Do a short informal dictation with students at their desks or at the board writing the numbers.

1D Subject Pronoun + Present of *Be*

STUDENT BOOK P. 8

Notes on the Photo and Warm-up Activities

This photo shows two people — a male and a female. They are teenagers or young adults. It looks like they are probably close friends. They look happy.

Describe the People
- Put students in pairs to discuss the people in this photo. Ask them to decide who these people are, how they know each other, what they do, and where they live. Although the Student Book gives some ideas about the people, students should feel free to come up with their own ideas.
- Have each pair share their ideas with the class.

Describe a Friend
Ask students to discuss these questions in small groups or as a class:
Describe a good friend. How old is he or she? What does this person look like? What does he or she like to do? Where does he or she live? Why is this person your friend? What do friends usually do together?

Notes on Usage: titles

Review titles (*Mr., Mrs., Ms., Miss*) with students.

6 Practice

1. am	3. are	5. are	7. is	9. are
2. are	4. is	6. is	8. are	10. is

7 Practice

A.
1. 's	3. 're	5. 's	7. 're	9. 's
2. 're	4. 's	6. 'm	8. 're	10. 's

 CD1/4, 5   B.   Play tracks 4 and 5 so students can check their answers. Then play track 5 again so they can listen and repeat the sentences.

8   Unit 1

Frequently Asked Questions (FAQs)

✦ Why do we say "He's **a** doctor" instead of "He's doctor," like in some other languages?
In English, a singular count noun, even if it denotes a profession, is preceded by an article, e.g., *He's a soldier; She's a nurse; It's a plane.*

✦ Why do we say "I'm Italian" and "They're Italian," not "They're Italians," like in some other languages?
Adjectives do not have singular and plural forms in English, like they do in some languages. We say "They're hungry," **not** "They're hungrys." While it is possible to say "They're Italians" (meaning "They're Italian citizens"), it's more common to say "They're Italian" (that is, "Their nationality is Italian").

1E Negative of *Be*

STUDENT BOOK P. 10

Notes on the Photo and Warm-up Activity

This woman is standing in front of a chalkboard. Many teachers rely on classroom chalkboards, whiteboards, or overhead projectors as they conduct lessons.

Discuss Teachers

✦ Ask students to discuss these questions in groups or in pairs:
Do you have a favorite teacher? Think of a teacher you have now or a teacher from your past. Why is this person a favorite teacher? Explain what he or she does well.
What do good teachers usually do? What do bad teachers usually do?
What is a good classroom like? What is a bad classroom like?

✦ Have students create a chart for each group like the one that follows. Remind them to use *they* when they talk about teachers, and *it* when they talk about a classroom. Encourage students to use *is* or *are not* and contractions.

✦ Ask students to share their charts with the class. Create a master chart on the board and have each group come up and add their ideas, or write the students' ideas in the chart yourself. Have students listen and check the board for the correct use of subject pronouns. For example:

Good Teachers	Bad Teachers	A Good Classroom	A Bad Classroom
They are ready for the lesson. They are helpful. They listen.	They're not on time to class. They aren't helpful. They're not organized.	It is comfortable. It's not dark. It's bright. It has windows.	It smells. It isn't clean. It's not big. It's small. It doesn't have windows.

The Present of *Be*

8 Practice

1.	is not	3.	are not	5.	are not	7.	is not
2.	am not	4.	is not	6.	are not	8.	is not

9 Practice

A.
1.	'm not	3.	aren't	5.	aren't	7.	isn't/'s not	9.	'm not
2.	isn't	4.	isn't	6.	aren't	8.	isn't	10.	aren't/'re not

CD1/6, 7 B. Play tracks 6 and 7 so students can check their answers. Then play track 7 again so they can listen and repeat the sentences.

CD1/8 C. Answer: B

10 Practice

1.	is, isn't	3.	is, isn't	5.	are, are
2.	is, is	4.	isn't, is	6.	aren't, aren't

Introductions Activity

♦ To give students practice in spelling their names, ask each one to spell his/her name, as you write it in a column on the board. Write the letters as they say them, even if they are incorrect. If they try to correct you, allow classmates to help them. For example, Jorge might say *G-O-R-G-A*, but other students may say the correct letters.

♦ Write *NAME* over the column you just completed. Then write the other activity headings: *AGE* and *OCCUPATION*. After the students talk, ask them to look at the board. Write your name, age, and occupation. Then ask students to fill in the columns on the board with their age and occupation.

♦ Ask each student in turn to make one affirmative and one negative sentence with the information. For example, *Amalia is from Brazil. She's not from Italy.* For variety, point to a name and an item in one of the other columns, and let the student decide if the sentence is affirmative or negative. For example, point to *Abdul* and *42*, and the student will say, *Abdul isn't 42. He's 22.*

1F Be + Adjective

STUDENT BOOK P. 12

Notes on the Photo and Warm-up Activity

This photo shows two little girls hugging. They are about three or four years old. They look happy.

Discuss Childhood and Adulthood

Ask students to discuss these questions in small groups or as a class:

What things are true about most children? Describe children, or childhood, using adjectives and the verb *be*. Use both positive and negative sentences.

When does childhood end? In your culture, is there a year or a life event that marks the end of childhood?

11 Practice

Answers will vary. Possible answers:

1. She is sad.
2. She is happy.
3. She is angry.
4. He is strong.
5. They are young.
6. He is old.

12 Practice

1. Korean
2. Peruvian
3. Swedish
4. Sudanese
5. Polish
6. French

13 Practice

Answers will vary. Possible answers:

1. is sour
2. are red
3. are salty/crunchy
4. is sweet/heavy/fresh
5. is cold
6. is red/sweet/crunchy/hard
7. is sweet/white
8. are sweet/soft
9. is hot/salty
10. are crunchy/hard/orange/fresh
11. is brown/sweet
12. is chewy/sweet

14 Practice

1. 's rich
2. 's short
3. 's happy
4. 's not/isn't shy
5. 's not/isn't sick
6. 's single
7. 's lazy
8. 's thin

The Present of *Be* 11

Notes on Vocabulary: countries and nationalities

✦ It is important for students to know how to pronounce the name of their country and their nationality correctly in English, so they are reviewed here. Note that while there are some general patterns, it is difficult to predict whether the nationality adjective will be based on the country name.

✦ Many countries and nationalities are listed on Student Book page 13. Here is a list of more countries and nationalities. Add those of your students if they are not listed here.

✦ Put the list on the board for pronunciation practice. Point out that the words in the second column with an asterisk (*) have a stress shift. For example, in <u>Ca</u>nada, the first syllable is stressed, but in Ca<u>na</u>dian, the stress shifts to the second syllable.

✦ For a fun review, call on a student and toss a ball or a beanbag. Say the name of a country and elicit the adjective form. Continue until everyone has had a chance to participate.

✦ For variety, you can put a map on the wall. The students can take turns pointing to their countries and introducing themselves; for example, *I'm Rigoberta from Guatemala. I'm Guatemalan.*

Australia	Australian	Malawi	Malawian
<u>Ca</u>nada	Ca<u>na</u>dian*	<u>Pa</u>raguay	Para<u>gua</u>yan*
Colombia	Colombian	Peru	Peruvian
<u>Con</u>go	Congo<u>lese</u>*	Puerto Rico	Puerto Rican
<u>E</u>cuador	Ecua<u>do</u>rian*	Slovak Republic	Slovak
<u>E</u>gypt	E<u>gyp</u>tian*	Slovenia	Slovene
El Salvador	Salvadoran	Spain	Spanish
Guatemala	Guatemalan	Switzerland	Swiss
Hong Kong	Chinese	The Netherlands	Dutch
Indonesia	Indonesian	Venezuela	Venezuelan
<u>Jor</u>dan	Jor<u>da</u>nian*	Viet<u>nam</u>	Vietna<u>mese</u>*

15 Practice

A. 1. She isn't Chinese. She's American.
   2. She isn't short. She's tall.
   3. She isn't lazy. She's hardworking.
   4. She isn't heavy. She's thin.
   5. She isn't old. She's young.
   6. She isn't married. She's single.

 CD1/9, 10 B. Play tracks 9 and 10 so students can check their answers. Then play track 10 again so they can listen and repeat the sentences.

16 Your Turn

Answers will vary. Sample answer:
My name is Eduardo Perez. I'm young, I'm single, and I'm shy. I'm not tall. I'm hardworking.

1G Possessive Adjectives

STUDENT BOOK P. 17

Notes on the Photo and Warm-up Activities

This young woman has probably not been teaching long. As part of her preparation to become a teacher, she spent some time as a "student teacher." A student teacher works alongside an experienced teacher in a classroom for part of the school year. In this way, student teachers can practice teaching before they have the responsibility of managing their own classrooms.

Compare Classrooms

Put students in small groups and give them this prompt:

Describe a typical children's classroom in your home country. Where is the teacher's desk? Where are the students' desks? Where are students' books and personal items? You can draw a picture to help describe the classroom to your classmates.

Write a Letter

- Have students write a letter to a friend and describe the class or the school that you are in now. They can describe their teacher, their classmates, the classrooms, and the neighborhood.
- Remind students to use possessive adjectives (*my, your, his, her, its, our, their*) as much as possible and to write at least six sentences.

17 Practice

1. My
2. My
3. His
4. my
5. Our
6. My
7. His
8. My
9. Her
10. Their
11. Its
12. Our

18 Pair Up and Talk

Conversations will vary. Possible conversation:

A: Look at Andrew. His favorite music is rock. My favorite music is rock, too.
B: Oh, my favorite music is jazz. His favorite sport is football. Do you like football?

Category Sort Activity

- Ask a question (for example, *What is your favorite sport?*). Have students walk around the room asking and answering the question and standing with other students who answer in the same way. After students are grouped, call on someone from each group to answer the question (for example, *soccer*).
- Continue the activity by asking other questions, for example: *What is your favorite type of music? What is your favorite food? What is your favorite television show?*

"Favorites" Activity

In this activity, a follow-up to **Pair Up and Talk 18B**, students find out each other's favorites in the categories listed: *Music, Sports, Food*.

✦ Ask students to make a four-column chart in their notebooks with the names of their classmates in the left-hand column and the three categories across the top of the page.

✦ Allow them to circulate, asking each other what his/her favorite is in each category. You may have to help with vocabulary.

✦ Have students sit in small groups. Because the possessive of nouns (*Raul's/Yuki's*) has not yet been introduced, the first student simply says a name and category to the second student; for example, "Raul – sports." The second student says, "His favorite sport is soccer," and turns to the third student and says, "Yuki – music." The third student says, "Her favorite music is pop," and so on. Tell groups to continue until they have made a sentence about all class members.

1H Demonstratives: *This, That, These*, and *Those*

STUDENT BOOK P. 19

Notes on the Photo and Warm-up Activity

This photo shows boats called *gondolas* in Venice, Italy. The gondolas travel up and down canals. The men standing up in the boats are called *gondoliers*. They steer the boats with long poles. They typically wear striped shirts and traditional hats. Many tourists like to ride in gondolas in Venice.

Discuss a Trip

✦ Ask students to bring in a postcard or photograph from their city, or from a place they have traveled to.

✦ Have each student explain what's in the picture to the group or the class. Encourage the class to ask follow-up questions for more information.

19 Practice

A.
1. This is
2. That is
3. This is
4. This is
5. That is
6. Those are
7. This is
8. These are

 CD1/11, 12

B. Play tracks 11 and 12 so students can check their answers. Then play track 12 again so they can listen and repeat the sentences.

14 Unit 1

Realia Activity

✦ Put items on your desk. Call on students, hold up one or more items, and ask questions (for example, *What is this?*). Elicit the answers (*That is a pen.*).

✦ Point out that we use *this/these* to refer to things that are near or appear to be near. We use *that/those* to refer to things that are farther away or appear to be farther away.

20 Pair Up and Talk

Conversations will vary. Possible conversation:
A: This is my dictionary. That is our blackboard.
B: And this is his chair, but that is her chair. This is her notebook.

1I Yes/No Questions with *Be*

STUDENT BOOK P. 21

Notes on the Photo and Warm-up Activity

This photo shows a mother and her son. They may be from India. The mother is wearing a traditional garment called a *sari*. There are different types of saris, but all of them involve wrapping and tying a long piece of fabric (almost like a scarf) around the body. Saris are only worn by women and girls.

Discuss Clothing
Have students draw a favorite piece of clothing and then describe them in small groups. Have the students ask and answer questions about the items.

Notes on Usage: long answers

Point out that the chart lists examples of short answers, but that long answers are also appropriate. Give examples: *No, I'm not from India. I'm from Indonesia.*

The Present of *Be*   15

21 Practice

A.
1. Is she
2. she is
3. she isn't
4. Is she
5. Is she
6. she is
7. Is he
8. Is he
9. he isn't
10. Is he
11. Are they
12. Are they
13. they are
14. Are they

 CD1/13, 14 **B.** Play tracks 13 and 14 so students can check their answers. Then play track 14 again so they can listen and repeat the questions and answers.

22 Practice

1. Is she a teacher? No, she isn't. She's a doctor.
2. Are they flowers? Yes, they are.
3. Is it a dog? No, it's not. It's a giraffe.
4. Is it a camera? Yes, it is.
5. Are they books? No, they're not. They're suitcases.
6. Are they glasses? No, they're not. They're shoes.
7. Are they peppers? Yes, they are.
8. Is it the Statue of Liberty? Yes, it is.

Photo Activity

Bring photos cut from magazines to class. Display each photo and have students ask and answer questions, following the models in **Practice 22**.

1J Questions with *What*, *Where*, and *Who*

STUDENT BOOK P. 24

Note: See page 247 of this Teacher's Manual for a supplementary Internet Activity Procedure and reproducible Worksheet for this section.

Notes on the Photo and Warm-up Activity

This photo shows a smiling young woman from Italy. She is probably in her late teens or early twenties. This photo looks like it could be from a student yearbook. Many high schools and colleges publish yearbooks, which include photos of the students by graduating year. People often save their yearbooks and look back at the photos of themselves and their friends.

16 Unit 1

Describe Yourself in the Future

Have students imagine their own lives in 10 years and write down their ideas, including their occupations, where they live, who they are married to (if they are married). Remind them to use the present of *be*. Then present the class with the following situation:

> You are at a 10-year reunion of this class. Ask each other questions with *what*, *where*, and *who* to find out what your classmates are doing now. Remember it's 10 years in the future.

Notes on Pronunciation: *wh-* words

Point out that most question words beginning with *wh-* are pronounced either as a *w* sound, or as an *hw* sound. *Who*, however, begins with an *h* sound.

23   Practice

1. Who is she?
2. What is she?
3. Where is she from?
4. Who is he?
5. Where is he from?
6. What is he?
7. Who are you?
8. Where are you from?
9. What are you?

Notes on Usage: asking about professions

To ask about a person's job or profession, we usually say "What do you do?" At this point, students can simply ask *Are you a doctor?* and get the response *No, I'm not. I'm a lawyer.* Or they can ask *What are you?* and get the response *I'm a lawyer.*

1K   Prepositions of Place

STUDENT BOOK P. 26

Notes on the Photos and Warm-up Activity

This series of photos aptly illustrates the most common prepositions of place.

Plan a "Photo Shoot"

✦ Explain to students that a *photo shoot* is when a photographer takes a series of pictures. Tell students that they are going to plan a photo shoot that illustrates the prepositions of place.

- ✦ Have students work in pairs or small groups. They should gather common supplies and items from around the classroom and set up scenes similar to the ones of the mouse and the boxes in their book.
- ✦ Have the pairs or small groups take turns describing their scenes to each other. You may also want students to write descriptions of their scenes.

24 Practice

1. in
2. at/in
3. on
4. on
5. above
6. behind/next to
7. on
8. on
9. on
10. in front of
11. in

25 Pair Up and Talk

Questions and answers will vary. Sample questions and answers:

A: Where is your backpack?   B: My backpack is on the floor.
A: Where is your book?   B: My book is on the desk.
A: Where is the clock?   B: The clock is above the door.

26 Read

Long or short answers are possible. Long answers are given below.

1. Emma and Bert are children.
2. Alfred is a man (with two children).
3. Emma is a gardener.
4. Bert is a brickmaker.
5. Emma is happy, but Bert isn't happy.
6. Yes, there is.
7. There is a lot of rain.
8. The father is confused.

Listening Puzzle

STUDENT BOOK P. 29

A. CD1, 15

Answer: A. Argentina

B. *Students might discuss the following*: Argentina is a huge country with big cattle ranches, and the tango is very popular there.

C. CD1, 16

18   Unit 1

Reading Challenge: Uluru

STUDENT BOOK P. 30

A. Answers will vary. Possible answers:
   1. in the Indian Ocean/south of Asia   2. kangaroos, the Outback

C.   The center of Australia <u>is</u> desert. For Australians this desert <u>is</u> the "Outback." Here in the desert, there <u>is</u> a very big stone. <u>It is</u> 1,143 feet high (348 meters), two miles long (3.2 kilometers), and ½ mile (804 meters) wide. This <u>is</u> "Uluru" or Ayer's Rock.

    The rock <u>is</u> famous for its colors in the day. In the morning <u>it is</u> pink, but at sunset <u>it is</u> orange. The color of the rock <u>is</u> different with the weather, too. After rain, the rock looks different. There <u>are</u> stripes of silver. There <u>are</u> waterfalls, too. These <u>are</u> about 700 feet (213 meters) high.

    Over 400,000 visitors come to the Outback every year. <u>They</u> come to see Uluru. Uluru <u>is</u> a special place for the native Australians or Aborigines. <u>It is</u> a sacred or religious place for them.

Note: Some students may recognize that *This* in paragraph 1 and *These* in paragraph 2 are demonstrative pronouns.

D. 1. B   2. B   3. C   4. B   5. C

Writing: Describe Yourself

STUDENT BOOK P. 32

Writing Expansion
Have students also complete the information and write about a partner.

Self-Test

STUDENT BOOK P. 33

A. 1. A   2. B   3. D   4. D   5. B   6. C   7. D   8. C   9. A   10. A
B. 1. B   2. C   3. D   4. D   5. C   6. B   7. D   8. A   9. A   10. B

The Present of *Be*   19

Unit 2

Be: It, There, and the Simple Past of Be

Unit Sections		Notes/Activities	SB page	TM page
2A	*It* to Talk about the Weather	Internet Activity; Notes on Usage: *What is the weather like?*; Weather Activity	36	21
2B	*It* to Tell the Time	Notes on Vocabulary: time expressions; Clock Activity	38	22
2C	Questions with *When, What Day,* and *What Time*; Prepositions of Time	Personalization Activity; Notes on Numbers and Prepositions	40	24
2D	Statements with *There + Be*	Notes on Usage: homophones; Frequently Asked Question	43	26
2E	Questions with *There + Be*	Number Activity	46	28
2F	The Conjunctions *And, But,* and *Or*	Map Activity	49	30
2G	The Simple Past of *Be*: Affirmative and Negative Statements	Notes on Culture	52	32
2H	The Simple Past of *Be*: Questions	Guessing Activity	55	34
✦	Listening Puzzle: Cities		59	36
✦	Reading Challenge: Hawaii		60	37
✦	Writing: Describe a Place	Writing Expansion	62	37
✦	Self-Test	Answer Key	63	37

Unit 2 continues with the present of *be* by introducing weather and time expressions with *it*. The section on weather includes descriptive adjectives and the names of cities in the United States. The section on time includes numbers, days of the week, holidays, months, and seasons of the year.

Sections **2D** and **2E** teach and practice *there* in its affirmative and negative forms, enabling students to expand their vocabulary and talk about a variety of places, including their homes, schools, cities, and countries.

The introduction of conjunctions in section **2F** allows students to join ideas in a logical manner and practice new words.

The past of *be*, which is taught and practiced in sections **2G** and **2H**, enables students to contrast present and past activities and discuss people and events of the past.

2A *It* to Talk about the Weather

STUDENT BOOK P. 36

Note: See page 249 of this Teacher's Manual for a supplementary Internet Activity Procedure and reproducible Worksheet for this section.

Notes on the Photo and Warm-up Activity

This picture shows a child in a swimming pool. She is wearing sunglasses and floating in an inflatable pool toy.

Discuss Activities

- Have students work in small groups or pairs to discuss these questions and list activities for different types of weather:

    In the photo, the girl is in a swimming pool. What else do people do when it's sunny and hot? What do they do when it's cold? When it's raining? When it's windy? When it's snowing?

- After the groups have made their lists of activities, have them share their ideas with the class. Call out a type of weather or a temperature and ask each group to describe an activity.

Notes on Usage: *What is the weather like?*

Point out that the question *What is the weather like?* is asking for a description, it is not asking *What weather do you like?* An appropriate answer would be *It's sunny and warm.*

1 Practice

A. 1. It's cloudy.
    2. It's sunny.
    3. It's sunny.
    4. It's windy.
    5. It's hot.
    6. It's rainy.
    7. It's windy.
    8. It's cloudy.

 CD1/17, 18   B. Play tracks 17 and 18 so students can check their answers. Then play track 18 again so they can listen and repeat the questions and answers.

Be: It, There, and the Simple Past of *Be*   21

Weather Activity

✦ This activity should be done before students go on to section **2B** or **2C**. Write the months of the year on the board, indicating the stressed syllables, and ask students to listen and repeat.

Ja<u>nu</u>ary	March	May	Ju<u>ly</u>	Sep<u>tem</u>ber	No<u>vem</u>ber
<u>Feb</u>ruary	<u>A</u>pril	June	<u>Au</u>gust	Oc<u>to</u>ber	De<u>cem</u>ber

✦ After going over the list several times, put the seasons of the year on the board with drawings like flowers, a lake and swimmers, falling leaves, and a snowman. After practicing them, write the months in the abbreviated form and say *March, April, and May are in spring*, and so on.

spring	summer	fall (autumn)	winter
Mar.	June	Sept.	Dec.
Apr.	July	Oct.	Jan.
May	Aug.	Nov.	Feb.

✦ Play a word game by saying either a month or a season. The next person has to say the corresponding season or month. For example, student A says *fall* and student B says *October*. Then student B says *April*, and student C says *spring*, and so on.

✦ Draw a globe on the board and explain in simple terms that these are the seasons in the northern hemisphere; the seasons in the southern hemisphere are the opposite. You can also explain that some countries around the equator have only two seasons, *rainy* and *dry*. This vocabulary will help them do **Pair Up and Talk 2**.

2 Pair Up and Talk

Questions and answers will vary. Sample question and answer:

A: How's the weather in Miami?
B: It's sunny.

2B *It* to Tell the Time

STUDENT BOOK P. 38

Notes on the Photo and Warm-up Activity

This picture shows someone winding his watch. This is an analog watch, although many people now use digital watches. It looks like the person is probably wearing a suit jacket and a nice shirt. He may be a businessperson.

The time on his watch is 10:11. Punctuality is seen differently in different countries. If you have a meeting in the United States, for example, it's important to arrive on time or even 5 to 10 minutes early.

Role Play

Have students work in pairs. Present them with the following situation:

> Imagine that one of you in each pair has been asleep for a long, long time. When you finally wake up, you need to find out what year it is, what month it is, what day of the week it is, what the date and time are, and what the weather is like. Ask your partner questions to find out this information. Your partner can give you real or imagined information.

Notes on Vocabulary: time expressions

Point out that we also use the expression *after* to mean "past," and *before* or *until/'til* to mean "to":
It's a quarter **after** two. It's ten **before/until/'til** noon.

3 Practice

A.
1. It's six o' five. OR It's five past six.
2. It's twelve forty-five. OR It's a quarter to one.
3. It's five fifteen. OR It's a quarter past five.
4. It's one o'clock.
5. It's ten o' five. OR It's five past ten.
6. It's three forty. OR It's twenty to four.

 CD1/19, 20 B. Play tracks 19 and 20 so students can check their answers. Then play track 20 again so they can listen and repeat the times.

Clock Activity

- Have students make clocks in class. Bring in paper plates, plastic bag ties, and pipe cleaners. Students can write the numbers around the clock, poke a hole in the middle, and attach one or two pipe cleaners to a big tie. They will be able to move the hands and ask their partner what time it is.
- For variety, draw vertical lines representing time zones and write the capitals of students' countries on the board and +6, +8, +10, depending upon the time zones. You can find this information in the first section of the telephone directory.
- Students either stand at the board or sit in the order of their zones. Set your clock to 8:00 A.M. EST (or whatever time zone you're in) and say *In New York, it's 8:00. What time is it in Paris?* Then move eastward.

Be: It, There, and the Simple Past of *Be*

> The student from France will say *It's 2:00. What time is it in Riyadh?* The student from Saudi Arabia will say *It's 4:00. What time is it in Moscow?*, and so on.
> + When you finish one round, another student starts over again with a different time, moving eastward.

4 Practice

1. e   2. c   3. b   4. a   5. d

5 Pair Up and Talk

Answers will vary. Sample answers:
1. What time is it? It's noon.
2. What month is it? It's June.
3. What year is it? It's 2009.
4. What day is it? It's Tuesday.
5. What's the date today? It's June 2nd.

2c Questions with *When*, *What Day*, and *What Time*; Prepositions of Time

STUDENT BOOK P. 40

Notes on the Photo and Warm-up Activities

Because of the way the cake in this photo is decorated, it is probably for a child. In many countries, a cake is a regular part of a birthday celebration, especially for children. Different cultures may have different ideas about which birthdays are the most significant, or which ones are milestones. For example, 16 is considered an important birthday in the United States, perhaps because that is the age when people can get a driver's license. In Jewish culture, 13 is an important birthday; this is the year that a girl or boy is considered an adult in the community. In Latin American cultures, 15 is an important birthday for girls. In Japan, the ages of three and seven are important for girls, while three and five are important for boys.

Plan a Party
+ Ask students to discuss these questions in groups or as a class:
    When is your birthday? What do you like to do on your birthday? What birthdays are important in your culture? What do you think are the most important birthdays? Would you want a birthday cake at age 16 like the one pictured? At 21? 30? 80? Why or why not?
+ Put students in small groups to plan a birthday party for someone in the group. They must decide if the

party is in the morning, afternoon, or evening. They should then decide what day the party will be, and what time it will start and end.
- Ask one person in the group to take notes on the group's ideas. Each group can then announce their party to the class.

Write an Invitation
- Distribute paper to students. Direct students to cut or fold the paper to make an invitation to a birthday party.
- Have students determine who the party will be for and write the invitation, including information about the month, the date, the day of the week, the location, and the time the party will start and end. Suggest students make the card look interesting with colored markers or pencils.
- Have students exchange party invitations with a partner. Have students write an email or a letter to their partner and accept or decline the invitation. Remind students to give a reason if they can't go.

6 Practice

1. in
2. in
3. on
4. at
5. at
6. on
7. in
8. from, to
9. at
10. at

Personalization Activity

- Have students write sentences about themselves, using **Practice 6** as a model.
- Put students in pairs to read their sentences aloud.

Notes on Numbers and Prepositions

- In most languages, ordinal numbers differ from cardinal numbers, so students should not have difficulty with the concept. The ordinal numbers can be taught by writing them on the board along with the days of the week for practice. For example, *the first day of the week is Sunday, the second day of the week is Monday*, and so on. You can also write the numbers with superscripts (*1st, 2nd, 3rd, 4th*), so students are aware of that form.
- To help students remember prepositions, draw a triangular shape like this on the board. Explain that the more general the time, the lower the position on the triangle. The more specific the time, the higher the position on the triangle. For example,

The wedding is **at** 2:00 P.M.
The wedding is **on** June 22nd.
The wedding is **in** the summer.

Be: It, There, and the Simple Past of *Be*

7 Practice

1. It's on January 1st.
2. It's on Wednesday.
3. It's on May 13th.
4. It's on Sunday.
5. It's on February 14th. It's on Friday.
6. It's on November 26th. It's on Thursday.

8 Pair Up and Talk

Conversations will vary. Sample conversation:

A: When is your birthday?
B: It's on December 2nd.

2D Statements with *There + Be*

STUDENT BOOK P. 43

Notes on the Photo and Warm-up Activities

This photo is of someone sitting at a table with two coffee cups. The coffee cups are small, so she or he may be drinking espresso, and is probably sitting and talking with someone else. Many people begin their day with a cup of coffee, but it is a popular beverage for any time of the day. A common social activity is to "meet for coffee."

Discuss the Photo

- Ask students to discuss these questions in small groups or as a class:
    How does this photo make you feel? Why?
    Is the person in the photo a woman or a man? Do you think he or she is married?
    How do you think the person in the photo feels? Why?

Describe and Draw

- Have students discuss this scenario in groups or pairs:
    Describe either a happy scene or a sad scene at a restaurant. How many people are there at the table? What is on the table? What isn't on the table? Have one person in the group write down your ideas. It may help to draw the scene that you are describing.
- Call on each group or pair to describe their restaurant scene to the class. Tell students to listen carefully and draw the scene that is being described. Then ask the class to decide if the scene is happy or sad, and explain why.

Notes on Usage: homophones

Write *there*, *their*, and *they're* on the board. Explain the differences between these homophones and use them in sentences, so students do not confuse these words.

9 Practice

A.
1. There is, There are
2. There are
3. There are, There is
4. There is
5. There are
6. There is, There is

 CD1/21, 22

B. Play tracks 21 and 22 so students can check their answers. Then play track 22 again so they can listen and repeat the sentences.

10 Practice

1. There's
2. There's
3. There's
4. There's
5. There are
6. There aren't
7. There isn't
8. There are
9. There are
10. There aren't

Frequently Asked Question

In some languages, there is only one form of the "existential" *there*. Why is there a singular and plural form in English?

Although German (*es gibt*), French (*il y a*), and Spanish (*hay*) use the same form for both singular and plural, English employs different verbs (*is/are*) to indicate whether the following noun (notional subject) is singular or plural. Students simply have to remember this rule.

11 Practice

Things in the classroom (may vary)
1. There are desks.
2. There are boards.
3. There are students.
4. There are chairs.
5. There are windows.

Things not in the classroom (may vary)
6. There aren't any computers.
7. There aren't any apples.
8. There aren't any animals.
9. There aren't any babies.
10. There aren't any pots and dishes.

2E Questions with *There + Be*

STUDENT BOOK P. 46

Notes on the Photo and Warm-up Activities

This photo looks like a scene in the American West, with flat plains and snow-capped mountains. The mountains in the western United States are the Rocky Mountains.

Role-play

+ Have students work in small groups or with a partner and imagine that they are travel agents. Ask them to consider the following questions about the photo:

  What city, state, and country is this? What else is around this place? Is it a nice place to visit?

+ Then ask groups to answer questions from another group, taking turns being *travelers* and *travel agents*. The *travelers* will ask questions with *Is there*, *Are there*, and *How many?* The *travel agents* will answer. Students could also ask about the weather and temperature (section **2A**) or times and dates (sections **2B** and **2C**).

Write about a Favorite Place

+ Have students write a list of questions to find out about a place they don't know well. Remind students to use *Is there*, *Are there*, and *How many*.

+ Have students think of their favorite places to go. Have students write at least six statements about their favorite place. Remind students not to say the name of the place.

+ Put students in pairs or small groups. Have students take turns asking questions about each other's favorite place. Suggest students use the questions they wrote down in the first step. Elicit guesses.

12 Practice

B.
1. Is there a view from the hotel? Yes, there is.
2. Are there mountains near the hotel? Yes, there are.
3. Is there an exercise center? Yes, there is.
4. Is there a train service to the town? Yes, there is.
5. Is there an underground parking lot? Yes, there is.
6. Is there a town near the hotel? No, there isn't.
7. Is there a movie theater? Yes, there is.
8. How many swimming pools are there? There are two swimming pools.
9. How many restaurants are there? There are three restaurants.
10. How many shops are there? There are over 20 shops.

 CD1/23, 24

C. Play tracks 23 and 24 so students can check their answers. Then play track 24 again so they can listen and repeat the questions and answers.

Number Activity

This activity can be done with almost any section of **Unit 2**, but students need to know these numbers before they do **Pair Up and Talk 13**.

- Review the numbers, asking each student to count in groups of 10; for example, the first student counts from 1 to 10, the second from 11 to 20, and so on.
- Put the rest of the numbers on the board in rows like this:
   101, 102, 103, 104, 105, 106, 107, 108, 109, 110
   200, 300, 400, 500, 600, 700, 800, 900
   1,000, 2,000, 3,000, 4,000, 5,000, 6,000, 7,000, 8,000, 9,000, 10,000
- Say the numbers as you point to them, with students joining in if they know them.
- Next, point to certain numbers and call on different students to say them individually.
- Put a list of numbers on the board and ask the students to say them, first together as a class and then individually.
   101 244 365 450 523 652 748 829 963
   1,756 3,578 5,604 7,059 9,120 10,248
- Explain that in the United States, we usually use a comma to separate every three digits in numbers over a thousand, unlike in other countries where they use a period (8,000 vs 8.000). When we write dates, however, we do not use a comma, and we say the numbers in groups of two. For example, we say "seventeen seventy-six" (1776) or "nineteen fifty" (1950), but we say "two thousand nine" (2009), not "twenty-oh-nine."
- Do a short dictation with students sitting at their desks or standing at the board writing the numbers. To check answers, ask students to read the numbers aloud.

13   Pair Up and Talk

How many minutes are there in an hour?	There are 60.
How many hours are there in a day?	There are 24.
How many days are there in a week?	There are seven.
How many days are there in a year?	There are 365. (Every four years, there are 366. This is called a "leap year.")
How many weeks are there in a year?	There are 52.
How many hours are there in a week?	There are 168.
How many centimeters are there in a meter?	There are 100.
How many inches are there in a foot?	There are 12.

14 Practice

- To begin this activity, model it by giving one student a slip of paper with a word on it and asking questions such as *Are there five letters in the word? Is there a t?*
- Then pass out slips of paper to each student for the first round of the game. When they finish, they can think up words themselves for the second round.
- For variety, play Hangman. As the class guesses letters, have a student at the board write them down. For each letter that is not in the word, he/she crosses it out and draws a part of a stick figure (such as a head or arm). If they are in the word, he/she leaves them there until someone guesses the correct word. Students must guess the correct word before the drawing is finished.

15 Practice

For variety, ask the students to summarize their partner's answers and present the information to another pair of students orally or in writing. For example,

In Fatima's hometown, Cairo, there are many tall buildings, some parks for children, an outdoor market, and many tourists. There isn't a beach, but there is a river. There is also a desert outside the city. In the desert, there are pyramids and a sphinx.

2F The Conjunctions *And*, *But*, and *Or*

STUDENT BOOK P. 49

Notes on the Photo and Warm-up Activities

This picture shows a man in a car talking on a cellular phone. He's using a headset. In some states, it's illegal to talk on a cell phone while driving unless you are using a "hands-free" phone. In other states, it's illegal to talk on a cell phone at all while driving. Some laws restrict cell phone use by young drivers.

Discuss the Photo

Have students discuss these questions in groups or as a class:

The man in the photo is talking on a cellular (cell) phone. Do you have a cell phone, a land-line phone, or both? Which type of phone do you prefer? Do you talk on the phone a lot? Do you use it for work? For other reasons? Who do you talk to?

Discuss Cell Phone Etiquette

✦ Put students in groups to discuss and write guidelines for cell phone etiquette. Each group should write in a two-column chart and talk about where and when to use and not use cell phones. For example,

Where and When to Use Cell Phones	Where and When Not to Use Cell Phones
In a parked car Walking down the street (talking quietly)	Driving a car In a restaurant In a movie theater

✦ Have groups explain their guidelines to the class using *and*, *but*, and *or*. For example,
Use cell phones in a parked car, but don't use them when you are driving a car.
Don't use cell phones in a restaurant or a movie theater.

16   Practice

A. 1. but   3. and   5. and   7. and   9. but
        2. and   4. but   6. and   8. or   10. or

CD1/25, 26   **B.** Play tracks 25 and 26 so students can check their answers. Then play track 26 again so they can listen and repeat the sentences.

CD1/27   **C.** 1. False   2. True   3. False

Map Activity

✦ To practice prepositions and conjunctions, draw a simple map of a college campus on the board or photocopy a portion of it for this activity.

✦ Tell students to make up five questions in the singular and five questions in the plural about places on campus. Then they will exchange papers with a partner who will answer the questions adding *and*, *but*, or *or* in the answer. For example,

A: Is there a bank on campus?   B: No, **but** there's a bank near campus.
A: Is there a lake on campus?   B: Yes, **and** it's very beautiful.
A: Are there shops in the Student Union? B: Yes, **but** they're expensive.
A: Are there study rooms in the dorms?   B: Yes, **and** they're very quiet.

17 Your Turn

To introduce this activity, ask the students to draw a floor plan of their dorm room, apartment, or house. Have them label the items and write four sentences about their floor plans.

18 Practice

A. 1. c   2. a   3. b   4. h   5. f   6. e   7. d   8. g

B. 1. He's not rich, but he has an expensive car.
2. It's winter, but it's warm today.
3. What's the best time for you? Morning or afternoon?
4. It's late, and I'm tired. Let's go home.
5. Is tomato a fruit or a vegetable?
6. Is this milk good or bad?
7. She speaks Spanish, French, and Italian.
8. The restaurant is clean, and the food is very good.

2G The Simple Past of *Be*: Affirmative and Negative Statements

STUDENT BOOK P. 52

Notes on the Photos and Warm-up Activities

These are two photos of the same couple. The photo on the right is a recent one; the photo on the left is a wedding picture of the couple from 50 years ago.

The issue of aging is an important one in North America, particularly as people in the baby-boomer generation reach middle age and care for their elderly parents. Different cultures may have very different ideas about aging and caring for older relatives, or about how elderly people are treated in the community. They may even have different concepts of when someone is considered old, or what it means to be young or "young at heart."

Discuss Aging

Ask students to discuss these questions in groups or as a class:
- Do you know any senior citizens? How old are they? Where do they live?
- At what age do you think someone is old?
- Do you know any older people who are young at heart? Describe them.
- What do you think is the secret to staying young at heart?

Discuss the Past and Present

✦ Ask students to discuss this scenario in groups or pairs:

How are young couples different today from couples in the past? Think of movies or TV shows that show couples in the past, or think of stories you might know from your parents, your grandparents, or other older people. What things did they do? Where did they go? What did they wear on a date? What did they bring on a date? Write your ideas in a two-column chart. Use complete sentences and put the simple past in the first column and the simple present in the second column.

✦ Call on groups to share their ideas with the class. Ask one group to start by giving a fact about couples in the past. Then go around the room and ask other groups to give contrasting ideas about couples today.

EXAMPLE

Couples in the Past	Couples Today
The men always paid for meals and other activities.	Sometimes the women pay.
Men and women dressed up for dates.	Men and women often wear casual clothes.
Couples went to drive-in movie theaters.	Couples go to cinemas.

19 Practice

A. 1. is 2. was 3. was 4. is 5. were 6. are 7. were 8. are

CD1/28, 29 **B.** Play tracks 28 and 29 so students can check their answers. Then play track 29 again so they can listen and repeat the sentences.

CD1/30 **C.** Answer: C

20 Practice

1. were   3. wasn't   5. were   7. wasn't   9. wasn't   11. was
2. were   4. was   6. was   8. was   10. was   12. weren't

Notes on Culture

Talk briefly about weddings and graduations in North America.

✦ Some people get married in a simple, quick ceremony at city hall. They go before a Justice of the Peace who performs the rite. They sign a legal document in front of two witnesses and are declared married.

✦ Other people get married in a religious ceremony in their church, synagogue, or temple. They wear special clothing and have a lot of flowers. They invite their family and friends to see the ceremony, and afterwards, they have a party in a house, restaurant, hotel, or other special place.

- ✦ After the party, the couple usually goes on a trip for a few days or a longer time. This is called the *honeymoon*, and it is usually very romantic.
- ✦ Graduations can also be simple or elaborate affairs. Sometimes there is only a small group of students graduating and the ceremony takes place in the high school, college, or university. Students may wear formal clothes or the traditional cap and gown.
- ✦ At large universities, hundreds or thousands of people attend the ceremony, which may be held in an auditorium or in a football stadium. There is usually a band, many speeches, and finally, the diplomas. Students are happy when this day finally arrives.

2H The Simple Past of *Be*: Questions

STUDENT BOOK P. 55

Notes on the Photo and Warm-up Activity

Wolfgang Amadeus Mozart was a famous Austrian composer who lived in the 18th century. He died in 1791 at the age of 35. He is known for his classical music, including the operas *Don Giovanni*, *The Marriage of Figaro*, and *The Magic Flute*.

Discuss Famous People
Put students in small groups to talk about famous musicians, artists, or writers from their native countries.

21 Practice

A.
1. Was the food good?
2. Was the food expensive?
3. Were the servers polite?
4. Was the restaurant clean?
5. Was the place busy?
6. Was the restaurant convenient?
7. Were the plates full?
8. Was the service good?
9. Was the restaurant big?
10. Was the food tasty?

CD1/31, 32

B. Play tracks 31 and 32 so students can check their answers. Then play track 32 again so they can listen and repeat the questions.

22 Pair Up and Talk

A: Was Napoleon a musician?   B: No, he wasn't.
A: Was Mozart a painter?   B: No, he wasn't.
A: Was Elvis Presley a singer?   B: Yes, he was.
A: Was Marilyn Monroe Chinese?   B: No, she wasn't.

34 Unit 2

A:	Were the Beatles French?		B:	No, they weren't.
A:	Was Picasso a politician?		B:	No, he wasn't.
A:	Was Princess Diana American?		B:	No, she wasn't.
A:	Was Cleopatra Egyptian?		B:	Yes, she was.
A:	Were Mozart and Beethoven musicians?		B:	Yes, they were.
A:	Were George Washington and John F. Kennedy presidents of the United States?		B:	Yes, they were.

Guessing Activity

+ To introduce this activity, first model it with the class. You can either pass out slips of paper with names on them or have the students think of a famous person. Tell them it should be a person who is well known outside his/her country.
+ In pairs, have students practice asking and answering questions about the famous people that they each thought of. They should use the present or the past of *be*.
+ For variety, expand the game into a role-play of a party. Bring name tags with adhesive (or just use paper and tape) and write the names of famous people on them.
+ Stick the name tags to the backs of the students. Then the students circulate around the classroom, asking questions about themselves to guess who they are. They should use the present or past of *be*. For example, *Am I a baseball player? Was I a movie star?*

23 Practice

1. c   2. d   3. a   4. f   5. b   6. e

24 Your Turn

+ Students can simply start to ask and answer the questions, or you can ask each student to write one question on the board and work in pairs to answer them.
+ For variety, you can also have students write six questions on a piece of paper with their name on it.
+ Collect the papers and distribute them at random. The students write the answers.
+ Then collect the papers again, return them to the student who wrote the questions, and ask him/her to guess who wrote the answers.

25　Pair Up and Talk

Answers will vary. Sample questions:

Where were you born? Where were you on your birthday? How many people were at your party? When was your last birthday? How old are you? Who was at the party?

26　Read

Long or short answers are possible. Long answers are given below.
1. A mule is the child of a horse and a donkey.
2. It was happy because it was very energetic.
3. The mule's mother was a racehorse.
4. The mule was very, very tired.
5. The mule's father was a donkey.

Listening Puzzle

STUDENT BOOK P. 59

A. CD1, 33

   Answer: B. New York City

B. Students might discuss the following: *While all three cities are large and near the ocean, the famous landmarks listed, including Central Park, Broadway, and the Empire State Building, make it clear the city is New York.*

C. CD1, 34

Reading Challenge: Hawaii

STUDENT BOOK P. 60

A. Answers will vary. Possible answers:
   1. in the Pacific Ocean   2. 132

C.   There <u>are</u> 132 islands in the state of Hawaii. There <u>are</u> people on eight of the islands. There <u>are</u> four main Hawaiian Islands. These <u>are</u> Maui, Oahu, Kauai, and Big Island. Hawaii <u>is</u> about 2,000 miles (3,219 kilometers) from California. It <u>is</u> in the Pacific Ocean.

   The first people in Hawaii <u>were</u> from islands in the South Pacific. Today, the people of Hawaii <u>are</u> from different countries. There <u>are</u> Asians, Americans, and Europeans. About one percent of them <u>are</u> pure Hawaiian.

   The Hawaiian language <u>is</u> important for Hawaiians. It has 18 letters. There <u>are</u> ten vowels and eight consonants. The word *aloha* <u>is</u> hello or goodbye or love. The word *mahalo* <u>is</u> thank you. They also speak English. It <u>is</u> the language of the state.

   Hawaii <u>is</u> famous for surfing and pineapples. Of course, many people go there for vacations, too.

   Note: Some students may recognise that *These* in paragraph 1 is a demonstrative pronoun and *them* in paragraph 2 is an object pronoun.

D. 1. B   2. C   3. B   4. B   5. A   6. C

Writing: Describe a Place

STUDENT BOOK P. 62

Writing Expansion
✦ If you have old postcards at home, bring them to class to use for this writing activity.
✦ If you don't have postcards, cut photos out of a travel magazine (try to make them the size of a postcard and glue white paper to the back) to distribute to students.
✦ Tell them to imagine they are on vacation in that place as they proceed to follow the instructions.

Self-Test

STUDENT BOOK P. 63

A. 1. C   2. C   3. B   4. A   5. C   6. B   7. D   8. A   9. C   10. B
B. 1. A   2. B   3. A   4. C   5. B   6. A   7. D   8. D   9. B   10. B

Be: It, There, and the Simple Past of *Be*   37

Unit 3

The Simple Present

Unit Sections		Notes/Activities	SB page	TM page
3A	The Simple Present	Weekday/Weekend Activity	66	39
3B	Adverbs of Frequency	Notes on Usage: position of *sometimes* and *usually*; Find Someone Who	68	40
3C	Spelling and Pronunciation of Final *-s* and *-es*	Notes on Pronunciation: voiced and voiceless sounds	71	43
3D	Irregular Verbs: *Have*, *Do*, and *Go*	Notes on Usage: expressions with *do*; Illness/Remedies Activity	74	45
3E	The Simple Present: Negative	Animal Alphabet Activity	77	46
3F	The Simple Present: *Yes/No* Questions	Frequently Asked Question	80	48
3G	The Simple Present: *Wh-* Questions	Internet Activity; Workplace Activity; Guessing Game	82	49
✦	Listening Puzzle: Sea Animals		89	52
✦	Reading Challenge: Camels		90	53
✦	Writing: Describe a Person	Writing Expansion	92	53
✦	Self-Test	Answer Key	93	53

Unit 3 introduces the simple present, illustrating the correct form, explaining how and when we use it, and providing plenty of practice. Students learn a variety of adverbs of frequency and how and when we use them in sentences with *be* and other verbs. The section highlighting the spelling and pronunciation of the final *-s* and *-es* increases students' accuracy and fluency in speaking.

Section **3D** teaches and practices the simple present of the common irregular verbs *have*, *do*, and *go*, emphasizing their pronunciation in the third person.

The unit completes coverage of the simple present by teaching and practicing the negative form, *yes/no* questions, and *wh-* questions. For each of these cases, the unit illustrates the correct form, explains how and when we use it, and provides ample practice.

3A The Simple Present

STUDENT BOOK P. 66

Notes on the Photo and Warm-up Activities

This woman is talking on the phone in an office. Some people in offices use headsets so their hands are free to type or write. This phone has a cord. Many phones now are cordless.

Role-play

Put students in pairs to discuss the photo. Ask them to imagine what kind of company this woman works for, why people call her, and how she helps them. Have them role-play a conversation between this customer service representative and a customer. Ask them to perform their role-play for the class.

Write about a Job

✦ Have students imagine that they are the person in this photograph and that they work as a customer service representative or hold some other office position in a company.

✦ Have students write an email to a friend and talk about the job. Suggest students say if they like the job or not and give reasons. Have students write at least six sentences.

1 Practice

A. 1. rings   3. takes   5. puts   7. watch   9. say   11. waits
    2. gets   4. brush   6. eats   8. stays   10. locks 12. gets

 CD1/35, 36   B. Play tracks 35 and 36 so students can check their answers. Then play track 36 again so they can listen and repeat the sentences.

2 Your Turn

Answers will vary. Sample answers:

Five things you do
1. I get up at 7:30.
2. I go to the bathroom.
3. I take a shower.
4. I eat breakfast.
5. I listen to the radio.

Five things your partner does
6. Liu gets up at 8:00.
7. She gets dressed.
8. She drinks coffee.
9. She brushes her teeth.
10. She reads the newspaper.

The Simple Present   39

Weekday/Weekend Activity

✦ Write the words *Weekdays* and *Weekends* on the board and elicit activities from students. The chart might look like this:

WEEKDAYS	WEEKENDS
go to school	go dancing
do homework	do housework
watch TV	watch movies

✦ Tell students to write at least six sentences. You can revisit this activity to practice adverbs of frequency, which are introduced in the next section. For example:

On weekdays, I always go to school.

On weekends, I often go dancing.

On weekends, I sometimes do homework.

3B Adverbs of Frequency

STUDENT BOOK P. 68

Notes on the Photos and Warm-up Activities

✦ The **penguins** are standing on an ice floe or a glacier. Penguins usually live in colder climates. They are often found in places like Antarctica, New Zealand, and Australia. They don't fly.

✦ This **businessman** is at a train station. The sign behind him shows arrival and departure times for trains, as well as which tracks they arrive and depart from. He looks frustrated. He may have just missed a train and is calling someone to say that he will be late. Yukio is a Japanese name. Punctuality is very important in Japan. In the United States, it is also important to be punctual for work and meetings.

✦ This woman looks like she is **a college student**. Most Americans attend college after high school when they are about 18. Colleges and universities are usually four years. Older students are sometimes called non-traditional students because they go back to school after they have been working for a while or after starting their families. This student is carrying a book bag. Some students leave their books in lockers or, if they live on a college campus, in their dorm rooms. Others carry everything with them in a backpack or book bag.

Talk about Penguins

Have students work in small groups or pairs. Present them with the following situation:

Imagine that you are experts on penguins, the birds pictured in this photo. You are appearing on a TV show about animal life. Tell viewers facts about penguins, using adverbs of frequency. What do they eat? Where do they live? What do they look like? Do they all look the same? What things do penguins like to do? If you don't know anything about penguins, use your imagination, or choose a different animal.

Role-play

- Pair up students and ask them to imagine where the man in the photo is, where he is going, what happened to him, and whom he is calling. Then ask one student in each pair to be the man in the photo; the partner will be the person he is calling.
- Have students role-play the phone conversation and perform their role-plays for the class. Make sure they use adverbs of frequency.

Discuss Transportation

Have students discuss these questions in small groups or as a class:

How do you usually get to work or school? Do you take a train, a subway, a bus, or a taxi? Do you walk? Do you drive?

How often are you late? How often are you early? How often are you on time?

Which type of transportation do you prefer: public transportation (trains, buses, and subways), driving, or walking? Why?

Write Directions

Tell students to write directions for a friend, telling the friend how to get to their house, school, or place of work using public transportation. Students should state when the transportation arrives and departs, and how often it is on time. Remind students to use at least three adverbs of frequency in their directions.

Talk about College Students

Have students work in small groups or pairs. Present them with the following situation:

Imagine that you are experts on students. You are appearing on a TV show about student life. Tell viewers several facts about students using adverbs of frequency. What do they usually eat? Where do they live? What do they look like? Do they all look the same? What things do students like to do?

Tell What's in Your Backpack

- Ask students to discuss this question in groups or as a class:

    What do you usually, often, sometimes, rarely, and never carry in your backpack, bag, or purse?
- Go around the room or the group and have each student say one or more things that they do (or don't) carry.

Notes on Usage: position of *sometimes* and *usually*

Sometimes and *usually* can also appear at the beginning of a sentence. For example, **Sometimes** *I sleep late on Saturdays.* **Usually** *my sister makes the family breakfast.*

3 Practice

1. I always get up at 7:00.
2. I usually have breakfast at 7:30.
3. I often drink two cups of tea for breakfast.
4. I never eat eggs for breakfast.
5. I sometimes watch the news on television.
6. I rarely listen to the radio at home.
7. I usually read the newspaper in the morning.
8. I always lock my door.

4 Practice

1. Yukio is always on time.
2. Yukio always comes to work on time.
3. Yukio is never sick.
4. He usually works on Saturday.
5. He sometimes feels tired.
6. He is rarely home early.
7. He often works late at the office.
8. He never misses a meeting.

5 Pair Up and Talk

Sentences will vary. Sample sentences:

1. I rarely eat dinner early.
2. I often watch TV.
3. I sometimes go to bed late.
4. I never read magazines.
5. I often go to the movies.
6. I always do homework.
7. I sometimes stay at home.
8. I usually see friends.

Find Someone Who

- On the board, write _____ *always eats dinner early*.
- Ask the class, *Do you always eat dinner early?* Write the name of one of the students who answers *yes* on the line on the board. On the board, you may want to write *Do you* _____ ?
- Have students add an adverb to each phrase in **Pair Up and Talk 5**.
- Have students stand and walk around the room to talk to their classmates. Remind students to use *Do you* before the phrase to ask questions. Have students write names next to each phrase to make a true complete sentence.
- Call on students to tell the class about one of their classmates.

3c Spelling and Pronunciation of Final -s and -es

STUDENT BOOK P. 71

Notes on the Photo and Warm-up Activities

This picture shows a man watching TV and holding a remote. He is using the remote control to change the TV stations. A useful expression to teach here might be *couch potato*, which is someone who sits on a couch or a chair in front of the TV for many hours. The average number of hours an American spends each week watching TV is 19.

Talk about the Photo

Have students work in small groups or as a class. Present them with the following situation:

> Look at the picture of Ken, the man on the couch. Imagine what he does during the day. Does he have a job? What is his job? Why is he usually tired in the evening? Describe a typical day for Ken before he comes home to watch TV. Is he a "couch potato"? Share your ideas with the class or your group.

Write about Habits

- Have students interview someone—a classmate or somebody outside of class—to find out what they usually do every day and every evening. Suggest students find out what the person usually does to relax at the end of the day.
- Have students write a paragraph about this person's habits. Instruct students to write at least six sentences, using the simple present.
- Call on students to read their paragraph to the class.

6 Practice

/s/	/ɪz/	/z/
asks	brushes	begins
eats	catches	buys
likes	dances	flies
looks	fixes	opens
puts	kisses	plays
speaks	misses	says
stops	passes	sees
walks	teaches	stays
writes	wishes	tries

The Simple Present

Notes on Pronunciation: voiced and voiceless sounds

✦ Show students the difference between voiced and voiceless sounds by placing your fingers on either side of your vocal chords and asking them to do the same.
✦ Make the /s/ sound, and ask students to join in. Draw a snake on the board, and refer to it when they mispronounce this sound. Practice the first column in **Practice 6** again.
✦ Make the /z/ sound, and ask students to join in. Draw a bee on the board, and refer to it when they mispronounce this sound. Practice the third column in Practice 6 again.
✦ To practice the /iz/ sound, count the vowels in the word before and after adding the final -s. Practice the second column in Practice 6 again.
✦ Review the list from time to time to reinforce these sounds.

7 Practice

A.
1. comes /z/
2. lives /z/
3. teaches /iz/
4. likes /s/
5. walks /s/
6. arrives /z/
7. enjoys /z/
8. loves /z/
9. forgets /s/
10. gives /z/

CD1/37, 38

B. Play tracks 37 and 38 so students can check their answers. Then play track 38 again so they can listen and repeat the sentences.

C. Answers will vary. Sample answer:
I think Dan Thomas is a good teacher. He enjoys his job, and he really likes his students.

8 Practice

1. always tries
2. usually studies
3. often worries
4. never stays
5. rarely enjoys
6. sometimes cries
7. usually says
8. often looks

9 Your Turn

Answers will vary. Sample answers:
1. I usually drink tea in the morning.
2. I rarely exercise.
3. I am often late to school.
4. I always do my homework.

3D Irregular Verbs: *Have, Do,* and *Go*

STUDENT BOOK P. 74

Notes on the Photo and Warm-up Activity

This woman is sitting at her kitchen table. She might be what is called a "non-traditional student." For example, she might be returning to school or completing a degree program later in life. The ideas of continuing education, adult education, or university extension schools may or may not be common in students' own cultures.

Survey Classmates

✦ Have students work in pairs or small groups to conduct an informal survey within or outside of class. Instruct students to interview people about their study habits and write down the results. Suggest students each interview one person.

✦ If students have a hard time thinking of questions to ask, here are some suggestions:
  Where do you usually study and do your homework?
  Do you study at home or someplace else? Where are some good places to study?
  How do you usually study? What do you do first? What do you do last?
  Do you have any food or drink while you study?

✦ Have students share what they found out in their small groups or with the class.

Notes on Usage: expressions with *do*

Explain to students that we use *do* with specific expressions: *do homework, do chores, do dishes, do laundry*.

10 Practice

1. goes, goes   2. have   3. has, has   4. do   5. does, does

11 Practice

1. has
2. finishes
3. goes
4. eats
5. usually studies
6. often give
7. takes
8. has
9. fixes
10. talks
11. does
12. pays
13. closes
14. goes
15. is
16. always tries
17. cook
18. eat
19. always do
20. usually watch
21. like
22. often go

The Simple Present

12 Practice

A. 1. has   3. have   5. have   7. has   9. has
    2. has   4. has   6. have   8. has   10. have

 CD1/39, 40 B. Play tracks 39 and 40 so students can check their answers. Then play track 40 again so they can listen and repeat the sentences.

13 Practice

1. is   2. is   3. is   4. has   5. is   6. has   7. has   8. is

Illness/Remedies Activity

- Ask students how they feel. Tell them you don't feel well. Mime these different illnesses and ask them to repeat; then write the words on the board:
  backache, cold, cough, flu, headache, stomachache, toothache, virus.
- Be sure to point out that the *ch* in *ache* is pronounced /k/ and that all the words are preceded by the indefinite article (*a cold*) except *flu* (*the flu*).
- Mime the illnesses again and elicit the words from students. Elicit remedies and write them on the board.
- Have students practice the vocabulary with short dialogues like the following:
  A: I have the flu.
  B: Hot tea is good for the flu.

3E The Simple Present: Negative   STUDENT BOOK P. 77

Notes on the Photo and Warm-up Activities

This picture shows an overweight man eating potato chips and watching TV. If it was not presented with the photo in **3C**, a useful expression to teach here might be *couch potato*.

Discuss Healthy and Unhealthy Habits

Have students work in pairs or small groups. Present them with the following situation:

Len, the man in the photo, isn't healthy. On the other hand, Len's brother Leo is very healthy. Discuss what Len does or doesn't do and why he is unhealthy. Discuss what Leo does or doesn't do and why he is healthy.

Discuss Your TV Viewing Habits

Ask students to share their TV viewing habits. Have them discuss the following questions in small groups:

How many hours a day do you watch TV? What TV shows do you like? What TV shows don't you like?

14 Practice

1. don't understand
2. doesn't want
3. doesn't talk
4. don't go
5. doesn't eat
6. doesn't drink
7. doesn't like
8. don't have
9. doesn't see
10. don't know

15 Practice

A.
1. Birds don't give milk.
2. Fish swim.
3. A chicken comes from an egg.
4. Plants need water to grow.
5. Penguins don't live in Italy.
6. Elephants don't eat chickens.
7. Rice doesn't grow on trees.
8. The Chinese drink tea.

 CD1/41, 42 B. Play tracks 41 and 42 so students can check their answers. Then play track 42 again so they can listen and repeat the sentences.

Animal Alphabet Activity

✦ Elicit the alphabet and put the letters on the board in vertical rows as students say them.
✦ Say an animal, like *A - ape*. The first student says *B - baboon*. The second student says *C - cat*, and so on. Write the names of the animals on the board so students can copy them.
✦ Go over the list, repeating the letters and animals so students repeat with correct pronunciation.

16 Practice

A.
1. aren't
2. doesn't get up
3. doesn't put on
4. doesn't go
5. doesn't wait
6. don't sit
7. don't talk
8. don't eat
9. don't look at
10. doesn't worry

 CD1/43, 44 B. Play tracks 43 and 44 so students can check their answers. Then play track 44 again so they can listen and repeat the sentences.

17 Pair Up and Talk

For variety, have students face each other. One student can say an affirmative or negative sentence like "I get up early" and the other student can say the corresponding negative or affirmative sentence, "I don't get up early." Continue until each student has had a chance to make up a sentence.

3F The Simple Present: *Yes/No* Questions

STUDENT BOOK P. 80

Notes on the Photo and Warm-up Activity

This photo shows a man wearing glasses. He may be nearsighted or farsighted or both.

Take a Survey
- Take a class survey about glasses and contact lenses. Have students work in small groups. They should ask each other the following questions: *Do you wear glasses? Do you wear contact lenses?*
- As a class, compile the results on the board.

18 Practice

A.
1. A: Do you love him?   B: Yes, I do.
2. A: Do you know his family?   B: Yes, I do.
3. A: Does he have a good job?   B: Yes, he does.
4. A: Does he live in a nice apartment? B: Yes, he does.
5. A: Does he drive a nice car?   B: Yes, he does.
6. A: Does he wear nice clothes?   B: Yes, he does.
7. A: Does he smoke?   B: Yes, he does.
8. A: Does he buy you nice gifts? B: Yes, he does.
9. A: Does he take you out?   B: Yes, he does.
10. A: Does he want to marry you?   B: No, he doesn't.

 CD1/45, 46

B. Play tracks 45 and 46 so students can check their answers. Then play track 46 again so they can listen and repeat the questions and answers.

 CD1/47

C. Answer: C

48 Unit 3

Frequently Asked Question

Why do we put an -s on nouns to make them plural, yet put an -s on verbs for third-person singular?
This will often confuse students who have recently learned plurals and are now learning the simple present. The -s comes from an older -th form (*doth, giveth, taketh*) found in ancient books. There is little a teacher can say to students except to keep practicing this form. Putting a large *S* on the board and pointing to it when students make this mistake can help.

19 Pair Up and Talk

Students may do this exercise in pairs orally. A second alternative is for students to write questions first, and then practice asking and answering with a partner.

Conversations will vary. Sample conversation:
A: Do you go to bed late?
B: Yes, I do. Do you?
A: No, I don't.

3G The Simple Present: *Wh-* Questions

STUDENT BOOK P. 82

Note: See page 251 of this Teacher's Manual for a supplementary Internet Activity Procedure and reproducible Worksheet for this section.

Notes on the Photo and Warm-up Activity

This photo shows a kangaroo. They live in Australia, Tasmania, and New Guinea. They have powerful hind legs for hopping or leaping, and they can travel great distances very quickly. Female kangaroos carry their babies in a pouch until they are too large to carry anymore.

Discuss Unusual Animals
- Ask students to discuss the following questions in small groups or as a class:
    Have you seen a kangaroo in a zoo, in a movie, on TV, or in person? Why is this animal unusual?
- Now ask students if they know of other unusual or interesting animals. Instruct students to tell their group or the class about another unusual animal and answer questions about it. Encourage them to draw a picture of the animal to help explain it.

20 Practice

1. c   2. b   3. e   4. a   5. f   6. d

21 Read

1. Where does Linda live? She lives in Toronto.
2. What does Tom do? He is an accountant.
3. How many children do they have? They have one daughter.
4. What does Nancy do? She goes to the university.
5. What does Linda do? She is a nurse.
6. Where does Linda work? She works in a big hospital.
7. When does Linda start and finish work? She starts work at 9:30 in the evening and finishes at 6:30 in the morning.
8. What does she do after breakfast? She usually watches television and goes to bed at about 9:00.
9. What do they do after dinner? They talk and watch television together.
10. What does Linda do then? She goes to work.

22 Your Turn

Answers will vary. Sample answers:

She wants to change her hours because she doesn't spend much time with her husband/because she doesn't like to sleep during the day/because she doesn't get to go out at night.

Workplace Activity

- Elicit different jobs from students; you can start by asking where members of their family work.
- Write the jobs and the places of work on the board:

ac<u>coun</u>tant	accounting office	me<u>chan</u>ic	garage
<u>ar</u>chitect	studio	nurse	clinic/hospital/office
<u>bank</u>er	bank	poli<u>ti</u>cian	government office
<u>bus</u>inessman/woman	company	<u>sail</u>or	ship (on)
engi<u>neer</u>	construction site (at)	<u>sol</u>dier	army base (on)
<u>law</u>yer	law office		

- Pronounce the words and ask students to repeat. Point out the stress in each word, and the sound /k/ in *architect* and *mechanic*.

- Say a sentence that includes the occupation and the typical job site, for example: *An accountant works in an accounting office.* Ask students to repeat.
- Go around the room, asking each student to say a sentence.
- When finished, go around again, this time using a question – answer format. For example:
  - A: Where does a sailor work?
  - B: A sailor works on a ship.

23 Practice

A.
1. is
2. does
3. does
4. does
5. Are
6. Do
7. are
8. are
9. Does
10. Do

 CD1/48, 49

B. Play tracks 48 and 49 so students can check their answers. Then play track 49 again so they can listen and repeat the questions and answers.

24 Practice

1. Is Gina Louisa's sister?
2. How old is Gina?
3. What does Gina do?
4. Is she famous?
5. Is she married to a TV producer?
6. Why is she unhappy?
7. Is Louisa happy?
8. Where does she live?

25 Pair Up and Talk

A. Conversations will vary. Sample conversation:
   - A: When do you have breakfast?
   - B: I have breakfast at 7:00 every morning.
   - A: Who do you usually see on your way to class?
   - B: I usually see Jan and Renae on my way to class.

B. Sentences will vary. Sample sentences:
   1. Paul has breakfast at 7:00 every morning.
   2. Paul usually sees Jan and Renae on his way to class.

The Simple Present

Guessing Game

- Have students write their sentences from **Pair Up and Talk 25B** on a piece of paper. Instruct students to use pronouns only (*he, she*), not names in the sentences.
- Collect the papers and redistribute them.
- Call on students to read the sentences they received. Elicit guesses from the class as to which student the sentences describe.

26 Read

Long or short answers are possible. Long answers are given below.
1. This man loves his gold.
2. He melts the gold into a big brick.
3. He buries the gold behind his house.
4. He digs it up, looks at it, and buries it again.
5. A thief sees him.
6. He takes the gold brick and puts an ordinary brick in its place.
7. He finds an ordinary brick.
8. No, he doesn't.

Listening Puzzle

STUDENT BOOK P. 89

A. CD1, 50

Answer: C. dolphin

B. Students may discuss the following:

Penguins lay eggs. While the seal and dolphin share some characteristics, the seal is not part of the whale family.

C. CD1, 51

52 Unit 3

Reading Challenge: Camels

STUDENT BOOK P. 90

A. Answers will vary. Possible answers:
1. They live in the desert.
2. Its hump.

C. Some people <u>think</u> that a camel <u>stores</u> water in its hump, but this <u>isn't</u> true. A camel's hump <u>is</u> really fat. When there <u>is</u> no food or water, the camel's body <u>makes</u> the fat into food. After it <u>uses</u> the fat in its hump, the hump <u>gets</u> soft and <u>bounces</u> around from side to side. Arabian camels <u>have</u> one hump. These camels <u>live</u> mainly in the Sahara desert and the Middle East. Bactrian camels <u>have</u> two humps, and they <u>live</u> in Asia.

People <u>call</u> camels "ships of the desert." Camels often <u>go</u> many days or sometimes months with no water. When a camel <u>finds</u> water, it <u>drinks</u> 50 gallons (220 liters) at a time! The camel's body temperature <u>rises</u> from 95 to 104 degrees Fahrenheit (35 to 40 degrees Celsius) during the day. We rarely <u>see</u> this in other animals. For the desert sand, camels <u>have</u> a double set of eyelashes. This <u>gives</u> the camel a gentle look, but be careful!

D. 1. C
E. 2. C   3. C   4. A   5. C
F. 6. A
G. 7. B

Writing: Describe a Person

STUDENT BOOK P. 92

Writing Expansion

These paragraphs can be:
- displayed on a bulletin board,
- collated into a class booklet, or
- incorporated into a webpage.

Self-Test

STUDENT BOOK P. 93

A. 1. B   2. A   3. C   4. D   5. B   6. A   7. A   8. C   9. A   10. C
B. 1. C   2. B   3. C   4. A   5. B   6. C   7. A   8. A   9. D   10. D

Unit 4

The Present Progressive

Unit Sections		Notes/Activities	SB page	TM page
4A	The Present Progressive: Affirmative Statements	*Yes* or *No* Activity; Sentence Activity	96	55
4B	The Spelling of Verbs Ending in *-ing*	Sentence Activity; Dictation Activity	101	57
4C	The Present Progressive: Negative Statements	Description Activity	104	59
4D	The Present Progressive: *Yes/No* Questions	Mime Game	106	60
4E	The Present Progressive: *Wh-* Questions	Photo Activity	108	62
4F	Nonaction or Stative Verbs	Internet Activity; Notes on Usage: exceptions; Notes on Vocabulary: non-action verbs	109	63
4G	The Simple Present and the Present Progressive	Contrast Activity	112	65
✦	Listening Puzzle: Holidays		117	67
✦	Reading Challenge: Water Festival		118	68
✦	Writing: Describe Experiences	Writing Expansion	120	68
✦	Self-Test	Answer Key	121	68

Unit 4 introduces the present progressive in affirmative and negative statements, and in *yes/no* and *wh-* questions. For each of these cases, the unit illustrates the correct form, explains how and when we use it, and provides ample practice. Additional practice in the spelling of verbs ending in *-ing* is provided.

The text explains and practices the difference between dynamic verbs (verbs that can be used in both present progressive and simple present) and stative verbs (verbs that can be used only in simple present).

Finally, the present progressive is contrasted with the simple present to clearly illustrate the difference in usage more firmly in the minds of the students.

4A The Present Progressive: Affirmative Statements

STUDENT BOOK P. 96

Notes on the Photos and Warm-up Activities

- In the photo on page 96, **a teenage girl** is lying on the grass and wearing a hat. The hat is made of straw and is a cowboy style. Many people in the western part of the United States wear hats like this in the summer.
- In the photo on the left on page 97, **two students** are studying in a library. Many middle-school and high-school students have a time during their day, usually called "study hall" or "study period," when they can go to the school library and do their homework or conduct research.
- In the photo on the right, the **woman** is skiing. In the United States people often go skiing in the New England or in the Rocky Mountain states, such as Colorado.

Discuss the Girl with the Hat

- Put students in small groups and ask them to say as much as they can about the girl in the photo. Give them a time limit.
- Have one person in each group write down the group's ideas. Then have each group present their ideas.
- To make the activity into a contest, award a point for each sentence that correctly uses the present progressive. The group with the most points wins. For an additional challenge, require groups to use a different verb in each sentence.

Describe a Public Place

- Put students in groups or in pairs. Ask them to think of a specific place at or near their school (the library, the cafeteria, a student center, the campus bookstore).
- Lead them in a discussion of ways to describe what is going on there without actually stating the place.
- Tell them to write down at least three "clues" to this place using the present progressive; then have each group present their clues to the class. The class must guess what place on campus is being described.
- To practice the question form, you can also allow class members to ask each group questions about the place they are giving clues to using the present progressive.

Act It Out

Put students in groups or pairs. Explain that they are going to pantomime (act out) an activity that people do during certain seasons of the year and then ask the class, "What are we doing?" The class must guess what activity is being demonstrated, phrasing their guesses in the present progressive (*You're flying a kite*). To give a little extra help, each group can tell the class in what season their activity takes place. Or for an extra challenge, the class can guess the season.

1 Practice

A.
1. are singing 4. is eating 7. are going 10. is waiting
2. is working 5. are playing 8. is fixing 11. is flying
3. are talking 6. is washing 9. is reading 12. are watching

 CD2/2, 3 B. Play tracks 2 and 3 so students can check their answers. Then play track 3 again so they can listen and repeat the sentences.

Yes or No Activity

Say statements about an activity in the classroom or the environment, using the present progressive (for example, *The sun is shining*). Some sentences should be true and some false. Elicit *yes* or *no* from the students.

2 Practice

1. Paul is playing the guitar.
2. The girls are eating ice cream.
3. The baby is crying.
4. Linda is talking on the phone.
5. Tim is opening the door.
6. Peter is carrying bags and suitcases.

3 Practice

Answers will vary. Possible answers:
1. He's wearing a shirt.
2. She's carrying/holding an umbrella.
3. The man is carrying a briefcase.
4. He's wearing a suit.
5. She's wearing a skirt.
6. He's wearing a tie.
7. The woman is wearing boots.
8. He is wearing a hat.
9. He is walking.
10. The man and the woman are walking/smiling.

4 Practice

Answers will vary. Sample answer:
A: The student is wearing glasses. The student is sitting at a desk and writing in a notebook.
B: Is it Michiko?
A: Yes, it is.

56 Unit 4

5 Pair Up and Talk

Answers will vary. Sample answers:
A: Yumi is reading a book.
B: Our teacher is writing on the board.

Sentence Activity

✦ Put either or both sets of words on the board, depending on the number of students in class.

university	department store	laboratory	restaurant
movie theater	classrooms	hotel	sports center
auditorium	gas station	library	supermarket
dance club	dormitory	laundromat	town/city
cafeteria		office	

✦ Send students to the board, individually or in pairs, to write a few sentences beside each word. You can write these as examples:

Auditorium: A professor is giving a lecture. Students are listening to her and taking notes.

Movie theater: People are watching a movie. Children are eating popcorn and drinking soda.

✦ When they are finished, go over the sentences with the class, making corrections.

4B The Spelling of Verbs Ending in *-ing*

STUDENT BOOK P. 101

Notes on the Photo and Warm-up Activities

This photo shows a woman sitting in a deck chair on the beach. She is typing on a laptop computer. This photo might illustrate the problem people have balancing life and work in North America and other parts of the world. It is difficult for many people to leave their work behind and take a vacation. The woman in this photo might be a *workaholic*, which is someone who is always thinking about work and cannot stop working.

Discuss the Photo

Ask students to discuss some or all of these questions in small groups or as a class:

Do you think the woman in this photo is a workaholic? Why or why not?

What do you think she is doing on her laptop computer? What is she working on?

Are you a workaholic, or do you know someone who is?

Is it difficult for you (or for this person) to stop working and take a vacation? Why or why not?

Write a Letter or Email

✦ Tell students to imagine that they are the woman in the photograph. Alternatively, tell students to think of a place that they would love to visit, and imagine that they are there on vacation.

✦ Have students write a postcard or email to a friend or family member, telling this person where they are and what is going on around them. Encourage students to write at least six sentences.

6 Practice

A.
1. save
2. make
3. type
4. study
5. hope
6. plan
7. add
8. smile
9. hurry
10. drive
11. agree
12. give

 CD2/4, 5 B. Play tracks 4 and 5 so students can check their answers. Then play track 5 again so they can listen and repeat the words.

Sentence Activity

Have students write sentences for each word in **Practice 6** and then read their sentences to a partner.

7 Practice

Add -ing	Drop e, add -ing	Double the consonant, add -ing
crying	dancing	getting
fixing	hoping	putting
playing	moving	running
raining	saving	shopping
reading	smiling	stopping
showing	taking	swimming
washing	writing	
wearing		

58   Unit 4

8 Practice

A.
1. is raining
2. am sitting
3. am watching
4. am thinking
5. is reading
6. eating
7. is playing
8. is making
9. is doing
10. is listening to
11. is ringing
12. is calling

 CD2/6, 7   B. Play tracks 6 and 7 so students can check their answers. Then play track 7 again so they can listen and repeat the sentences.

 CD2/8   C. Answer: B

Dictation Activity

- Divide the class into two and tell them that there will be a dictation.
- While one half of the class goes to the board, the other half dictates the present progressive form of the verbs in **Practice 6 and 8** to them. The students at the board may help each other.
- Then the groups change places; those seated should dictate the base form of the verbs in **Practice 7** to the students at the board.
- After a few rounds, check the answers. As an additional challenge, students can write both the base form and the present progressive form of the verbs.

4C The Present Progressive: Negative Statements

STUDENT BOOK P. 104

Notes on the Photo and Warm-up Activity

This man is resting his arms and head on the table. He may be at work. Recent research suggests that a nap in the middle of the day can help concentration. Some North American companies have started to provide "nap rooms" for their employees.

Discuss the Photo
- Ask students to discuss this situation in small groups or as a class:
    How do you think the man in this photo feels? Why? What isn't going well for him these days? Talk about the problems he is having. Say as much as you can about him. Have someone write down the group's ideas.
- Invite each group to read their sentences to the rest of the class.
- You can have students work as a class to brainstorm possible solutions to this man's problems.

The Present Progressive 59

9 Practice

A. Answers will vary. Probable answers:
1. The man and the woman aren't standing in an office. They are standing in the street.
2. The man isn't talking on the phone. The woman is talking on the phone.
3. The man isn't holding a book. He's holding an umbrella.
4. The man isn't looking at the cars. He's looking at the woman.
5. The man isn't wearing a raincoat. He's wearing a jacket.
6. The woman isn't holding her handbag. She's holding a telephone.
7. It isn't sunny. It's raining.
8. The woman isn't working on her computer. She's talking on the phone.

 CD2/9, 10 B. Play tracks 9 and 10 so students can check their answers. Then play track 10 again so they can listen and repeat the sentences.

Description Activity

✦ Make a negative and an affirmative statement in the present progressive about a student. For example:
Josep isn't wearing a blue sweater. He's wearing a green sweater.
Vanessa isn't listening to the teacher. She's talking to Miyako.

✦ Tell the students to continue, one by one, until all the students have said a pair of sentences.

4D The Present Progressive: Yes/No Questions

STUDENT BOOK P. 106

Notes on the Photo and Warm-up Activities

In this photo, a woman cyclist is standing next to her bicycle. She has a mountain bike. Mountain bikes have thicker tires and handlebars that go straight across. The woman is wearing bicycle leggings.

Discuss Exercise Activities

Ask students to discuss these questions in small groups or as a class:
What kind of exercise or activity do you enjoy doing? How often do you do it? When did you start doing it?

Role-play

✦ Put students in pairs. Present them with the following situation:
The cyclist in the photo is in the middle of a very long bicycle ride. She and many other cyclists are riding 100 miles together. The woman is taking a break. She has 25 miles remaining to the finish.

60 Unit 4

A newspaper reporter wants to interview her about the ride. Work with a partner and role-play the interview. One person is the reporter, and one person is the cyclist. Ask the cyclist *yes/no* questions about what she is doing now.

✦ Have students perform their role-plays for the class.

10 Practice

A. 1. d   2. f   3. a   4. e   5. c   6. b

  CD2/11, 12

B. Play tracks 11 and 12 so students can check their answers. Then play track 12 again so they can listen and repeat the questions and answers.

11 Pair Up and Talk

Is the bride wearing a white dress?	Yes, she is.
Is the bride holding flowers?	Yes, she is.
Is the mother standing next to the groom?	No, she isn't.
Are the people sitting?	No, they aren't.
Is the father wearing a suit?	Yes, he is.
Is the bride crying?	No, she isn't.
Is the mother crying?	No, she isn't.
Is the groom wearing a flower on his jacket?	Yes, he is.
Are the mother and father smiling?	Yes, they are.
Are the mother and father wearing hats?	No, they aren't.

Mime Game

✦ Write actions on separate slips of paper. Here is a partial list that you can add to:

frying eggs	making toast	making coffee	eating breakfast
changing a baby's diaper	bathing a baby	feeding a baby	rocking a baby
driving a car	riding a bicycle	riding a motorcycle	riding a surfboard
windsurfing	riding jet skis	downhill skiing	rollerblading
reading a newspaper	making a telephone call	watching a sad movie	

✦ Put them in a box or on the desk. Pick one and demonstrate the action to the students.

✦ Tell them to ask questions in the present progressive, for example, *Are you cooking something? Are you frying eggs?* Shake your head if the answer is wrong; nod if it is right, but don't talk until someone has guessed the action. Write the form of the question on the board so they get the idea.

The Present Progressive

♦ Have the students take turns miming the actions and asking questions. If the word is unfamiliar, tell the student who was miming it to write it on the board. Students can copy the list after the game is over.

♦ To practice the vocabulary, you can mime the actions the next day to see how many words they remember.

4E The Present Progressive: *Wh-* Questions

STUDENT BOOK P. 108

Notes on the Photo and Warm-up Activities

This man is talking on a cell phone and walking. Some people think there should be restrictions on how cell phones are used in public. Some people don't like to hear ringers on cell phones or conversations. In many places, there are already laws prohibiting cell phone use on public transportation or in restaurants and theaters.

Discuss the Photo

Put students in pairs. Ask them to discuss the following questions about the man in the photo:

Who is he talking to? Where is he walking? When is he having this conversation?
Why is he talking on his cell phone? How is he feeling?

Role-play

Instruct students to role-play a phone conversation between the man and the person he is talking to. Tell them to imagine that the man in the photo is trying to invite someone to lunch. In each role-play, the characters should say what they are doing at the moment. Invite students to perform their role-plays for the class.

12   Practice

A. 1. What is she watching?   5. Who is Peter talking to?
    2. What are you drinking?   6. How is Linda feeling?
    3. When is Sandra coming?   7. Where are the children playing?
    4. Why are you taking an umbrella? 8. Who are you talking to?

 CD2/13, 14   B. Play tracks 13 and 14 so students can check their answers. Then play track 14 again so they can listen and repeat the questions and answers.

62   Unit 4

Photo Activity

- Tell students the day before to bring some photos of their family or country to class. Have some photos on hand from magazines in case they forget.
- Have them exchange photos with a partner. Have the students think of a few *wh-* questions to ask their partner about the photo. They can write them down and give them to their partner.
- Each one answers the questions and then gives the paper back to their partner. Allow them to talk about the photos for a few more minutes.

4F Nonaction or Stative Verbs

STUDENT BOOK P. 109

Note: See page 253 of this Teacher's Manual for a supplementary Internet Activity Procedure and reproducible Worksheet for this section.

Notes on the Photo and Warm-up Activities

This photo shows the Eiffel Tower in Paris, France. This famous landmark was designed by A.G. Eiffel and built in 1889 for the Paris Exposition. A *landmark* is a building or monument that has historical, artistic, or cultural importance. The Eiffel Tower is made of iron and contains three platforms accessed by stairs and elevators. The tower is 984 feet (300 meters) high, excluding the antennae, and has 1,665 steps. Over 6 million people visit the Eiffel Tower every year.

Discuss Landmarks

- Ask the class if anyone has been to the Eiffel Tower.
- Introduce the term *landmark*, and explain that it is a building or monument that has historical, artistic, or cultural importance. Add that we usually think of landmarks as structures made by humans, rather than those created by nature.
- Brainstorm other famous landmarks, or have small groups brainstorm landmarks, and write the results on the board. Put students in groups to discuss the landmarks listed. Ask them to discuss these questions:

    Have you been to any of these places? If so, what do you remember about them? Have you seen any of these places in movies, on TV, or in books?

    Imagine you are at one of these places now. What do you think of it? What do you see, hear, smell, or taste there?

The Present Progressive

> **Write about a Landmark**
> - As an out-of-class assignment, have students visit a landmark or some other popular place in your city or town and take notes. Suggest students write down what they think of this place, including what they see, smell, hear, taste, and feel at this place. Suggest students write down what they like and don't like about the place.
> - Have students use their notes to write a short paragraph about this landmark.

Notes on Usage: exceptions

Point out that there are many exceptions to the list of non-action verbs on Student Book page 109. For example, we say *The roses smell wonderful*. This means that the roses have the quality of smelling wonderful. However, we can also say *I am smelling the roses now*. This sentence refers to the action of smelling rather than the quality.

13 Practice

A. 1. b 2. a 3. b 4. b 5. b 6. b 7. b 8. b

 CD2/15, 16 **B.** Play tracks 15 and 16 so students can check their answers. Then play track 16 again so they can listen and repeat the sentences.

14 Practice

A.
1. has
2. is wearing
3. is sitting
4. is reading
5. has
6. loves
7. buys

 CD2/17, 18 **B.** Play tracks 17 and 18 so students can check their answers. Then play track 18 again so they can listen and repeat the sentences.

 CD2/19 **C.** Answer: C

Notes on Vocabulary: non-action verbs

Here is a more complete list of non-action verbs in case you feel students are ready for them. You can write them on the board or give them examples in sentences.

Senses	Emotions	Descriptions	Mental Processes
feel	desire	be	believe *
hear *	dislike	cost	forget
look	hate *	have *	guess
see *	like *	look	imagine
smell *	love *	own	know *
sound	need *	seem	mean
taste *	want *	weigh	prefer *
	wish		remember *
			think *
			understand *

* Already mentioned in section 4F.

4G The Simple Present and the Present Progressive

STUDENT BOOK P. 112

Notes on the Photos and Warm-up Activity

These photos show a man and a woman stretching. They may be dancers. Fitness experts say that it's important for people to stretch their muscles before or after they exercise. Stretching makes people more flexible; more importantly, stretching helps to prevent injuries such as pulled muscles, strains, and sprains.

Discuss Exercise Practices

Have students talk about their exercise habits in small groups. Ask them to discuss these questions:
  What kind of exercise do you do? Where do you usually exercise?
  How often do you exercise? Do you stretch before you exercise? Why or why not?
  Do you do other things to prepare for exercise? Demonstrate some of these activities. For example, if you stretch, show how you stretch. Explain what you are doing.

15 Practice

A. A 1. Are
   2. studying
   3. 'm/am not studying
   B 1. are
   2. sitting

4. 'm/am cleaning
5. Do
6. wash
3. sit
4. don't/do not have

7. like

C	1. Do	3. speak	5. mean
	2. speak	4. does	6. means

D	1. do	3. don't/do not like
	2. write	4. call

E	1. are	3. 'm/am going	5. need
	2. going	4. Do	

F	1. Are	4. Do	7. write
	2. working	5. like	
	3. 'm/am sitting	6. love	

G	1. are	3. 'm/am going	5. want
	2. putting	4. Do	

H	1. Are	3. 'm/am waiting	5. know
	2. waiting	4. opens	6. want

I	1. are	3. don't walk	5. 's/is waiting
	2. walking	4. 'm/am hurrying	

J	1. Do	3. always take	5. don't have
	2. usually take	4. like	

K	1. Do	3. Is	5. 's/is working
	2. remember	4. still studying	6. has

 CD2/20, 21   **B.**   Play tracks 20 and 21 so students can check their answers. Then play track 21 again so they can listen and repeat the questions and answers.

Contrast Activity

✦ Tell the students to think of things they usually do and what they are doing right now.
✦ Write some examples on the board and have students talk to a partner about their ideas. They should include both affirmative and negative sentences. Here are some examples:

I usually wear red, but I'm not wearing red now.
I don't usually wear red, but I'm wearing red now.
I listen to the news every morning, but I'm not listening to it now.

✦ After they talk, they should write five sentences with their partner.

Note: Students may want to use present progressive for activities they are not presently doing. Try to keep them on track by focusing on activities going on in the classroom right now.

16 Practice

A. Answers will vary. Sample answers:
Maybe she is riding her bike now.
She is probably riding her bike now.
She always rides her bike to and from work.

B. Answers will vary. Sample answers:
1. Maybe her friend is studying now.
2. Her friend is probably studying now.
3. Her friend always studies in the afternoon.

17 Read

Long or short answers are possible. Long answers are given below.
1. The traveler is starting a journey soon.
2. The traveler has a dog.
3. The dog is by the door.
4. The dog is stretching and wagging its tail.
5. He thinks the dog is yawning.
6. He wants his dog to hurry up and get ready.
7. It is wagging its tail.
8. It is waiting for its master.

Listening Puzzle

STUDENT BOOK P. 117

A. CD2, 22

Answer: B. Thanksgiving

B. Students might discuss the following:
Turkeys are a well-known symbol of Thanksgiving. Usually people give their mothers gifts on Mother's Day.

C. CD2, 23

Reading Challenge: Water Festival

STUDENT BOOK P. 118

A. Answers will vary. Possible answers:
1. They are spraying water on each other.
2. They are celebrating the New Year.
3. It's a country in Asia.

C. **Paragraph 2:** are splashing and spraying, are singing and spraying, are spraying, are celebrating, are washing, are making

D. 1. D
E. 2. B   3. D   4. D   5. D
F. 6. A
G. 7. B

Writing: Describe Experiences

STUDENT BOOK P. 120

Step 1: Answers:
1. Rima is writing it.
2. They're staying in a big hotel on Waikiki beach.
3. They're writing the email from the hotel.
4. Tony is lying on the beach, and Jerry is swimming in the pool.
5. They're enjoying the vacation very much.

Writing Expansion

- If you have extra postcards, bring them to class for this activity. If you don't, bring index cards to class along with old magazines or travel brochures, scissors, and glue or tape.
- Pass out the items and tell students to cut out a photo from a magazine or travel brochure to glue onto the index card.
- They should use the photo as a basis for the writing assignment, i.e., if it is a mountain, they write about a mountain vacation; if it is a cruise ship, they write about a cruise vacation, and so on.
- When they are finished, they can put the cards on a bulletin board or make a mobile to hang from the ceiling so other students can read them.

Self-Test

STUDENT BOOK P. 121

A. 1. C   2. D   3. C   4. B   5. D   6. C   7. C   8. B   9. A   10. C
B. 1. A   2. B   3. C   4. A   5. B   6. C   7. A   8. B   9. A   10. B

Unit 5

Nouns and Pronouns

Unit Sections	Notes/Activities	SB page	TM page
5A Count and Noncount Nouns	Internet Activity; Notes on Usage: new uses of noncount nouns; Alphabet Activity	124	70
5B *A/An* and *Some*	Notes on Pronunciation: unstressed articles	125	71
5C *A/An* or *The*	Conversation Activity; Notes on Usage: exceptions with *a/an*	127	73
5D Generalizations	Dictation Activity	129	74
5E *Some* and *Any*	Country Activity	130	76
5F Measurement Words	Vocabulary Activity; Notes on Usage: *some*	132	77
5G Quantifying Expressions	Rhythm Activity	134	78
5H Quantity Questions	Tongue Twister Activity	136	80
5I *Whose* and Possessive Nouns	Notes on Usage: forming possessives; Frequently Asked Question	137	81
✦ Listening Puzzle: Food		141	83
✦ Reading Challenge: Penguins		142	83
✦ Writing: Describe Objects	Writing Expansion	144	83
✦ Self-Test	Answer Key	145	83

In **Unit 5**, count and noncount nouns are introduced, along with the definite (*the*) and indefinite (*a/an*) articles. *Some* and *any* are practiced and measurement words are taught with new vocabulary. A variety of quantifying expressions and quantity questions are introduced and practiced through exercises that encourage reinforcement of the structures. The final section presents possessive nouns and the *wh-* question word *whose*.

5A Count and Noncount Nouns

STUDENT BOOK P. 124

Note: See page 255 of this Teacher's Manual for a supplementary Internet Activity Procedure and reproducible Worksheet for this section.

Notes on the Photo and Warm-up Activities

Pizza is such a popular food in North America that many people think of it as American. Others believe that Italians invented pizza because it's very popular there as well. It's not really possible to pinpoint exactly where pizza was born because many countries contributed to its creation. People in ancient Egypt, Greece, the Middle East, and Rome all ate a flat bread with seasoning on top. Mozzarella cheese, which is widely used on pizza, was originally made in India from the milk of water buffalo. The tomato is from South America. In the late 1800s, Italians from the city of Naples invented something that looks much like the pizza we know today. Italian immigrants brought this delight to cities in the U.S. in the early 1900s.

Discuss Preferences

Have students work in small groups or as a class to discuss these questions:

What do you like on your pizza? What don't you like on your pizza?

Design a "Perfect Pizza"

✦ Ask students to design a "perfect pizza" that everyone in the group would like. Everyone must agree on the toppings. Ask these questions:

What do you want to put on top of it? What don't you want to put on top of it? What do you want to drink or eat with the pizza?

✦ Invite each group to share their perfect pizza with the class.

1 Practice

1. N   4. N   7. C   10. N   13. N   16. N   19. C
2. C   5. N   8. N   11. N   14. C   17. C   20. N
3. C   6. C   9. C   12. N   15. N   18. N

2 Your Turn

Answers will vary. Possible answers:

Count
1. apples
2. eggs
3. tomatoes

Noncount
4. milk
5. bread
6. coffee

Notes on Usage: new uses of noncount nouns

In recent years, some noncount nouns have also come into use as count nouns. Students may ask about the following informal uses of noncount nouns.

✦ At fast-food restaurants, people usually order *two coffees*, *three juices*, and *four milks* (instead of *two cups of coffee*, *three containers of juice*, and *four cartons of milk*).

✦ In college classrooms, professors sometimes say that the students have to turn in *ten homeworks* (instead of *ten homework assignments*) during the semester or they'll lose points.

✦ In offices, people may say that they have a lot of *emails* to answer (instead of *email messages*). *Email* is a noncount noun — we use *email* in the way that we use *mail*. For example, "I got a lot of email yesterday." Once in a while, students may hear *email* used as a count noun, in the way that we use *letter*. For example, "I sent four emails before lunch."

✦ In sports clubs, members frequently say, "Hey, let's play *a little/some* basketball/soccer/table tennis!" This means that they'd like to play the sport for a limited amount of time.

Alphabet Activity

✦ Write *a* on the board and elicit examples of count and noncount food nouns that begin with *a* (for example, *apple*, *apple juice*).

✦ Put students in pairs or small groups. Set a time limit of five minutes. Have students list count and noncount food nouns for each letter of the alphabet.

✦ Award the groups points for each letter of the alphabet for which they were able to list at least one count and one noncount food noun.

5B *A/An* and *Some*

STUDENT BOOK P. 125

Notes on the Photo and Warm-up Activities

This photo shows a typical lunch. There are also two straws and some napkins in the photo. Different cultures have different ideas about lunch. Some people eat a big sit-down meal at lunch; others prefer a small meal "on the go." Some eat lunch early in the day, some late in the day. Some people take one hour or more for lunch; some take fifteen minutes or have no lunch at all.

Discuss Lunch Habits

Invite students to discuss their lunch habits in small groups or as a class. Ask these questions:

What do you usually eat for lunch?

Do you think you eat healthy food or unhealthy food for lunch?

Do you usually buy lunch at a restaurant or make your own? If you buy lunch, where do you go?

Do you prefer a small lunch or a large one?

Do you like to eat early in the day, in the middle of the day, or late in the day?

How much time do you usually have for lunch?

Do you like to eat lunch alone or with friends?

Play a Memory Game

- Tell students they are going to play a memory game. Ask them to name different foods that are often eaten for lunch using *a/an* and *some*.
- Start with one student and go around in a circle, creating a list of food. Alternatively, toss a bean bag or some object to a student to start; that student will then toss the bean bag to another student, and so on.
- Each student must remember, in order, the previous foods that were stated, and then add a new food to the list. They must also remember to use *a/an* and *some* correctly.

Write a List

Tell students that they are going to make a big picnic lunch for their friends. Have them write a list of things they need to buy, using *a/an* and *some*. Remind them to list food items as well as other things they might want to take. Encourage them to include at least ten items.

3 Practice

1. some	5. some	9. some	13. some
2. some	6. an	10. some	14. an
3. a	7. some	11. some	15. some
4. a	8. a	12. some	16. a

4 Practice

A.
1. some 3. some 5. some 7. an 9. a
2. some 4. some 6. some 8. a

 CD2/24, 25 B. Play tracks 24 and 25 so students can check their answers. Then play track 25 again so they can listen and repeat the sentences.

 CD2/26 C. Answer: C

72 Unit 5

Notes on Pronunciation: unstressed articles

✦ Point out that the definite article *the* and the indefinite article *a* are rarely stressed. Their pronunciation is the schwa vowel /ə/ or "uh" sound.

✦ Often, *the* is pronounced as a simple lingual flap before consonants. For example:
  th'**cor**ner   th'**dog**   th'**kit**chen   th'**pan**da

✦ However, before vowels, it is longer and pronounced like /ði/ or "thee" sound. For example:
  /ði/ **ap**ple   /ði/ **egg**   /ði/ **oil**   /ði/ um**bre**lla

✦ *Some* also contains the schwa vowel /ə/ or "uh" sound, and it is rarely stressed. For example:
  s'm **cups**   s'm **but**ter   s'm **forks**   s'm **nap**kins

5c *A/An* or *The*

STUDENT BOOK P. 127

Notes on the Photo and Warm-up Activity

This is a type of dog called a bulldog. There are two primary breeds of bulldog: American and English. People used to use these dogs for work, but now they are kept as pets, and they can be expensive to buy. People own dogs for many different reasons. Some keep dogs for practical uses, such as to guard a home or to help people with disabilities. Some dogs receive special training to guide blind or deaf people. Some people keep dogs as companions. In some countries, dogs are not seen as pets, and they would never be allowed inside a house.

Talk about Pets

Students may have talked about dogs in **Unit 1**. Here is an opportunity for them to revisit and expand on the topic. Ask students to discuss some or all of these questions in small groups or as a class:

   Do you want a dog like the one in this picture? Why or why not?
   What kinds of dogs do you like? What kinds of dogs don't you like?
   Do you think dogs make good pets? Why or why not?
   Do you want a pet dog that lives in your home? Sleeps in your bed? Why or why not?
   Do you have a dog now, or did you have one in the past? Do you know someone who has a dog? Tell your group or the class about a dog that you know.

5 Practice

A. A 1. an   3. a   5. a   7. The   9. the   11. the
       2. The   4. The 6. a   8. the   10. a

    B 1. a   3. the 5. a   7. The   9. a
       2. a   4. the 6. a   8. a

    C 1. a   3. a   5. The 7. a
       2. an   4. an   6. the 8. a

 CD2/27, 28   B. Play tracks 27 and 28 so students can check their answers. Then play track 28 again so they can listen and repeat the sentences in A and the conversations in B and C.

Conversation Activity

✦ Put students in pairs to create new conversations. Encourage students to use *a/an* and *the* at least twice.
✦ Have volunteer pairs perform their conversations in front of the class. Have the class write down the articles + nouns that they hear.

Notes on Usage: exceptions with *a/an*

Most teachers tell students the general rule that *a* is used before consonants and *an* is used before vowels, but there are a few exceptions that you may want to review.

✦ The article *a* is used before the vowel *u* when it is long, or pronounced with a *y* sound before it; for example, *a university, a universal right, a unique opportunity*.
✦ The article *an* is used before the consonant *h* when it is silent; for example, *an hour, an herbal medicine, an honest man*.

5D Generalizations

STUDENT BOOK P. 129

Notes on the Photo and Warm-up Activity

These pink roses may be part of a bouquet of a dozen (12) roses. Sometimes people give a dozen roses on very special occasions, like weddings, anniversaries, or birthdays. In North America and in some other countries, red roses represent love and are usually given to girlfriends, boyfriends, or spouses. Yellow, white, or pink roses usually indicate friendship. However, different kinds and colors of flowers may have varying meanings in other cultures. In addition, different cultures might have separate ideas about when to give flowers to someone.

Discuss When to Give Flowers

Ask students to discuss some or all of these questions in small groups or as a class:

Have you ever given or received flowers as a gift? What was the occasion? What did the flowers look like?

Do you like giving or receiving flowers as a gift? Why or why not?

When should men buy flowers for women?

When should women buy flowers for men?

6 Practice

1. X, the   2. X, X, X   3. X, X, The   4. X, The

Dictation Activity

- To review nouns that are count and noncount (mass, abstract, others), put the following chart on the board:

Count	Noncount		
	Mass	Abstract	Others
banana	bread	beauty	advice

You can fill in a noun in each category to give students a hint in case they've forgotten.

- Divide the class into two groups and tell them that there will be a dictation.
- While one half of the class goes to the board, the other half dictates some of the nouns in the Form/Function box in **5A** to them. Tell students to say the words in random order.
- The students at the board may help each other, but they may not receive help from those sitting down.
- Then the groups change places; those seated should dictate the nouns in **Practice 1** to the students at the board, trying not to repeat the words already dictated from **5A**.
- After a few rounds, check the answers. You can keep score between the two groups, depending upon how competitive the students are.
- For an optional added challenge, announce that there will be a dictation test on count and noncount nouns the next day.

5E Some and Any

STUDENT BOOK P. 130

Notes on the Photo and Warm-up Activity

This lovely tropical scene looks like one that would be featured on the pages of a travel brochure or vacation resort website. Looking at it, one can almost feel the warm air, the gentle breeze, and the refreshing blue water. Many people, especially those who live in climates with cold, snowy winters, visit such places, ideally sometime during those long winter months. Some people come to just relax and soak up the sun, while others seek out water-related activities such as snorkeling, scuba diving, windsurfing, and deep-sea fishing.

Discuss Vacations

✦ Put students in pairs or small groups and ask them to imagine and discuss their personal dream vacation.

✦ Tell students that each partner or group should ask follow-up questions using *any*, and the person speaking should answer the questions with *any* or *some*. They can begin with these questions:

Where do you want to go to relax? What kind of vacation do you want? Do you want a relaxing vacation or an active vacation? Would you prefer a vacation alone, with friends, or with family?

7 Practice

1. any, any   2. any, any   3. any, some   4. any, any   5. any, some

8 Pair Up and Talk

Questions and answers will vary. Possible questions and answers:

A: Are there any bananas on the table?   B: Yes, there are (some bananas).
A: Are there any eggs?   B: Yes, there are (some eggs).
A: Is there any fish?   B: No, there isn't (any fish).
A: Are there any carrots?   B: No, there aren't (any carrots).

Country Activity

✦ Ask students to draw rough outlines of their countries, or bring a world map to class and tape it to the wall.

✦ Tell each student to think of the products of their countries, such as oil (petroleum), fish, rice, fruit, vegetables, flowers, gold, silver, and so on. Students from the same country or region can sit together and make a list.

✦ Tell the other students to take turns asking them questions, such as "Is there any oil (petroleum) in your country?" "Are there any flowers in your country?," while they give the answers.

- After all the students have finished, they can write a few sentences, some affirmative and some negative, about the products of their countries, such as "There's a lot of oil (petroleum) in Kuwait." "There aren't a lot of flowers in Kuwait."

5F Measurement Words

STUDENT BOOK P. 132

Notes on the Photo and Warm-up Activities

This photo shows a tall glass of water. Sometimes people drink strong coffee with a glass of water.

Take a Survey

- Write these questions on the board:
  How many cups of coffee do you drink each day? When is your favorite time of day to drink coffee?
- Have students stand and walk around the room to ask each question of 10 classmates. Remind students to record their classmates' answers.
- Have students tally the results. For example, they might write *0 cups – 2 (people), 1 cup – 4 (people), 2 cups – 3 (people), 3 or more cups – 2 (people)*.
- Discuss the results. Elicit answers to the questions from the class.

Discuss Alternatives to Coffee

- Point out that some people worry that they drink too much coffee.
- Ask students to work in groups and discuss what else people could drink, eat, or do for energy instead of drinking coffee. Choose one person in each group to write down the group's ideas.
- Ask each group to report their ideas to the class. The group with the most ideas should read their list first. The other groups should listen and check off items that they have also. Ask the other groups to read any items from their lists that the first group did not have.

9 Practice

A.
1. a bar of soap
2. a roll of toilet paper
3. a can of tomatoes
4. a carton of milk
5. a loaf of bread
6. a <u>box</u>/a bowl of cereal
7. a box/<u>bag</u>/pound of sugar
8. a <u>bottle</u>/tube of shampoo
9. a pack of batteries
10. a tube of toothpaste
11. a jar of mayonnaise
12. a bottle of olive oil
13. a pound/<u>piece</u>/slice of cheese
14. a carton/can/<u>bottle</u> of juice

CD2/29, 30   **B.** Play tracks 29 and 30 so students can check their answers. Then play track 30 again so they can listen and repeat the phrases.

Note: While all of the options in **Part A** are correct, students will hear only one option.

10 Pair Up and Talk

Conversations will vary. Possible items:

I have a carton of juice.   I have a jar of sauce.   I have a loaf of bread.

Vocabulary Activity

- Put the students into pairs. Tell Student A to make a list of 10 measurement words, such as *a bar of* _____ , *a sheet of* _____ , *a bowl of* _____ , on a piece of paper.
- Tell Student B to make a list of 10 food or drink items, such as _____ *milk*, _____ *toothpaste*, _____ *tea*, on a piece of paper. Write some examples on the board.
- Have them exchange lists and fill in the blanks, and then exchange again to check their partner's answers.

Notes on Usage: *some*

Point out that people would be just as likely to say *I have some salt* as to use a measurement word. Measurement words allow speakers to specify amounts of noncount nouns.

5G Quantifying Expressions

STUDENT BOOK P. 134

Notes on the Photo and Warm-up Activities

This young man is jogging or running. Jogging is a little slower than running, but both are aerobic activities that help people build endurance and increase their energy levels. A lot of people like running and jogging because they are inexpensive compared to other sports and forms of exercise.

Discuss Healthy and Unhealthy Habits

Have students discuss these questions in small groups or as a class:

What are some of your healthy habits? What do you do and eat to stay healthy?

What are some of your unhealthy habits? What unhealthy things do you sometimes do and eat?

78 Unit 5

	11	**Practice**						

A. 1. much 3. many 5. much 7. much
   2. much 4. many 6. much 8. much

 CD2/31, 32 B. Play tracks 31 and 32 so students can check their answers. Then play track 32 again so they can listen and repeat the sentences.

	12	**Practice**

A. 1. a few   3. a few   5. a little   7. a few
   2. a few   4. a little 6. a little   8. a few

 CD2/33, 34 B. Play tracks 33 and 34 so students can check their answers. Then play track 34 again so they can listen and repeat the sentences.

 CD2/35 C. Answers: 1. True 2. False 3. False 4. True

Rhythm Activity

✦ This is a game to practice the quantifying expressions. It works best when students are in a circle.

✦ Tell students that they are going on a trip to the country. Elicit things they might see, like *grass*, *trees*, *flowers*, *water*, *birds*, *woods*, *horses*, and write them on the board in columns of count and noncount nouns.

✦ Start by tapping your hands to establish a rhythm and say each line, having students repeat it after you:

T: Goin' on a field trip.	S: Goin' on a field trip.
T: There's a lot of grass.	S: There's a lot of grass.
T: Can't go over it.	S: Can't go over it.
T: Can't go under it.	S: Can't go under it.
T: Can't go around it.	S: Can't go around it.
T: Gotta go through it.	S: Gotta go through it.

✦ The game continues with the next set of phrases, like *many trees, a lot of flowers, a little water, a few birds, some woods, some horses,* and so on, making sure to differentiate between singular and plural phrases (*There's a little water* vs *There are a few birds*). Allow students to try leading a round.

Nouns and Pronouns 79

5H Quantity Questions

STUDENT BOOK P. 136

Notes on the Photo and Warm-up Activities

Orange juice, coffee, milk—these are all typical breakfast drinks in the United States. Popular breakfast foods include cereal and milk, toast, bagels, pancakes, and eggs. A walk down the "cereal aisle" in a typical U.S. supermarket shows just how popular and convenient dry cereal is. From the sweet varieties designed to appeal to children, to the health-conscious choices made from whole grains, there seems to be a type of cereal for everyone.

Discuss Breakfast in Different Cultures

- Put students in pairs or groups to list the food and drink that people typically have for breakfast in countries they know about.
- Elicit ideas and write them on the board. Ask quantity questions (for example, *how many eggs do people often eat?*) and add quantity words to the food nouns on the board.

13 Pair Up and Talk

Conversations will vary. Sample conversation:
A: How many apples do you eat?
B: I eat a lot of apples.

Tongue Twister Activity

- Write the two tongue twisters below on the board and explain them to the students.
- Say them slowly, line by line, stressing the words in boldface (you can tap or clap to show the stress). Have students repeat them, tapping or clapping the stressed syllables with you.
- Ask students to say them as a class and then as individuals, as fast as they can.
- Put students in language groups (all Chinese speakers, all Spanish speakers, and so forth) and ask them to think of a tongue twister in their native language and say it for the class.

How much **wood** would a **wood**chuck **chuck**,
If a **wood**chuck **could** chuck **wood**?

If **Pe**ter **Pi**per **pick**ed a **peck** of **pick**led **pep**pers,
How many **pick**led **pep**pers did **Pe**ter **Pi**per **pick**?

80   Unit 5

51   *Whose* and Possessive Nouns

STUDENT BOOK P. 137

Notes on the Photo and Warm-up Activity

This man and woman are enjoying a walk on the beach. Dogs are not always allowed on public beaches in the U.S., especially during the summer.

Practice Asking Questions with *Whose*

- Collect personal belongings—for example, a backpack, pens, books, a jacket—from the students in your class. Try to gather one item from each student.
- Call on students and ask questions with *whose*. For example, *Whose backpack is this?* If necessary, cue students by pointing to the object's owner.
- Continue until everyone has had a chance to answer. Then call volunteers to the front of the room to ask questions of their classmates.

14   Practice

A.
1. Whose bicycle is this?   It's Mike's.
2. Whose sneakers are these?   They're Ted's.
3. Whose hat is this?   It's Jane's.
4. Whose house is this?   It's Sandra's.
5. Whose ball is this?   It's Timmy's.
6. Whose car is this?   It's my parents'.

 CD2/36, 37

B. Play tracks 36 and 37 so students can check their answers. Then play track 37 again so they can listen and repeat the questions and answers.

Notes on Usage: forming possessives

Even native speakers are often confused when they need to make possessives of nouns ending in *-s*. Point out that if it's a plural noun (e.g., *boys*), we only add an apostrophe, but if it is a singular noun ending in *-s* (e.g., *recess*, *floss*), we add an apostrophe and an *s*. This is true for names ending in *s* also (e.g., *Smiths'* and *Bliss's*).

- Do not confuse *'s = is* with *'s = possessive*.
- We can use *whose* with or without a noun: *Whose jacket is this? Whose is this?*

15 Practice

1. mother's
2. parents'
3. husband's
4. girls'
5. Kate's
6. children's

16 Practice

1. What's your teacher's name?
2. What's your school's name?
3. What's your partner's name?
4. What's your best friend's name?
5. What's your mother's/father's name?
6. What's your parents' address?

17 Your Turn

Answers will vary. Answers should begin as follows:

My teacher's name is …
My school's name is …
My partner's name is …

My best friend's name is …
My mother's name is … /My father's name is …
My parents' address is …

18 Read

Long or short answers are possible. Long answers are given below.

1. They talk about many things.
2. He invites his friends for dinner.
3. No, there isn't.
4. They bring a big pot of food.
5. He says, "The sound of dishes when you are hungry — is the best sound!"

Frequently Asked Question

Students may ask about the difference between the *'s* possessive and the *of the* _____ possessive.

✦ The ***'s*** possessive is usually used for:

personal nouns:	the teacher**'s** book	places:	Japan**'s** future
collective nouns:	the nation**'s** security	time words:	today**'s** news

✦ The ***of the*** _____ possessive is usually used for:

inanimate nouns: the roof **of the** house   the title **of the** movie

82 Unit 5

Listening Puzzle

STUDENT BOOK P. 141

A. CD2, 38

Answer: B. pizza

B. Students might discuss the following points:
Sandwiches are usually not baked in an oven. Pizza is a popular food around the world.

C. CD2, 39

Reading Challenge: Penguins

STUDENT BOOK P. 142

A. **1.** where it's cold/in Antarctica/south of the equator **2.** 18

C. **Paragraph 1:** snow, ice; **Paragraph 2:** skin, cold, food, food, sea

D. **1.** C **2.** A
E. **3.** B **4.** D **5.** B **6.** A
F. **7.** A
G. **8.** A

Writing: Describe Objects

STUDENT BOOK P. 144

Writing Expansion

✦ Have students ask and answer questions about the picture using the quantifying expressions and quantity questions from this unit. They may work in pairs or small groups.

✦ Have students write a paragraph about what is on the table. They should write the sentences that they just practiced with their partners or groups.

Self-Test

STUDENT BOOK P. 145

A. **1.** C **2.** B **3.** D **4.** A **5.** C **6.** B **7.** C **8.** A **9.** B **10.** A
B. **1.** B **2.** D **3.** D **4.** C **5.** A **6.** D **7.** D **8.** B **9.** A **10.** B

Nouns and Pronouns

Unit 6
The Simple Past

Unit Sections		Notes/Activities	SB page	TM page
6A	The Simple Past: Regular Verbs	Photo Activity	148	85
6B	Past Time Expressions	Frequently Asked Questions	151	87
6C	Spelling of Regular Simple Past Verbs	Alphabet Activity	154	88
6D	Pronunciation of -ed: /t/, /d/, and /id/	Notes on Pronunciation: linking and reductions	160	90
6E	The Simple Past: Irregular Verbs	Story Activity	163	92
6F	The Simple Past: Negative	Previewing Activity	167	94
6G	The Simple Past: Yes/No Questions	Chant Activity	170	96
6H	The Simple Past: Wh- Questions	Internet Activity	173	98
6I	The Simple Past: Time Clauses with Before and After	Timeline Activity	179	100
✦	Listening Puzzle: Appliances		183	102
✦	Reading Challenge: The Terracotta Army		184	103
✦	Writing: Narrate Events	Writing Expansion	186	103
✦	Self-Test	Answer Key	187	103

Unit 6 introduces the simple past, starting with the spelling and pronunciation of regular verbs. The unit teaches and practices important past time expressions that serve as markers for the simple past, such as *yesterday*, *last night*, or *two hours ago*. The text provides extra practice in simple past spelling and pronunciation, focusing on the contrast between the /t/, the /d/, and the /id/ endings.

The unit then introduces irregular verbs, negatives, *yes/no* questions, and *wh-* questions. For each section, the text illustrates the correct form, explains how and when we use it, and provides ample practice.

The unit concludes with time clauses using *before* and *after*.

6A The Simple Past: Regular Verbs

STUDENT BOOK P. 148

Notes on the Photos and Warm-up Activities

- The top photo shows **a smiling nurse**. Around her neck she is wearing a stethoscope, which is used to check heart rate. The profession of nursing has changed a lot over the years. Nurses now take on many responsibilities that used to be reserved for doctors. In addition to checking blood pressure, temperature, and weight, nurses also give physical examinations and injections, and use various kinds of medical equipment and machines. Nurses work in many different places, from small doctors' offices, to schools, to large hospitals. And nursing is not an occupation just for women. In North America and elsewhere, men are increasingly becoming registered nurses.

- In the bottom photo **a man** is standing in the rain. In the background people are walking down the street carrying umbrellas. Umbrellas have been around for a long time—over 4,000 years! The first umbrellas were actually paper parasols. These parasols were designed to shade people from the sun. The Chinese were the first to use parasols as protection from the rain by putting wax on the paper parasols.

Role-play Injuries

- Ask students to brainstorm types of injuries or reasons people go to see a doctor. Write these injuries and reasons on the board.
- Next, put students in groups of three. Present them with the following situation:

    One of you is the nurse in this photo. One of you is a patient with an injury, and one of you is a doctor. Role-play a conversation. First, the patient will tell the nurse what happened. The nurse will take notes. The doctor will be standing outside the room where he or she cannot hear. The nurse will then tell the patient's information to the doctor while the patient stands outside the room. Finally, the doctor will tell the patient what the nurse said and ask if the information is correct.

EXAMPLE

Patient (to the nurse): I hurt my ankle. This morning I fell down the stairs and I twisted it. It turned red and it swelled up. After that, I put ice on it.

Nurse (to the doctor): The man in Room 2 hurt his ankle. This morning he fell down the stairs and twisted it. It turned red and swelled up. After that, he put ice on it.

Doctor (to the patient): Let me see if I understand what happened. You hurt your ankle. This morning you fell down the stairs and twisted it. It turned red and swelled up. After that, you put ice on it. Is that correct?

Memory Game

- Ask students to answer these questions in small groups or as a class:

    What do you like to do when it rains? What did you do the last time it rained?

- Call on a student to say one sentence about what he or she did the last time it rained. Ask another student to repeat what each previous student said and then add his or her own sentence. Continue around the room. The information can be factual or creative.

The Simple Past

1 Practice

A.
1. rained   4. opened   7. worked   10. stayed
2. waited   5. listened   8. called   11. called
3. walked   6. talked   9. ordered   12. boarded, arrived

B. Answers will vary. Sample answer:
Peter is going on vacation. He is meeting his girlfriend in Rio de Janeiro.

2 Practice

1. worked   4. received   7. wasn't/was not   9. solved
2. works   5. listens   8. plays, stayed   10. called
3. call   6. answers, asked

3 Pair Up and Talk

Conversations will vary. Sample conversation:
A: What did you do last week?
B: Last week, I cleaned my apartment. I played tennis with a friend. I listened to jazz music. What did you do?
A: I worked on homework all weekend!

Photo Activity

- Ask students to look at the top photo on page 148 again.
- Write the words on the board and elicit sentences from students. Write the sentences correctly next to the words.

talk/doctors	Erika talked to doctors.
ask/patients/questions	She asked the patients many questions.
listen to/answers	She listened to their answers.
give/medicine/patients	She gave some medicine to the patients.
type/comments/computer	She typed some comments on the computer.

6B Past Time Expressions

STUDENT BOOK P. 151

Notes on the Photo and Warm-up Activities

This photo is a winter scene of snow on trees and grass. Snow can be beautiful and fun, but a heavy snowfall can shut down an entire city for days. The train in the picture is a freight train, not a passenger train.

Report on a Snowstorm

Put students in pairs. Present them with the following situation:

Look at the photo. Imagine that a big snowstorm just hit your city or town. One of you is a TV news reporter, and the other is a person who lives in the city and has had problems because of the storm. The TV news reporter will talk about the snowstorm and mention when things happened. The reporter will then ask the citizen to describe what happened and when. After discussing ideas for your conversation, work together to write down what each of you will say. Practice your news interview, then perform it for the class.

Write about a Weather Event

Present your students with the following prompt:

Think of a big weather event that you experienced in the past. For example, were you ever in a big snowstorm, a rainstorm, a hurricane, a tornado, a heat wave, an earthquake, or something else? What happened? When did it happen? What did you do? What did other people do? Write at least six sentences about your experience.

4 Practice

A.
1. last
2. last
3. yesterday
4. ago
5. ago
6. last
7. yesterday
8. Yesterday
9. last
10. ago
11. ago
12. ago
13. yesterday
14. last
15. ago
16. last

 CD3/2, 3

B. Play tracks 2 and 3 so students can check their answers. Then play track 3 again so they can listen and repeat the conversation.

C. She's surprised Mary Jane is marrying Tony.

5 Practice

A. Answers will vary. Sample answers:
Three months ago, I was in California.
Last year, I graduated from high school.
Last night, I watched a movie on TV.

B. Answers will vary. Sample answers:

Yesterday morning, there was a fire alarm in her/his dorm.

One hour ago, she/he had breakfast.

Twenty minutes ago, she/he drank some coffee.

Frequently Asked Questions

✦ Students may ask, "Why don't you say *ago three days*, *since three days*, or *before three days* like in other languages?"

In some other languages, a preposition comes before the time words, so *three days ago* is *hace tres días* in Spanish or *seit drei Tage* in German. In English, we say *three days ago* (not *since* or *before*), so this difference should be pointed out to make students aware of the construction.

✦ Students may also ask, "Why don't you say *night last* or *month next*, like in Latinate languages?"

In English, we say the adjective before the noun, so it's *last night* or *next month*.

6c Spelling of Regular Simple Past Verbs

STUDENT BOOK P. 154

Notes on the Photo and Warm-up Activity

This is a photo of a baby who has just stopped crying. Babies usually cry when they are hungry, when they don't want to be alone, when they are ill or in pain, or when they are uncomfortable. Crying is a baby's way of telling the parents or caretaker what he or she needs.

Write about Caring for a Child

✦ Have students think about a time they cared for a child or they were cared for. Ask questions:

Did you ever take care of a baby or a small child? Did you ever have a problem with a child crying or behaving badly? What happened? What did you do? How did you try to solve the problem?

✦ Have students write at least six sentences about their experience. If they have never taken care of a baby or small child, have students write about the experience of someone they know, or write about a time in their childhood when someone took care of them.

6 Practice

A.
1. added
2. carried
3. allowed
4. showed
5. counted
6. erased
7. fitted
8. married
9. died
10. failed
11. stopped
12. hurried

13.	waited	15.	cried	17.	studied	19.	cooked
14.	stayed	16.	dropped	18.	tasted	20.	worried

CD3/4, 5 B. Play tracks 4 and 5 so students can check their answers. Then play track 5 again so they can listen and repeat the words.

7 Practice

List A
1. listened
2. mixed
3. smiled
4. kissed
5. picked
6. shopped
7. tipped
8. replied
9. admitted

List B
1. started
2. studied
3. fixed
4. referred
5. hugged
6. touched
7. lived
8. clapped
9. offered

8 Practice

Add -ed: listened, mixed, picked, started, fixed, touched, offered, kissed
Add -d: smiled, lived
Change y to i and add -ed: studied, replied
Double the consonant and add -ed: hugged, shopped, tipped, admitted, referred, clapped

9 Your Turn

Answers will vary.

10 Practice

A.
1. arrived
2. rained
3. carried
4. shopped
5. preferred
6. visited
7. entered
8. climbed
9. walked
10. watched
11. decided
12. enjoyed

CD3/6, 7 B. Play tracks 6 and 7 so students can check their answers. Then play track 7 again so they can listen and repeat the sentences.

The Simple Past 89

11 Practice

A.
1.	are	11.	called	21.	has
2.	'm/am	12.	asked	22.	was
3.	arrived	13.	wanted	23.	was
4.	'm/am walking	14.	are	24.	walked
5.	'm/am talking	15.	are	25.	offered
6.	sounds	16.	staying	26.	allowed
7.	Are	17.	'm/am staying	27.	danced
8.	thinking	18.	have	28.	enjoyed
9.	'm/am thinking	19.	Does	29.	danced
10.	have	20.	have		

CD3/8, 9 B. Play tracks 8 and 9 so students can check their answers. Then play track 9 again so they can listen and repeat the conversation.

CD3/10 C. Answer: C

D. Conversations will vary.

Alphabet Activity

✦ Divide the students into groups of three or four. Have one person take a piece of paper and write the alphabet down the left margin.

✦ Have the other students look at the lists of verbs in sections **6c** and **6d** and try to find a verb for each letter, writing it in the simple past, for example, *acted, baked, carried, dipped,* and so forth.

6D Pronunciation of -*ed*: /t/, /d/, and /id/

STUDENT BOOK P. 160

Notes on the Photo and Warm-up Activity

This photo shows students graduating from high school or from college. They are wearing their graduation *regalia*. It consists of a *gown*, or robe, which is usually either black or one of the school colors, and a *cap*, which is flat and square on top. A *tassel* is worn on the top of the hat, and is made of colored threads. Traditionally, students graduating from North American high schools and colleges wear the tassel to one side before they graduate. After the ceremony, they move the tassel to the other side to show that they have graduated.

> **Discuss Graduations**
>
> Ask students to discuss these questions in small groups or as a class:
>
> Have you ever participated in a graduation ceremony, or do you know someone who has? Who graduated? What did they graduate from? What happened before, during, and after the ceremony? What did the graduating students wear? How did they celebrate?

12 Practice

A.
1. opened /d/
2. pointed /id/
3. yawned /d/
4. stayed /d/
5. showered /d/
6. shaved /d/
7. dressed /t/
8. finished /t/
9. walked /t/
10. ordered /d/
11. enjoyed /d/
12. started /id/
13. called /d/
14. invited /id/
15. arrived /d/
16. watched /t/
17. laughed /t/
18. stopped /t/
19. wanted /id/
20. returned /d/

CD3/11, 12   B. Play tracks 11 and 12 so students can check their answers. Then play track 12 again so they can listen and repeat the sentences.

13 Practice

A.
1. played /d/
2. washed /t/
3. dried /d/
4. folded /id/
5. cooked /t/
6. turned on /d/
7. answered /d/
8. talked /t/
9. needed /id/
10. shopped /t/
11. picked /t/
12. watched /t/

CD3/13, 14   B. Play tracks 13 and 14 so students can check their answers. Then play track 14 again so they can listen and repeat the sentences.

14 Pair Up and Talk

Conversations will vary. Sample conversation:
A: What did you do yesterday?
B: Yesterday, I finished Practice 10 in my grammar book. Then I enjoyed a soccer game in the park. What did you do yesterday?
A: Yesterday, I needed to call my family. Then I watched TV.

Notes on Pronunciation: linking and reductions

Explain two features of pronunciation to the students regarding the simple past:

✦ **Linking:** The /t/ or /d/ sound at the end of some simple past forms should be linked to the following sound if it is a vowel sound or a similar /t/ or /d/ sound. For example:

We **bought a** ticket to Washington.   We **paid in** cash.
We **got to** the train station on time.   We **rode to** Washington.

✦ **Reductions:** When native speakers use *did* in questions, they sometimes reduce it. For example:

| Did you eat? | **Jeet**? | Did you see that? | **Didja** see that? |
| No, did you? | No, **ju**? | Did he call you? | **Didi** call ya? |

6E The Simple Past: Irregular Verbs

STUDENT BOOK P. 163

Notes on the Photo and Warm-up Activity

This is a photo of a chimpanzee, which is a type of great ape. Chimpanzees are the closest relatives of humans, sharing 99 percent of our genetic make-up! Chimps are well known for being intelligent, social, communicative, and even entertaining, often appearing in movies or circus acts. They have a variety of facial expressions and can learn certain behaviors. Wild chimps live in Africa, primarily in rain forests or in the open savannah, but they are an endangered species in their native environment. One reason they're endangered is that their habitat, the rain forest, is being destroyed. Only 100,000 to 200,000 chimpanzees exist in the wild today.

Role-play

Divide students into three groups. Each group represents a different organization and wants to use the chimp on page 163 for specific reasons. In their groups, have students discuss why they want the chimp and list the reasons they should have it. They can imagine that they have worked with chimpanzees in the past and talk about what happened with those experiences. Ask each group to share their reasons and examples with the other two groups.

GROUP A - *Researchers who want to save the chimpanzee:* You want to leave this chimp in Africa, in the wild.
GROUP B - *Movie studio executives:* You want to bring the chimp to the United States and use it in Hollywood movies.
GROUP C - *Zoo officials:* You want to take the chimp to the United States and put it in a zoo.

15 Practice

A.
1. flew
2. found
3. wasn't / was not
4. was
5. ate
6. drank
7. took
8. heard
9. made
10. were
11. spoke
12. told
13. taught
14. took
15. saw
16. went
17. bought
18. sat
19. had
20. spent
21. thought

 CD3/15, 16 **B.** Play tracks 15 and 16 so students can check their answers. Then play track 16 again so they can listen and repeat the sentences.

 CD3/17 **C.** Answer: B

16 Practice

A.
1. loved
2. finished
3. worked
4. invited
5. saved
6. went
7. was
8. met
9. was
10. became
11. traveled
12. began
13. lived
14. went
15. saw
16. stood
17. came
18. began
19. gave
20. discovered
21. eat/ate
22. kill/are killing
23. cut/are cutting
24. studied
25. travels/traveling
26. talks/talking

CD3/18, 19 **B.** Play tracks 18 and 19 so students can check their answers. Then play track 19 again so they can listen and repeat the sentences.

17 Practice

1. travels
2. talks
3. heard
4. went
5. began
6. lived
7. came
8. became

Story Activity

✦ Tell the students you are going to write a class story on the board in the simple past. You can either pass out slips of paper with verbs on them that students have to use, or simply let them choose their own verbs.

✦ Begin by writing the first sentence on the board, using the name of a student in the class. For example:
Yesterday, Yoshi went to the bank and took out some money.

✦ The next student might write a sentence like the following:
He walked down the street to a travel agency and bought a ticket.

The Simple Past 93

- ✦ Have the students continue the story, reminding them that it has to be logical.
- ✦ After all the students write their sentences, make corrections and then ask the students to read each one in turn. You can also ask them to make up questions—written or oral—in pairs for more practice.

6F The Simple Past: Negative

STUDENT BOOK P. 167

Notes on the Photo and Warm-up Activities

In this old 1940s photo, a woman is washing dishes in the sink and drying them by hand. In North America, dishwashers didn't start becoming part of people's homes until the 1950s. Many types of inventions have been created to make our home lives easier. However, some people think that they actually create even more work for us!

Brainstorm Inventions

- ✦ Write the word *invention* on the board and be sure that students understand the meaning.
- ✦ Put students in groups and ask them to brainstorm as many inventions used in or around the home as possible (for example, *dishwasher, vacuum cleaner, clothes dryer, lawn mower, leaf blower, personal computer*). One person in each group should write down the group's ideas. Then ask the groups to rank the items on their list from least to most useful; the number 1 item should be the most useful.
- ✦ Ask each group to share their top three inventions and explain why they chose them. They should explain what people did in the past and how these inventions changed that behavior.
- ✦ Next, ask students to work in groups and discuss these questions:

    Does this invention give us more free time? Why or why not? Is there anything negative about it?

Write about Chores

The woman in the photo is smiling cheerfully as she washes and dries dishes. Everyone seems to have dreaded chores, and chores they rather enjoy. Point this out to students, and then present the following situation:

What housework or chores did you do when you were younger? What chores didn't you do? Did you like doing these chores? Why or why not? Write at least six sentences about your responsibilities at home in the past.

18 Practice

A.
1. Children didn't wear jeans.
2. People didn't watch a lot of television.
3. Many mothers stayed at home.
4. Many mothers didn't work outside the home.
5. People didn't eat fast food.
6. Homes didn't have computers.
7. Children didn't play video games.
8. People didn't use microwaves.
9. People didn't drink a lot of soda.
10. Mothers read books to their children.

B. Answers will vary. Sample answers:
Women didn't wear jeans. Women wore dresses. Life was not good because people had to do more physical work. They didn't have modern machines like today. But life was good because people appreciated simpler things.

19 Practice

Answers will vary. Possible answers:
1. said, didn't say hello to her
2. asked, he didn't answer her
3. called, he didn't call her back
4. wrote, he didn't say anything about it
5. gave, he didn't thank her for it
6. went, he wasn't happy to see her
7. smiled, he didn't smile at her
8. waited, he didn't show up
9. kissed, he turned away
10. invited, he said *no*

Previewing Activity

To preview **Practice 20,** put some or all of the following statements on the board and elicit answers. As a class or in small groups, brainstorm more statements and answers. Encourage students to explore a wide range of topics: science and technology, the arts, nature, current events. You can also have them do this previewing activity and **Practice 20** in the computer lab using an online encyclopedia.

STATEMENT: Diego Rivera painted small paintings.
ANSWER: False. Diego Rivera painted murals. They were very big!

STATEMENT: Dinosaurs didn't eat meat.
ANSWER: False. The tyrannosaurus rex ate meat.

STATEMENT: J. K. Rowling wrote the Harry Potter series.
ANSWER: True.

STATEMENT: The United States hosted the 2008 Summer Olympics.
ANSWER: False. China hosted the 2008 Summer Olympics.

The Simple Past

20 Practice

Answers will vary.

21 Your Turn

Paragraphs will vary. Sample paragraph:

I was born in Cairo. My family lived in an apartment in the city. I studied at a school near my house. I played in the park with my friends after school. Sometimes they came to my house and stayed for dinner. When I passed my exams, I went to the university there and started to study biology.

6G The Simple Past: Yes/No Questions

STUDENT BOOK P. 170

Notes on the Photo and Warm-up Activity

This senior couple is walking in an area near the ocean. Many older people in the United States retire in warm places such as Florida and Arizona. Some senior citizens travel to sunny places only in the winter. They are called "snow birds." Older people sometimes face challenges both in their homes and when they leave, including occasional memory loss.

Role-play

Put students in pairs. Present them with the following situation:

> Imagine that you are the couple on page 170. One of you is having memory problems. You are having trouble remembering information from the past, such as people's names and places. You're also having trouble remembering whether or not you did basic things around the house, like lock the door. Your friend will ask you *yes/no* questions about what you did before you left the house to go for a walk. Because you are having problems with your memory, you will also ask your friend *yes/no* questions about what you did or didn't do before leaving the house. Perform your role-play for the class.

EXAMPLE

DORIS: Did you lock the door?
ALBERT: Yes, I did.
DORIS: Did you turn off the lights?
ALBERT: No, I didn't. Wait! Maybe I did. I'm sorry. I don't remember. Did I mail my letters?
DORIS: Yes, you did. I saw you mail them this morning.
ALBERT: Did I lose my glasses?
DORIS: No, you didn't. They're right here in your pocket.

22 Practice

A.
1. Did
2. enjoy
3. didn't
4. didn't /did not like
5. Did
6. like
7. didn't
8. Did
9. like
10. didn't
11. rained
12. Was
13. wasn't
14. called
15. answered
16. Did
17. visit
18. didn't
19. were
20. was
21. Did
22. go
23. did
24. didn't /did not buy
25. was
26. did
27. have
28. didn't
29. was
30. was
31. wasn't/was not
32. was

CD3/20, 21

B. Play tracks 20 and 21 so students can check their answers. Then play track 21 again so they can listen and repeat the conversation.

23 Pair Up and Talk

Questions and answers will vary. Sample questions and answers:
A: Did you cook a meal yesterday?   B: Yes, I did. I cooked dinner.
A: Did you go to the library yesterday?   B: No, I didn't. I worked all day.

24 Pair Up and Talk

Questions and answers will vary. Sample questions and answers:
A: Did you visit any museums?   B: Yes, we did. We visited the National Gallery.
A: Did you eat in restaurants?   B: Yes, we did. We ate some delicious food.
A: Did you go shopping?   B: Yes, we did. We bought a few souvenirs.

25 Practice

✦ Model the activity, which is based on the popular game "20 questions." First think of a famous person from the past. Then have students ask *yes/no* questions using the simple past to try to figure out who it is: *Did he or she live in the twentieth century? Was it a man? Did he play a sport?* Challenge students to guess the person in 20 questions or less.

✦ After students have guessed your famous person, call on a student to choose a famous person. Elicit *yes/no* questions from the class. Continue with several more students.

The Simple Past

✦ Here are a few suggestions of famous people. You can either put these names on slips of paper and pass them out to students, or have them think of famous people on their own.

Princess Diana	Marie Curie	John Lennon	Jane Austen
Mother Theresa	Leo Tolstoy	Napoleon	Indira Ghandi
Roberto Clemente	Audrey Hepburn	Juan Peron	Mao Zedong
Emperor Hirohito	Cleopatra	Walt Disney	Winston Churchill

Chant Activity

✦ Here is a simple chant that will encourage students to practice the simple past. Write the sentences below on the board, marking the syllables that are stressed.

✦ Tap or clap the rhythm as you say it, with students repeating each line, also tapping or clapping.

✦ Then tell the students to say it, pointing to each line. You can say it several times by asking different sides of the room to alternate questions and answers.

✦ The students can make up more sentences if they enjoy the activity.

Did you <u>buy</u> any <u>cheese</u>?	No, I <u>did</u>n't, I for<u>got</u>.
Did you <u>buy</u> some <u>bread</u>?	Yes, I <u>did</u>, yes, I <u>did</u>.
Did you <u>walk</u> the <u>dog</u>?	No, I <u>did</u>n't, I for<u>got</u>.
Did you <u>feed</u> the <u>cat</u>?	Yes, I <u>did</u>, yes, I <u>did</u>.
Did you <u>wash</u> the <u>car</u>?	No, I <u>did</u>n't, I for<u>got</u>.
Did you <u>get</u> some <u>gas</u>?	Yes, I <u>did</u>, yes, I <u>did</u>.
Did you <u>go</u> to the <u>bank</u>?	No, I <u>did</u>n't, I for<u>got</u>.
Did you <u>pay</u> the <u>bills</u>?	Yes, I <u>did</u>, yes, I <u>did</u>.
Did you <u>say</u> hel<u>lo</u>?	No, I <u>did</u>n't, I for<u>got</u>.
Did you <u>say</u> good<u>bye</u>?	No, I <u>did</u>n't, I for<u>got</u>.

6H The Simple Past: *Wh-* Questions

STUDENT BOOK P. 173

Note: See page 257 of this Teacher's Manual for a supplementary Internet Activity Procedure and reproducible Worksheet for this section.

Notes on the Photo and Warm-up Activity

In this photo, a surfer is carrying a surfboard into the water. Surfing is a popular sport in places like Hawaii, California, Australia, and parts of Europe. It involves riding the waves of the sea or the ocean on a long, narrow board and requires a lot of balance. Some waves can be very high and powerful. Point out to students that there are other uses for the word *surf*: *surfing the Internet*, or *channel-surfing* on TV. These uses of the word *surf* mean browsing, or visiting different websites or channels.

Role-play

- Write the word *lifeguard* on the board and ask students if they know what a lifeguard does.
- Put students in pairs or groups of three to brainstorm potential problems at a beach. For example, lifeguards might have to help people with *sunburn, a possible drowning, sharks, lightning storms*.
- Tell each group to choose one problem or danger and have them role-play a situation about that problem. One person should be a lifeguard and the other person or people will be witnesses. The lifeguard will ask the witnesses *wh-* questions in the simple past to find out what happened.
- Have students switch roles and role-play a conversation about another accident.

26 Practice

1. h   2. e   3. d   4. b   5. i   6. g   7. f   8. c   9. a

27 Practice

A.
1. Who did you see?
2. When did you see her?
3. Where did you see her?
4. How did she look?
5. What did she find?
6. How did she find it?
7. Who had a bad day yesterday?
8. When did he come home?
9. How did he feel?
10. Why did he come home so late?
11. Who did you see yesterday?
12. Where was she?
13. When did you see her?
14. How did she look?
15. What did she say?

CD3/22, 23 B. Play tracks 22 and 23 so students can check their answers. Then play track 23 again so they can listen and repeat the questions and answers.

28 Pair Up and Talk

Questions and answers will vary. Possible questions and answers:

A: Where did you go on vacation?   B: We went to the beach.
A: Did you listen to music?   B: Yes, I did.

The Simple Past

29 Read

Long or short answers are possible. Long answers are given below.

1. He had three sons.
2. He called his sons.
3. They promised to look for the money.
4. They started to look for the money after their father died.
5. They found nothing.
6. They felt upset.
7. Grapes started to grow on the vines.
8. They sold the grapes.
9. They had a lot of money.
10. They understood and lived happily.

30 Practice

Questions and answers will vary. Sample questions and answers:

A: What did you do yesterday? B: I went to work.
A: How long did you work? B: I worked for 10 hours.
A: Where did you go after work? B: I had school from 6:00 to 9:00.

61 The Simple Past: Time Clauses with *Before* and *After*

STUDENT BOOK P. 179

Notes on the Photos and Warm-up Activities

This pair of photos shows a watch and a cell phone. Different cultures have different values about time. Many have expressions or proverbs about time that reflect their cultural values. For example, the expressions "Time is money," "Lost time is never found again," and "The early bird catches the worm" are popular expressions in North American culture that reflect the value placed on time.

Discuss Proverbs

Ask students to discuss these questions in groups or as a class:

What proverbs or expressions about time do you know? (Lost time is never found again./ Haste makes waste./A watched pot never boils.)

In your culture, is it important to be on time? Is it important to be early? What happens if someone is late for an appointment or meeting?

Write about Your Schedule

Give students this prompt:

> Did you manage your time wisely yesterday? What did you do? Write a schedule showing each hour of the day: 8:00–9:00 A.M., 9:00–10:00 A.M., etc. Try to remember what activities you did yesterday and write them into the schedule. Then write sentences about what you did. Try to use at least two or three time clauses with *before* and two or three with *after*.

31 Practice

1. After she got up, she brushed her teeth. She brushed her teeth after she got up.
2. She took a shower before she had breakfast. Before she had breakfast, she took a shower.
3. She got dressed after she had breakfast. After she had breakfast, she got dressed.
4. Before she locked the door, she turned off the lights. She turned off the lights before she locked the door.
5. After she arrived at the office, she answered the phone. She answered the phone after she arrived at the office.
6. She finished her day's work before she left the office. Before she left the office, she finished her day's work.
7. She cooked dinner after she got home. After she got home, she cooked dinner.
8. After she ate dinner, she washed the dishes. She washed the dishes after she ate dinner.
9. She watched television before she went to bed. Before she went to bed, she watched television.
10. Before she went to sleep, she read a book. She read a book before she went to sleep.

32 Practice

1. After they got married, they had a baby.
   Before they had a baby, they got married.
2. After he learned to walk, he rode a bicycle.
   Before he rode a bicycle, he learned to walk.
3. After he graduated from college, he worked for a company.
   Before he worked for a company, he graduated from college.
4. (Answers will vary.) After he became the president of the company, he got a raise.
   Before he got a raise, he became the president of the company.

33 Pair Up and Talk

Sentences will vary. Possible sentences:

I had breakfast before I came to class today.

I put my books in my bag after I finished my homework.

I locked my door before I took the bus/train.

I talked to my classmates after I listened to the news.

Timeline Activity

- Write a timeline of your life on the board with the years as in the following:

1970	I was born in Chicago, Illinois.
1975–84	I was in elementary school.
1984	I traveled to Europe for the first time.
1984–88	I was in high school.
1988	I traveled to South America for the first time.
1988–92	I went to college in Los Angeles.
1992	I graduated from college and started working at a bank.
1994–96	I got a master's degree in teaching.
1996	I started teaching at this school.

- Tell the students about your life. Then have them ask you questions such as, "When did you go to Europe?" Answer them with *before/after* clauses if possible, "I went to Europe after I finished elementary school."
- After a few minutes of practice, have them make their own timelines. When they finish, they should give their timeline to a partner so she or he can write five questions about it.
- Students exchange papers again and answer their partner's questions with *before/after* clauses if possible. You can walk around and check the papers for accuracy.

Listening Puzzle

STUDENT BOOK P. 183

A. CD3, 24

Answer: A. microwave oven

B. Students might discuss the following:
   A blender can't make things hot. A toaster can't make popcorn.

C. CD3, 25

102   Unit 6

Reading Challenge: The Terracotta Army

STUDENT BOOK P. 184

A. 1. in China 2. to show that he was powerful in the next world (after he died)

C. In 1974 in China, some farmers <u>discovered</u> some figures under the ground. They <u>were</u> made of terracotta. Later, researchers <u>found</u> more figures. In all, they <u>found</u> over 8,000 figures. They <u>were</u> figures of soldiers and horses and <u>were</u> life-size. Each one is different from the other. Their hairstyles are different, too. They <u>were</u> all part of the tomb of Qin Shi Huangdi, (Ch'in shee hwahng-dee), the first emperor of China. Today, we call them the Terracotta Army.

Shi Huangdi <u>was</u> the first Qin emperor. The name China comes from the name Qin. He <u>started</u> to rule at the age of 13. This <u>was</u> over 2,225 years ago. Shi Huangdi <u>made</u> many changes in China. He <u>started</u> to build the Great Wall. He also <u>started</u> to build his tomb. It <u>took</u> over 700,000 people and 36 years to complete it. The emperor <u>wanted</u> to show that even in death, he <u>was</u> powerful in the next world.

D. 1. B 2. A
E. 3. B 4. C 5. B 6. A
F. 7. A
G. 8. C

Writing: Narrate Events

STUDENT BOOK P. 186

Writing Expansion
Students can give all the paragraphs to the teacher when they finish. She or he can read them aloud, one by one, omitting the name of the student. The other students have to guess whose vacation it was.

Self-Test

STUDENT BOOK P. 187

A. 1. C 2. B 3. C 4. A 5. D 6. C 7. A 8. B 9. A 10. B
B. 1. D 2. B 3. A 4. D 5. D 6. B 7. D 8. D 9. B 10. D

The Simple Past

Unit 7

The Past Progressive

Unit Sections		Notes/Activities	SB page	TM page
7A	The Past Progressive	Internet Activity; Chain Activity	190	105
7B	*While* and *When* with Past Time Clauses	Process Activity	195	107
7C	The Past Progressive and the Simple Past	Role-play Activity; Notes on Usage: *live*, *work*, *study*	198	108
✦	Listening Puzzle: Breakfast Foods		203	111
✦	Reading Challenge: The Titanic		204	111
✦	Writing: Narrate Events	Writing Expansion	206	111
✦	Self-Test	Answer Key	207	111

Unit 7 introduces the past progressive, illustrating the correct form of affirmative and negative statements, *yes/no* questions, and *wh-* questions. The text explains how and when we use the past progressive and provides practice in all forms.

The unit explains and illustrates the sometimes confusing use of *while* with the past progressive and *when* with the simple past in past time clauses. The writing section asks students and their partners to create timelines of events in their lives. They then write a paragraph using *while* and *when* to compare and connect their timeline with their partner's.

7A   The Past Progressive

STUDENT BOOK P. 190

Note: See page 259 of this Teacher's Manual for a supplementary Internet Activity Procedure and reproducible Worksheet for this section.

Notes on the Photos and Warm-up Activities

- In the photo on page 190, **three young women** are looking at something on a computer. They might be in an office setting or a library. The women look like they are enjoying whatever is on the computer. Many workplaces discourage the use of computers for personal activities, such as surfing the Internet.
- The photo on page 191 shows **a boy sleeping**. Children typically need between 10 and 12 hours of sleep each night.

Discuss Computer Use
- Ask students to brainstorm different reasons people use computers.
- Have students work in pairs or small groups to ask and answer questions like the following about the last time they used a computer:

    When was it? This morning? Last night? A week ago? Two months ago? What were you using the computer for? What kinds of things were you doing on the computer?

Write about Dreams
- As a class discuss these questions:

    Did you ever have a dream that you remembered for a long time?
    Can you remember a dream you had recently? What were you doing? What was happening?
- Ask students to write a paragraph that describes their dream using the simple past and the past progressive, and then share their paragraph with a partner.

1 Practice

1. What was Dad doing?   He was washing his car.
2. What was Karen doing?   She was playing the violin.
3. What was Bob doing?   He was getting dressed.
4. What was Nancy doing?   She was talking on the phone.
5. What was Mike doing?   He was driving his car.
6. What was the cat doing?   It was watching the birds.
7. What was Tim doing?   He was working on his computer.
8. What were Eric and Sherry doing? They were jogging.
9. What was Laurie doing?   She was swimming.

10. What was Ben doing?   He was shopping at the market.
11. What was Julio doing?   He was gardening.
12. What were Cheryl and Benny doing?   They were making cookies.

2 Pair Up and Talk

Conversations will vary. Sample conversation:

A: What were you doing an hour ago?
B: I was walking to class.

Chain Activity

- Write the students' names in a vertical column on the board. Ask them what they were doing on Saturday afternoon.
- Beside each student's name, put an activity; for example, *playing soccer, listening to music*.
- Walk around the classroom, getting students to ask and answer questions. For example:

TEACHER: What was Michiko doing on Saturday afternoon?
STUDENT A: She was making sushi. What was Raul doing?
STUDENT B: He was playing basketball.

3 Practice

A. 1. No, she wasn't doing her homework. She was cleaning the apartment.
2. No, they weren't talking about the basketball game. They were talking about the soccer game.
3. No, I wasn't trying to reach you. I was trying to reach your brother.
4. No, you weren't speaking too loudly. You were speaking too softly.
5. No, I wasn't reading *The New York Times*. I was reading *The Los Angeles Times*.
6. No, he wasn't explaining the present progressive. He was explaining the past progressive.

CD3/26, 27 B. Play tracks 26 and 27 so students can check their answers. Then play track 27 again so they can listen and repeat the conversations.

7B *While* and *When* with Past Time Clauses

STUDENT BOOK P. 195

Notes on the Photo and Warm-up Activities

This man is driving a car. Many people in the United States drive to work. The average commute time is about a half an hour, but it is increasing each year. These days, *road rage* (getting very angry while driving) is a common problem in cities in the United States.

Discuss Road Rage

Explain the meaning of *road rage* (getting very angry while driving) and ask the class why they think this happens. Put students in small groups or in pairs and present them with the following situation:

The man in the car had a difficult time while driving to work this morning. When he arrived at his office, he was in a very bad mood. Explain what was happening while he was driving. Then share your ideas with the class.

EXAMPLES

While he was driving to work, a big truck drove in front of him. He almost crashed!
When the crosswalk sign said "Don't Walk," a pedestrian walked in front of his car.
He had a flat tire when he was driving to work.

Write about a Travel Problem

Present students with this prompt:

Have you ever had problems while you were driving or taking public transportation? What happened? Write about your experience in at least six sentences. Use *while* and *when* with past time clauses.

4 Practice

1. f   2. e   3. h   4. d   5. g   6. a   7. b   8. c

5 Practice

A.
1. were talking
2. walked
3. was giving
4. sat
5. were taking
6. watched
7. was taking
8. talked
9. was talking
10. told
11. was finishing
12. said
13. was smiling
14. left
15. was walking
16. said

 CD3/28, 29

B. Play tracks 28 and 29 so students can check their answers. Then play track 29 again so they can listen and repeat the sentences.

CD3/30   **C.**   Answers: A. 1, 2   B. 2, 1   C. 2, 1   D. 2, 1   E. 1, 2

Process Activity

- To contrast the simple past and past progressive, either bring some ingredients to class to make some food or mime the process. For example, you could bring lettuce, a tomato, salad dressing, a bowl, a cutting board, and a knife to class to make salad, or you could draw them on the board.
- Tell the students to watch you and write down everything you do.
- Cut (or pretend to cut) the lettuce and look at the recipe. Slice (or pretend to slice) the tomato and sneeze. Put the ingredients in the bowl and drop the knife. Pour the dressing on the salad and taste some lettuce. Eat some salad and smile.
- Ask the students to tell you what you did and write their sentences on the board. For example:
  While you were cutting the lettuce, you looked at the recipe.
  While you were slicing the tomato, you sneezed.
- Then ask students to volunteer to come to the board and change the sentences into *when* clauses:
  You were cutting the lettuce when you looked at the recipe.
  You were slicing the tomato when you sneezed.
- Ask a few questions, alternating *while* and *when* clauses, to reinforce the structure.

7C   The Past Progressive and the Simple Past

Student Book p. 198

Notes on the Photo and Warm-up Activity

These students are studying at the library. Some students like to form "study groups," in which they meet regularly with the same classmates to review, ask and answer each other's questions, and study together.

Form a "Study Group"
- As a class, discuss the concept of study groups. Ask students if they have ever been in one or think they would like to join one.
- Tell students they are going to form mock study groups and then divide the class into small groups.
- Explain that the goal of this "meeting" of their study group is to review the material in the Form/Function box on page 198 of their Student Books. Give students a specific amount of time to review the material, allowing them to decide how they will proceed.
- To conclude, have groups take turns describing to the class how they worked together and if they think their study group meeting was helpful and why or why not.

6 Practice

A. A
1. was studying
2. saw
3. came
4. sat
5. put
6. started
7. was reading
8. looked
9. met
10. smiled
11. smiled

B
1. was reading
2. became
3. started
4. went
5. closed
6. turned
7. was watching
8. began
9. was blowing
10. were shaking
11. heard
12. woke

C
1. was getting
2. got
3. was walking
4. heard
5. began
6. got
7. began
8. got
9. got
10. was shaking
11. put
12. heard

 CD3/31, 32

B. Play tracks 31 and 32 so students can check their answers. Then play track 32 again so they can listen and repeat the sentences.

Role-play Activity

✦ Divide the students into groups in order to act out the situations in **Practice 5** and **Practice 6**. For **6A**, you need three students (one to read and two to act). For **6B**, you need two students (one to read and one to act). For **6C**, you need three students (one to read and two to act). The rest of the students can be in the role-play for **Practice 5**.

✦ Tell them that one student will be the reader, and the others will be the actors. Let them practice in different corners of the room. When they are ready, have them perform the role-plays for the class.

7 Practice

Answers will vary. Possible answers:

1. was living
2. arrived, was living
3. was living
4. studied
5. was living, was working
6. met
7. was working/ was living, met
8. was working
9. was working
10. was working

Notes on Usage: *live, work, study*

Point out that the verbs *live*, *work*, and *study* are often used in the simple past and past progressive interchangeably. For example, *I was working in New York in 1998* means almost the same thing as *I worked in New York in 1998*.

The Past Progressive 109

8 Practice

Answers will vary. Possible answers:
1. Maybe he was cooking when he burned his finger.
2. Maybe she was watching a sad movie when she started to cry.
3. Maybe he was running when he fell down.
4. Maybe he was moving the vase when it fell and broke to pieces.
5. Maybe he was on the train when he fell asleep.
6. Maybe someone was breaking into the house when we heard a strange noise.
7. Maybe I was dreaming when I saw a man's head in the window.
8. Maybe it was snowing when the lights went out.
9. Maybe she was reading a funny book when she laughed loudly.

9 Your Turn

Descriptions will vary. Sample description:

I had a very bad day last week. I was shopping when I lost my cell phone. While I was looking at the oranges, a woman accidentally bumped into me. I dropped my bag. When I dropped my bag, everything fell out. The phone fell under the counter. Someone found it and made a lot of expensive phone calls. When I went to the phone company to cancel it, they told me the bill was $500. I went to the bank to take out some money, but there wasn't much money left. While I was calling a friend from a pay phone to ask her if I could borrow some money, it started to rain on me. It was a terrible day!

10 Read

Long or short answers are possible. Long answers are given below.
1. He was walking sadly.
2. All he had in the whole world was a bag.
3. He took the bag and ran down the road.
4. He didn't have his bag.
5. He put it in the road.
6. He was happy.
7. He was watching from the bushes.

Listening Puzzle

STUDENT BOOK P. 203

A. CD3, 33

Answer: B. cornflakes

B. Students might discuss the following:

People eat yogurt at different times in the day. Cornflakes are a typical American breakfast.

C. CD3, 34

Reading Challenge: The Titanic

STUDENT BOOK P. 204

A. Answers will vary. Possible answers:

1. It's relaxing and you can meet people. 2. It's slow and you might get sick. 3. People who have a lot of time.

C. **Paragraph 3:** were sleeping, was sinking, were crying; were dancing, were praying, were saying

D. 1. C 2. A
E. 3. D 4. B 5. B 6. C
F. 7. B
G. 8. A

Writing: Narrate Events

STUDENT BOOK P. 206

Writing Expansion

Have one pair of students join another pair to compare dates and events. For example, one student can say, "In 2000, while I was studying in Mexico, Eunah was studying in Seoul." Another student can say, "Fabiola was working in Milan while I was working in Paris in 2002," and so on.

Self-Test

STUDENT BOOK P. 207

A. 1. A 2. B 3. D 4. C 5. B 6. D 7. A 8. D 9. A 10. A
B. 1. A 2. C 3. A 4. A 5. D 6. D 7. C 8. B 9. B 10. C

Unit 8
The Future

Unit Sections		Notes/Activities	SB page	TM page
8A	The Future with *Be Going To*	Prediction Activity; Notes on Pronunciation: *gonna*	210	113
8B	Future Time Expressions	Notes on Vocabulary: past time vs future time expressions	215	115
8C	The Present Progressive as the Future	Contrast Activity	217	116
8D	The Future with *Will*	Notes on Usage: *going to* vs *will*	220	117
8E	*May* and *Might*	Photo Activity	224	120
8F	Future Time Clauses with *Before*, *After*, and *When*	Internet Activity; Vacation Activity	227	121
8G	Future Conditional Sentences	Story Activity	230	123
8H	The Simple Present with Time Clauses and *If* Clauses	Chart Activity	233	124
✦	Listening Puzzle: Museums		237	126
✦	Reading Challenge: Global Warming		238	127
✦	Writing: Describe Future Plans	Writing Expansion	240	127
✦	Self-Test	Answer Key	241	127

Unit 8 introduces a variety of future forms. As with other units, for each of these future forms, the text illustrates the correct form, explains how and when we use it, and provides ample practice. It starts with *be going to* for predictions and plans, followed by future time expressions like *next* and *tomorrow*. The unit also teaches and practices the present progressive *be* + verb + *-ing* as a future form for schedules and plans. Section 8D provides comprehensive models and practice of the future with *will* for predictions and spontaneous decisions.

Next, the unit presents and practices the auxiliaries *may* and *might* for future possibility or permission.

Future time clauses with *before*, *after*, and *when* are reviewed. The text moves forward to teach the future conditional, which is comprised of an *if* clause in the simple present and a main clause in the future. Additional practice with time and *if* clauses is provided.

8A The Future with *Be Going To*

STUDENT BOOK P. 210

Notes on the Photos and Warm-up Activities

✦ This **little girl** is about to eat a cookie. Although children usually love cookies, candy, and other sweet things, most parents do not like their children to eat a lot of sugar. Children who eat a lot of sugar are more likely to have problems with their teeth and their behavior. Americans consume millions of bags of Oreos each year, and that's just one type of packaged cookie!

✦ There are different types of **clouds**: *cumulus* (big, puffy clouds), *stratus* (low level clouds that form in thin layers), *cirrus* (thin, wispy high clouds), and *nimbus*, or rain clouds. Weather forecasters study clouds carefully. However, you don't have to be a professional to identify typical storm clouds!

Predict

Have students work in pairs. Present them with the following situation:

> Imagine that you and your partner are babysitting the girl in the photo. Her parents have told you that she must not eat any cookies tonight. As you can see in the photo, she's probably going to eat a cookie. In fact, she has already eaten a whole bag of cookies, and this is the last one. What's going to happen next? What isn't going to happen? Make predictions. Share your predictions with the class.

Give a Weather Report

✦ Put students in pairs to make up the weather forecast for the next five days. Point out that their weather forecasts can be realistic, or purely invented.

✦ Call on students to read their weather reports to the class.

1 Practice

1. Jim is going to take a photo.
2. Brad is going to paint the wall.
3. Sue is going to buy some fruit.
4. Tony is going to drink a cup of coffee.
5. Mel is going to write a check.
6. Ted is going to order a meal.

Prediction Activity

✦ Bring in some everyday items, or use items in the classroom.

✦ Give each student an item and elicit what they are going to do with it. For example, *I have a pen. I'm going to do my homework.*

✦ For a greater challenge, go around the room, eliciting what students are going to do with their items. Each subsequent student must repeat what previous classmates said before adding their own. For example, *Martin has a pen. He is going to do his homework. I have an eraser. I'm going to clean the board.*

The Future

2 Practice

A.
1. 'm/am going to go
2. 're/are not going to work
3. are
4. going to stay
5. 'm/am going to stay
6. are
7. going to do
8. 'm/am going to see
9. 'm/am going to walk
10. 'm/am going to visit
11. 'm/am going to go
12. 'm/am going to shop
13. 'm/am going to buy
14. Are
15. going to eat
16. 'm/am not going to do
17. 'm/am going to eat

CD4/2, 3 B. Play tracks 2 and 3 so students can check their answers. Then play track 3 again so they can listen and repeat the conversation.

CD4/4 C. Monday – 2. walking in the parks; Tuesday – 4. visiting the Houses of Parliament; Wednesday – 1. going to museums; Thursday – 3. buying English tea

3 Practice

A. Questions are as follows. Answers will vary.
1. When are you going to have the party?
2. What kind of food are you going to have?
3. What food are you going to make?
4. What are you going to wear?
5. How many people are you going to invite?
6. Where are you going to have the party?
7. What time is the party going to start?
8. What kind of music are you going to have?

CD4/5, 6 B. Play tracks 5 and 6 so students can check their answers (to the questions they wrote). Then play track 6 again so they can work with a partner to ask and answer.

Notes on Pronunciation: *gonna*

◆ The future *be going to* + verb is often pronounced *gonna* in informal speech.

A: Are you going to fly to Chicago? B: Are you gonna fly to Chicago?
A: No, we're not going to fly. B: No, we're not gonna fly.

◆ When *going to* is used alone, we don't say *gonna*.

I'm going to the store.   I'm ~~gonna~~ the store.

◆ In writing, we always use *going to*, not *gonna*.

8B Future Time Expressions

STUDENT BOOK P. 215

Notes on the Photo and Warm-up Activity

The young woman in the photo is reading a handwritten letter. There are hearts drawn on the back of the envelope and she is smiling, so it is probably a love letter. Handwritten letters are not as common as they used to be. These days many people send email.

Discuss Letters vs Email

More and more people communicate by email rather than on paper. Have students work in small groups or as a class to discuss this topic. They can begin by answering some or all of the following questions:

- Do you prefer receiving/writing handwritten letters or emails?
- How do you think the woman in the photo feels about receiving this letter?
- When is it best to send a handwritten letter?
- In your opinion, how are people going to communicate with each other in two years? In 10 or 20 years?
- Is email ever going to replace handwritten letters completely? Why or why not?
- Who do you write letters/emails to?
- Who are you going to write to tonight? Tomorrow? Next week? Next month?

4 Your Turn

Answers will vary but should include the correct form of *be going to*.

5 Pair Up and Talk

Conversations will vary. Sample questions and answers:
- A: What are you going to do tomorrow morning?
- B: I'm going to visit my grandmother. What are you going to do?

Notes on Vocabulary: past time vs future time expressions

Write the chart below and on the top of page 116 on the board to contrast past time expressions and future time expressions:

Past Time	Future Time
yesterday	tomorrow
last night	tonight
the day before yesterday	the day after tomorrow

The Future 115

an hour/a week/a month ago	in an hour/a week/a month
last week/month/year	next week/month/year
a week/a month/a year ago today	a week/a month/a year from today

8c The Present Progressive as the Future

STUDENT BOOK P. 217

Notes on the Photos and Warm-up Activity

- The photo on page 217 shows **a man talking on the phone**. He looks tense, so he might be in a hurry or he might be worried about an important meeting or other aspect of his job.
- The photo on page 218 shows **a man waiting at the airport** and working on his laptop. In the United States, it is recommended that you arrive at the airport from one to one-and-a-half hours in advance for domestic flights and two hours in advance for international flights. In many airports there is access to the Internet; often wireless access is also available.

Role-play a Travel Agent

- Put students in pairs and present them with the following situation:

    Imagine that you work for a travel agency. You help businesspeople make their travel plans. Write a travel itinerary for a two-day business trip. Decide where the man in the photo set at the airport is traveling to and why. Consider these questions: What type of transportation is he taking? When is he leaving? When is he returning? Where is he staying while he is away?

- Call on one pair of students to present the man's itinerary while the class takes notes. Ask a volunteer to write the man's itinerary on the board. Check the itinerary against what the pair said.

6 Practice

A.
1. At 8:45 she's/she is arriving in New York.
2. Then she's/she is taking a taxi to the hotel.
3. At 9:30 she's/she is leaving the hotel.
4. At 10:00 she's/she is meeting Tim and Donna at the office.
5. From 10:00 to 12:00 she's/she is working with Tim and Donna.
6. From 12:00 to 2:00 she's/she is having lunch with Tim, Donna, and the boss.
7. At 2:30 she's/she is seeing Tod Cordel.
8. At 4:00 she's/she is returning to the office and working with Donna.
9. At 6:00 she's/she is going back to the hotel.
10. At 7:00 she's/she is waiting for Alex in the hotel lobby.

11. Then she's/she is going to dinner with him.
12. After 10:00 she's/she is preparing for the meeting on Tuesday.

B. 1. What time is Jan arriving in New York?
   She's/She is arriving in New York at 8:45.
2. Who is she meeting at 10:00?
   She's/She is meeting Tim and Donna at 10:00.
3. What is she doing between 12:00 and 2:00?
   She's/She is having lunch.
4. Where is she waiting for Alex?
   She's/She is waiting for Alex in the hotel lobby.
5. What is she doing at 4:00?
   She's/She is returning to the office and working with Donna.
6. When is she going back to the hotel?
   She's/She is going back to the hotel at 6:00.
7. Who is she having lunch with?
   She's/She is having lunch with Tim, Donna, and the boss.
8. Where is she preparing for Tuesday's meeting?
   She's/She is preparing for Tuesday's meeting in the hotel.

Contrast Activity

+ Have students continue asking questions using the present progressive as both the present and the future. For example:

   Who is Sara meeting now?   *Who is she meeting tomorrow?*
   What are we studying this semester? *What are we studying next semester?*
   Where are the children going now? *Where are they going this weekend?*

+ You can write a few verbs and question words on the board to help them think of questions:

   buy, call, drink, eat, read, type, wear, write   Who, What, Where

8D The Future with *Will*

Student Book p. 220

Notes on the Photos and Warm-up Activities

+ The photo on page 220 shows **a space shuttle** during lift-off. The astronauts will eventually return to Earth in the space shuttle attached to the top of the rocket. They will land it like an airplane. Currently, astronauts and scientists travel on space shuttle launches to do research. In the future, *space tourism*

- (flights into space for private citizens) may become more common. Some researchers predict that selling space flights to private citizens could one day be worth billions of dollars.
- In the top photo on page 221, **a scientist** is looking at a slide that will go under a microscope. Scientists work in a variety of places. They teach at universities and do research for large corporations that make medicine or products. They do research in hospitals. Lab technicians and medical doctors also use microscopes. This scientist is wearing protective gear, including goggles and a full face mask. Scientists often wear such protective gear when working with toxic, or biohazardous, materials.
- In the bottom photo, **a woman** is trying on shoes. The average American woman has 19 pairs of shoes, only four of which she wears regularly. Forty-three percent report having foot injuries caused by their shoes, especially their "high heels."

Make Predictions about Space Travel
- Ask students to discuss these questions in small groups:
    Will people go to the moon for vacations in the future? Why will they go or why won't they go?
    For what other reasons will people travel on space shuttles?
    What other things will people do in space?
- Have students work in groups to make as many predictions as they can about space travel and space exploration. Assign someone in each group to take notes. Set a time limit.
- Ask the group with the most predictions to read their list to the class. Students should check off items on their own lists as they hear them read and then share any other ideas from their lists.

Imagine Future Discoveries
- Put students in small groups and present them with the situation below:
    Imagine that you are a group of scientists. Decide exactly what it is you research. For example, do you do research for a company that makes sneakers? Do you work in a hospital and research possible cures for a disease? Imagine that you have just made an important discovery or found a cure for a disease. Make predictions about the changes that will happen as a result of your findings. Share your discovery and predictions with the class. Imagine you are talking to the public at a TV news conference. Be creative!
- Elicit from the class questions about the product.

Role-play
- Have students work in pairs. Present them with the following situation:
    The woman in the photo wants to buy good, but inexpensive dress shoes for a party. The sales clerk wants her to buy a pair of very expensive high heels. Role-play their conversation. One of you is the customer. The other is the sales clerk. Will the sales clerk successfully sell the customer more expensive shoes?
- Have volunteers perform their role-plays for the class.

7 Practice

A. Answers will vary, but all the sentences should contain *will* or *won't*.

B. Sentences will vary, but they all should contain *will* or *won't*.

8 Practice

A. A 1. 'm/am going OR am going to go
      2. 'll get
      3. 'll/will pick
      4. 'll/will be
      5. Will
      6. be
      7. 'm/am going to go OR 'm/am going
      8. 'll/will see
      9. are coming

   B 1. Are
      2. going
      3. 'm/am helping OR 'm/am going to help
      4. 's/is moving OR 's/is going to move
      5. are
      6. coming
      7. are
      8. going to go OR going
      9. 'll call/will call
     10. 'll/will tell
     11. 'll/will see/'m going to see
     12. 'll/will call

 CD4/7, 8 B. Play tracks 7 and 8 so students can check their answers. Then play track 8 again so they can listen and repeat the conversation.

Notes on Usage: *going to* vs *will*

Students may ask for a summary of the differences between ***going to*** and ***will***. You can write this chart on the board to help them remember.

Going To	Will
Plans for the future	Decisions at the moment of speaking
Predictions about the future	Predictions about the future
(what we see and feel sure is going to happen)	(what we think or imagine will happen)
	Requests and offers to help*
	Future promises*
	Facts about the future*

Some of the items (*) have not been taught in this unit, so you may want to omit them to avoid confusion. However, if students ask, you can tell them about these other differences.

The Future

8E *May* and *Might*

STUDENT BOOK P. 224

Notes on the Photo and Warm-up Activities

The man in the photo has a worried expression. It seems that he is looking at something that is causing him a lot of stress.

Discuss the Photo

Have students discuss the questions in small groups or pairs. Encourage them to use *might* or *may*.
What is the man in the photo looking at? What is he thinking about? Why is he worried? What does he think may or may not happen?

Write about Worries

Present students with this prompt:

> Sometimes writing down our worries can help us to worry less. Divide a piece of paper into two columns. In the left-hand column, write at least six worries. Consider this question: What things are you afraid might or might not happen? In the right-hand column, write down a positive thought about each worry. Write something you will do or think to help yourself stop worrying.

EXAMPLE

My Worries	Positive Thoughts
I might fail my exam tomorrow.	I will work with a tutor this afternoon.
My friends may forget my birthday next week.	I'll remind them about my birthday. I may throw a party for myself!

9 Practice

A. 1. will   3. may   5. will   7. will
    2. will   4. will   6. might   8. might

 CD4/9, 10

B. Play tracks 9 and 10 so students can check their answers. Then play track 10 again so they can listen and repeat the conversations.

10 Practice

1. 'm going   3. may go   5. 'll finish   7. will celebrate
2. 'm staying   4. won't spend 6. might see   8. may go

120   Unit 8

Photo Activity

✦ Tell students to look at the photos in **Practice 1** on page 212 and write sentences with *may* and *might*. For example:
   1. *It may be a digital camera.*   *It might be a video camera.*
   2. *He may paint the bedroom.*   *He might paint the bathroom.*

✦ Go around the room and elicit the sentences.

8F Future Time Clauses with *Before*, *After*, and *When*

STUDENT BOOK P. 227

Note: See page 261 of this Teacher's Manual for a supplementary Internet Activity Procedure and reproducible Worksheet for this section.

Notes on the Photo and Warm-up Activity

This woman is dressed in business attire. She's wearing a suit. Her appearance is serious and professional. In the United States, business attire means a suit and tie for men, and either a suit (with pants or skirt and jacket) or dress for women. Many workplaces have casual Fridays, which means that employees can wear neat but casual clothing on Fridays. Most workplaces have rules about work attire, including prohibitions against T-shirts, shorts, flip-flops, and torn clothing.

Role-play

✦ Put students in pairs and present the following situation:

   Think of the job that the woman in this photo will interview for. One person in each pair will be the woman in the photo (the job applicant); the other will interview her for a job. The interviewer has finished asking her about her past. Now she/he is interested in her career plans and goals for the future. The interviewer should ask questions about her plans and goals using *before*, *after*, and *when*.

✦ Call on students to perform their role-plays for the class.

11 Practice

1. before she goes to the interview
2. Before she leaves home
3. before she goes to the interview
4. When the interviewer asks questions
5. after the interview
6. When they meet
7. before she gets the news about her job
8. When she gets the job

Note: You can also have students rewrite the sentences changing the order of the clauses.

The Future 121

12 Practice

A.
1. 'll/will change
2. 'll/will make
3. get
4. 'll/will visit
5. won't/will not go
6. leave
7. visit
8. 'll/will buy
9. 'll/will take
10. stay
11. want
12. 'll/will get

 CD4/11, 12

B. Play tracks 11 and 12 so students can check their answers. Then play track 12 again so they can listen and repeat the conversations.

13 Pair Up and Talk

Conversations will vary. Sample questions and answers:
A: What are you doing before you eat dinner?
B: I'm going to study for an hour before I eat dinner.
A: What are you doing after you eat dinner?
B: I'm going to watch TV after I eat dinner.

14 Your Turn

Answers will vary.

Vacation Activity

- **Practice 2** is about a vacation in London, and **Practice 12** is about a vacation in Istanbul. You can talk about the following cities (or others if you prefer) and the tourist sites there.
- Write the following lists on the board, and say the names of the sites, asking the students to repeat them.

London	**New York**	**San Francisco**	**Washington, D.C.**
Buckingham Palace	Empire State Building	Golden Gate Bridge	White House
Houses of Parliament	Radio City Music Hall	Fisherman's Wharf	Washington Monument
Tate Museum	Central Park	Cable Cars	Capitol Building
Oxford Street	Statue of Liberty	Chinatown	Lincoln Memorial

- Have students make up sentences about their vacations using *before*, *after*, and *when*. For example:
  Before I go to the Empire State Building, I'll see the Statue of Liberty.
  After I visit the Empire State Building, I'll see a show at Radio City Music Hall.
  When I go to New York, I'll visit Central Park.
- You can ask them to write the sentences or simply say them to their partners.

8G Future Conditional Sentences

STUDENT BOOK P. 230

Notes on the Photo and Warm-up Activity

This photo shows a man and boy. They are hoping to go fishing. Fly-fishing requires a fishing rod (or pole) and a line. Special devices called *flies* are attached to the end of the line; these are meant to attract fish. Fly-fishing is usually done in lakes and ponds, and on rivers. Many people fish for recreation; they might not even eat the fish they catch. Others catch fish with the intent of eating them. Still others make a living by catching fish.

Make Predictions about the Photo

Have students work in small groups or pairs. Present them with the following situation:

Make predictions about what will happen if this father and son catch a really big fish, and what will happen if they don't catch any fish. Try to make as many predictions as you can.

15 Practice

A. 1. c   2. f   3. a   4. h   5. b   6. d   7. e   8. g

1. If you go out without a coat, you'll catch a cold.
2. If you lie in the sun, you'll get sunburned.
3. If you don't eat breakfast, you'll be hungry.
4. If you eat too many French fries, you'll get fat.
5. If you don't study hard, you won't pass your exam.
6. If you don't call home, you'll be lonely.
7. If you go to bed late, you'll be tired the next day.
8. If you get sick, you'll miss class.

CD4/13, 14

B. Play tracks 13 and 14 so students can check their answers. Then play track 14 again so they can listen and repeat the sentences.

16 Practice

1. will go/are going to go/are going
2. rains
3. 'll watch/'re going to watch/'re watching
4. 'll order/'m going to order/'m ordering
5. will make/'s going to make/'s making
6. 'll play/'re going to play/'re playing
7. get, 'll sit/'re going to sit/'re sitting
8. go, 'll have/'re going to have/'re having
9. 'll go/'m going to go/'m going, have
10. 'll have/'re going to have, go

The Future   123

Story Activity

- To practice the future conditional, start an oral or a written story with the class. You make up the first sentence, and each student adds to it. For example, you can say or write:

    T: If I have some extra money, I'll take a trip after this course.
    S1: If I go on a trip, I'll invite one of my classmates to go with me.
    S2: If she/he likes the sea, we'll go to Jamaica.
    S3: If she/he doesn't like the sea, we'll go to Mexico.
    S4: If we go to Mexico, we'll visit the Aztec ruins.

- It may be easier for students to follow if the story is written on the board. In that case, you can write the first sentence, and then allow the students to write the rest of the sentences.
- When the story is finished, you can ask each student to read his/her sentence aloud.

8H The Simple Present with Time Clauses and *If* Clauses

STUDENT BOOK P. 233

Notes on the Photos and Warm-up Activities

- The top photo shows **a woman drinking bottled water**. There are many varieties of bottled water on the market these days. If water has added chemicals or sweeteners, it is not pure water; it is a soft drink.
- The bottom photo shows **icebergs** in the sea. Icebergs are large, floating chunks of ice usually found in the sea near Greenland and Antarctica. In warmer weather, icebergs are formed when freshwater ice breaks off from glaciers or polar ice sheets.

Discuss Water

- Put students in small groups to talk about water. Challenge students to think of as many facts as they can about water. Ask them to consider the effects of water on plants, animals, and humans.
- One person from each group should write down the ideas generated. Each "water fact" should use the simple present with a time clause or an *if* clause. Set a time limit on the discussion and then have each group share their information with the class. Here are some examples:

    If you water plants, they grow.
    When people don't drink enough water, they become dehydrated.

Role-play

- Put students in small groups and present the following situation:

    You are officials on a large ship in the North Atlantic Ocean. You receive notice that an iceberg is nearby. You need to change the ship's course in the next 24 hours in order to avoid hitting the iceberg. Talk about the situation, your concerns, and your plans for preventing disaster. Use the simple present with time clauses and *if* clauses as much as possible.

17 Practice

1. c 2. d 3. e 4. f 5. b 6. a

1. If you don't water plants, they die.
2. If you put food in the refrigerator, it stays fresh.
3. If you put water in the freezer, it turns into ice.
4. If you walk in the rain, you get wet.
5. If you mix black and white, you get gray.
6. If you don't put milk in the refrigerator, it goes bad.

18 Practice

Answers will vary. Sample answers:

1. If have a headache, I take an aspirin.
2. If I eat too much, I feel full.
3. If I don't sleep, I feel tired the next day.
4. If I miss my class, the teacher gets angry.
5. If I get very angry, my face gets red.
6. When I am sad, I don't smile.
7. When I am happy, I smile a lot.
8. When I have a test, I get nervous.

19 Practice

A.
1. stays
2. 'll/will stay
3. sees
4. go
5. works
6. 'll/will go/is going to go
7. comes, will be
8. is, won't/will not make
9. 'll/will buy, comes
10. won't/will not turn, has
11. has, 'll/will go
12. works, will ask

 CD4/15, 16   B. Play tracks 15 and 16 so students can check their answers. Then play track 16 again so they can listen and repeat the sentences.

 CD4/17   C. Answer: D

Chart Activity

✦ To practice time clauses, put a chart on the board such as the one on the next page and elicit sentences from it. You can designate an actor or another famous person as the subject of the sentences. You can also make the verb phrases humorous.

The Future   125

Before	Roger Federer	plays a concert	invites famous people
After	Midori	makes a movie	buys new clothes
When	Halle Berry	plays a match	gets a lot of rest
If	Matt Damon	has a party	practices a lot

✦ Tell the students to watch the board carefully. Using a pointer or ruler, tap on one of the words or phrases from each column. Then call on a student to say the sentence that you just indicated. For example, *Before Halle Berry has a party, she buys new clothes.*

20 Read

1. The fox is walking in the forest.
2. He's going to eat the spider.
3. The spider hears some people.
4. The spider will go and see what the people are saying.
5. He is going to eat it.
6. The spider says that the fox will see everything, too.

Listening Puzzle

STUDENT BOOK P. 237

A. CD4, 18

Answer: C. The Smithsonian

B. Students might discuss the following:

The Louvre is an art museum in Paris. The British Museum is not named after a person.

C. CD4, 19

Reading Challenge: Global Warming

STUDENT BOOK P. 238

A. 1. Ice will melt. 2. Some places will flood.

C. **Paragraph 2:** will happen, will move, may become, may be, will move, might disappear, may be, will dry up, may become, will become; **Paragraph 3:** may/may not believe

D. 1. A 2. C
E. 3. D 4. C 5. B
F. 6. C
G. 7. D
H. 8. C

Writing: Describe Future Plans

STUDENT BOOK P. 240

Writing Expansion
Read students' paragraphs aloud, omitting the name of the student and the title of the paragraph. The other students have to guess which country or city it is.

Self-Test

STUDENT BOOK P. 241

A. 1. C 2. A 3. B 4. B 5. C 6. B 7. B 8. C 9. C 10. D
B. 1. C 2. C 3. A 4. C 5. D 6. C 7. D 8. A 9. C 10. A

Unit 9

Quantity and Degree Words

Unit Sections	Notes/Activities	SB page	TM page
9A *All Of, Almost All Of, Most Of, Some Of,* and *None Of*	Classroom Activity	244	129
9B *Every*	School Activity	247	130
9C *Very* and *Too*	Chant Activity	249	131
9D *Too Many* and *Too Much*	Internet Activity	252	133
9E *Too* + Adjective + Infinitive; *Too* + Adjective + *For* + Noun/Pronoun + Infinitive	Silly Sentence Activity	254	134
9F Adjective + *Enough*	Complaint Activity	256	135
9G *Enough* + Noun	Contrast Activity	258	136
✦ Listening Puzzle: Mountains		261	137
✦ Reading Challenge: The Sahara Desert		262	138
✦ Writing: Describe a Place	Writing Expansion	264	138
✦ Self-Test	Answer Key	265	138

Unit 9 introduces a variety of quantity and degree words to help students express themselves more accurately. *All of, almost all of, most of, some of,* and *none of* with nouns and pronouns are practiced in their singular and plural forms. The unit then moves to teach *every*, clearly illustrating the relationship between *all* and *every*. It teaches *very* and *too*, carefully explaining the subtle difference between the two words and providing practice to help solidify the difference in students' minds.

The text next explains how and when we use *too many* (with count nouns) and *too much* (with noncount nouns), and provides ample practice illustrating this difference.

The unit illustrates the correct forms of the sentence patterns using *too* with adjectives and infinitives—including the pattern that contains *for* plus a noun or pronoun—explains how and when we use them, and provides ample practice in the sentence patterns. The text also teaches use of *enough* with both adjectives and nouns.

Each section of the unit clearly differentiates between singular and plural nouns and between count and noncount nouns to avoid confusion and to aid the students in learning a variety of expressions.

9A All Of, Almost All Of, Most Of, Some Of, and None Of

STUDENT BOOK P. 244

Notes on the Photo and Warm-up Activity

This picture shows President Abraham Lincoln with a group of men, perhaps his Cabinet. It is interesting to note that none of the men are smiling. Matthew Brady was an important early photographer. Brady took many photographs during the Civil War, which was also the time of Lincoln's presidency. In the early days of photography, subjects had to sit or stand without moving for several seconds; otherwise, their image would blur on the film. Photography was not the instant art that it is today. These days, you can see many smiling faces in photographs, and it is common to take photos of people in action. In fact, photography has changed so much that now digital cameras are increasingly common, and people send photos in seconds over the Internet or cellular phones.

Compare and Contrast
- Ask each of the students to bring in a modern photo of a group of people. They can bring in a photo of friends, family, classmates, or strangers.
- Put students in small groups to describe their picture and the people in it.
- Still in their groups, students should then make comparisons between the old photo in the book and the modern group photo they brought in. Encourage them to say as much as they can about each photo, talking about what the people are wearing, how they look, and other objects in the photo. (If they don't have a photo, have them clip a picture of a group of people out of a magazine.)

1 Practice

1. All of the people
2. None of the men
3. All of the men
4. Almost all of/Most of the men
5. Some of the men
6. Some of the men
7. All of the men
8. None of the men

2 Practice

Answers may vary. Possible answers:

1. Some of the people
2. Some of the people
3. Most of the women
4. Some of the people
5. Almost all of the people
6. All of the women
7. Some of the people
8. Some of the people

Classroom Activity

- To practice using the expressions taught in this section, have students write sentences using each of the expressions to describe the people in your classroom. Have volunteers write sentences on the board.

3 Practice

A. 1. is   3. are   5. have   7. is   9. is
    2. come   4. are   6. are   8. is   10. are

CD4/20, 21   B.   Play tracks 20 and 21 so students can check their answers. Then play track 21 again so they can listen and repeat the sentences.

9B   *Every*

STUDENT BOOK P. 247

Notes on the Photo and Warm-up Activities

These young women are running in a race. The track and field outfits they are wearing are very modern. Students might be surprised to learn that as recently as the 1970s, girls did not participate in very many school sports in the United States. A law was passed in 1976 that made school sports open to both girls and boys.

Role-play an Interview

Tell students that they will role-play an interview with the runners in the photo. Ask them to first write interview questions in groups. Encourage them to write three questions with *every* plus a noun. Put students in pairs to ask and answer interview questions. One student is the interviewer. The other student is a runner on the track team. Then have them switch roles.

Write an Article

Present students with this prompt:

> Imagine that you are a sports reporter for a newspaper. You are writing about a sports team that did very well at a recent game or meet. Write a short article about this team. What's the sport? What is the team's name? When did they play? Write about what most of the team members did, what "almost all of" the team members did, what "some of" the team members did, and what "every" team member did. Write at least six sentences in your article.

4 Practice

A. 1. Every classroom has a number.
    2. Every person in this school is from my country.
    3. Every teacher speaks excellent English.
    4. Every teacher gives a lot of homework.
    5. Every student in this class is learning English.
    6. Every student has a grammar book.
    7. Every unit in the book has a test.

8. Every test has 20 questions.
9. Every question has four answers.
10. Every question is interesting.

 CD4/22, 23   **B.** Play tracks 22 and 23 so students can check their answers. Then play track 23 again so they can listen and repeat the sentences.

5 Your Turn

Answers will vary. Sample answer:
Every team has five players. The two teams wear different colors. Every player has a number. Every player has to dribble the ball, pass it, and try to make a basket. What is the game?

School Activity

Tell students to talk to a partner about their former schools or universities using the word *every*. For example:
Every student had to be in class at 8:00 in the morning.
Every student had to do all the homework **every** day.
Every student had to bow to the teacher in **every** class.
Every student had to wear a uniform.
Every boy had to wear a white shirt.
Every girl had to wear a gray skirt.

9C *Very* and *Too*

STUDENT BOOK P. 249

Notes on the Photo and Warm-up Activity

This photo shows a man standing in the snow in a city, perhaps New York City. It looks like it could be on Broadway or in Times Square because of the theater marquees. This young man looks happy about the snow. In some parts of the world, it snows so much that people are accustomed to it; they even celebrate the cold and the snow. For example, parts of Canada and Japan hold winter festivals with special activities like snow and ice carving. Many people in snowy parts of the world enjoy winter sports.

Role-play
Put students in pairs and present them with the following situation:
Imagine that you are the person in this photo. Where is this place? Do you live there or are you on vacation? Discuss different things to do. One of you will suggest things to do using the word *very* to talk about your ideas. The other person will not like any of these suggestions. Respond to your partner using *too* in your response. You can then switch roles with your partner.

Quantity and Degree Words   131

6 Practice

1. h   2. f   3. b   4. e   5. g   6. a   7. d   8. c

7 Pair Up and Talk

Conversations will vary. Possible conversation:

A: What's her problem?
B: She can't wear it because it's too big. What's her problem?
A: She can't finish it because she's too sleepy. What's their problem?
B: They can't drink it because it's too hot.

8 Practice

A.
1. very expensive
2. very intelligent
3. too sweet
4. too young
5. very tired
6. too small
7. too difficult
8. very fresh

CD4/24, 25   B. Play tracks 24 and 25 so students can check their answers. Then play track 25 again so they can listen and repeat the conversations.

Chant Activity

✦ Tell the students that they are going to do a chant about *rush hour*, which is noisy, and *nightfall*, which is quiet. Write the chants on the board, underlining the stressed syllables.

Rush Hour

There is lots of traffic.	Too much traffic!
There are lots of cars.	Too many cars!
There is lots of noise.	Too much noise!
There are lots of people.	Too many people!
Too much traffic!	Too many cars!
Too much noise!	Too many people!

Nightfall

There is so little traffic.	Very little ...
There are so few cars.	Very few ...
There is so little noise.	Very little ...
There are so few people.	Very few ...
Very little traffic ...	Very few cars ...
Very little noise ...	Very few people ...

✦ You say the words on the left side and the students respond with the words on the right. You can tap or clap on the stressed syllables, encouraging the students to do the same.

✦ You can repeat it in several different ways, having the right and left side of the classroom say it, having the men and women say it, having the students say it shouting and whispering, and so forth.

9D Too Many and Too Much

STUDENT BOOK P. 252

Note: See page 263 of this Teacher's Manual for a supplementary Internet Activity Procedure and reproducible Worksheet for this section.

Notes on the Photo and Warm-up Activity

In this photo, hundreds of cars and trucks are stuck in a traffic jam on a freeway. Traffic jams are a major problem in cities. They often occur at rush hour and when there is an accident or construction work. Traffic jams waste time and gas; they also contribute to noise and air pollution. People get angry when they sit in traffic for hours. City officials often encourage people to use other methods of transportation (buses or subways) or to carpool.

Discuss Transportation

- Divide the class in half and tell one group to prepare a list of reasons to use public transportation rather than cars; tell the other group to prepare reasons to use cars rather than public transportation.
- Then ask the groups to report their opinions and reasons to the class. Call on a person in one group to give a reason. Then ask someone in the other group to give a counter-reason.
- Keep a tally on the board of the reasons for and against using public transportation.

9 Practice

A. 1. too much 3. too much 5. too much 7. too many
    2. too many 4. too many 6. too much

 CD4/26, 27 B. Play tracks 26 and 27 so students can check their answers. Then play track 27 again so they can listen and repeat the sentences.

10 Practice

A. 1. too much   4. too many 7. too much 9. too many
    2. too many, too much 5. too many 8. too much 10. too many
    3. too many   6. too much

 CD4/28, 29 B. Play tracks 28 and 29 so students can check their answers. Then play track 29 again so they can listen and repeat the sentences.

11 Pair Up and Talk

Conversations will vary. Possible conversation:
A: What's wrong with our school?   B: There are too many rules.

9E Too + Adjective + Infinitive; Too + Adjective + For + Noun/Pronoun + Infinitive

STUDENT BOOK P. 254

Notes on the Photo and Warm-up Activity

The little boy in this photo is obviously wearing an adult's clothes. Children enjoy playing dress up. This kind of pretend play helps them prepare for their roles later when they are adults.

Write about Your Childhood

Present students with the following prompt:

> The boy in the photo is wearing clothes that are too big for him. He's too small to wear them, but he is probably having fun wearing his mom's or dad's clothes. Think about your childhood. Choose a specific age. What kinds of things did you want to do? What were you too small or too young to do? What was too difficult for you to do when you were younger? Write a paragraph of at least six sentences about your experiences.

12 Practice

A.
1. I'm/I am too tired to drive.
2. This room is too small to be comfortable.
3. This computer is too old to work well.
4. Peter is too sleepy to study.
5. Janet is too busy to go.
6. The children are too excited to sleep.

 CD4/30, 31

B. Play tracks 30 and 31 so students can check their answers. Then play track 31 again so they can listen and repeat the sentences.

13 Practice

1. The room was too cold for her to sit in.
2. The room was too dark for her to read.
3. The bed was too hard for her to sleep in.
4. The tea was too strong for her to drink.
5. The weather was too stormy for her to go out.
6. The bathroom was too cold for her to take a shower.

Silly Sentence Activity

✦ Have students make up five silly sentences with a partner. Then have each pair write one of their sentences on the board. Give a few examples:

The chicken is **too small** to ride.

The clouds are **too high** to wash.

The birds are **too fat** to sing.

The book is **too big** to bite.

✦ When all the sentences are written, have the students read them, changing them by adding *for [name]*. For example:

The chicken is too small **for Elvira** to ride. The clouds are too high **for Sook** to wash.

9F Adjective + *Enough*

STUDENT BOOK P. 256

Notes on the Photo and Warm-up Activity

This very young girl seems to be from Asia. She is wearing a kimono such as the ones worn in Japan.

Discuss the Photo

✦ Tell students they will discuss the photo. The girl in the photo can't do some things, but she can do other things.

✦ Put students in groups to write as many sentences as they can about what the girl can and can't do using an adjective + *enough*. Set a time limit.

✦ Ask the group with the most items to read them to the class. The other groups should listen and check off items on their own lists that are the same. Call on other groups to read items on their lists that were not read by the first group.

14 Practice

A.
1. The chair is too uncomfortable. It is not comfortable enough.
2. The water is too hot. It is not cold enough.
3. The soup is too warm. It is not cool enough.
4. The server is too slow. He is not fast enough.
5. The bread is too old. It is not fresh enough.
6. The portion is too small. It is not large enough.
7. The coffee is too weak. It is not strong enough.
8. The table is too small. It is not big enough.
9. The meat is too tough. It is not tender enough.
10. The meal is too expensive. It is not cheap enough.

CD4/32, 33 **B.** Play tracks 32 and 33 so students can check their answers. Then play track 33 again so they can listen and repeat the sentences.

Complaint Activity

✦ Tell the students to pretend they are Mrs. Parkway from **Practice 14**. Have them think about things to complain about at a language center. Write the sentences on the left on the board as examples:
The classroom is **too** cold. It's not warm **enough**.   Ask your teacher to turn up the heat.
The university is **too** far. It's not near **enough**.   Maybe you can buy a car and drive there.

✦ Then have them walk around the classroom and complain to each other. One person expresses a complaint and the other person offers a solution. Example solutions are listed above on the right.

9G *Enough* + Noun

STUDENT BOOK P. 258

Notes on the Photo and Warm-up Activity

These coworkers are getting ready for a meeting. They are planning to serve coffee. There is also a bowl of snacks on the table. More than 50 percent of Americans drink coffee every day, three to four cups each. That means more than 330 million cups a day. More than 500 billion cups of coffee are consumed worldwide each year.

Discuss Refreshments

✦ Brainstorm a list of occasions at work, school, and home when people serve refreshments.
✦ Put students in small groups to choose three events and plan refreshments for each.
✦ Call on representatives of each group to tell the class their events and their menus.

15 Practice

1. enough time   3. enough people   5. enough drinks   7. enough money
2. enough room   4. enough chairs   6. enough glasses   8. enough food

16 Practice

A. 1. enough people   3. enough time   5. enough CDs
    2. enough food   4. enough soda   6. enough chairs

136 Unit 9

CD4/34, 35   **B.** Play tracks 34 and 35 so students can check their answers. Then play track 35 again so they can listen and repeat the sentences.

17 Pair Up and Talk

Conversations will vary. Sample conversation:
A: Do you have enough money to buy a CD?
B: Yes, I have enough money to buy a CD.

Contrast Activity

✦ Tell students to think of things about their country that are good and bad. Have them write three sentences contrasting the good and bad things. For example:

There is **enough** water.	There are **not enough** jobs.
There are **enough** houses.	There is **not enough** good farmland.
There is **enough** electricity.	There are **not enough** buses in the city.

✦ Then have them share the sentences with a group of three or four other students and discuss them.

18 Read

Long or short answers are possible. Long answers are given below.

1. He was very hungry.
2. It was too simple.
3. It wasn't good enough.
4. It was very expensive.
5. There weren't enough eggs.
6. There aren't enough visits of kings.

Listening Puzzle

STUDENT BOOK P. 261

A.  CD4, 36
Answer: C. Mt. Fuji

B. Students might discuss the following:
Mt. Kilimanjaro is in Africa, not Asia. Mt. Everest was never a volcano; Mt. Fuji was.

C. CD4, 37

Quantity and Degree Words

Reading Challenge: The Sahara Desert

STUDENT BOOK P. 262

A. Answers will vary. Possible answers:
1. in Africa   2. camels, people, insects

C. **Paragraph 2**: <u>enough</u> water, <u>enough</u> water, <u>a few</u> palm trees, <u>enough</u> water; **Paragraph 3**: <u>Almost all of</u> the people, <u>Some</u> people; **Paragraph 4**: <u>Many</u> animals, <u>many</u> small creatures, <u>some</u> shade, <u>no</u> trees

D. 1. B   2. C
E. 3. D   4. A   5. C
F. 6. A
G. 7. C
H. 8. A

Writing: Describe a Place

STUDENT BOOK P. 264

Writing Expansion

Students can exchange paragraphs with a partner. They can use their paragraphs from this Writing activity or new ones. After reading the paragraph, the partner can offer solutions to the problems described, as in the **Complaint Activity** on Teacher's Manual page 136. She or he can write a few solutions on the back of the paper before handing it in to the teacher.

Self-Test

STUDENT BOOK P. 265

A. 1. A 2. A 3. B 4. C 5. D 6. B 7. A 8. A 9. C 10. B
B. 1. D 2. A 3. B 4. C 5. C 6. B 7. B 8. B 9. C 10. B

Unit 10

Objects and Pronouns

Unit Sections		Notes/Activities	SB page	TM page
10A	Object Pronouns	Substitution Activity	268	140
10B	Indirect Objects	Repetition Activity	272	141
10C	Indirect Objects with *For*	Notes on Usage: *to* vs *for*	275	143
10D	Indirect Objects with Certain Verbs	Internet Activity; Notes on Vocabulary: verbs with *to* and *for*	277	145
10E	Possessive Pronouns	Identifying Objects Activity; Chant Activity	280	147
10F	Indefinite Pronouns	Guessing Game Activities	286	149
✦	Listening Puzzle: Inventors		289	150
✦	Reading Challenge: Alexander Graham Bell		290	150
✦	Writing: Write an Expository Paragraph	Writing Expansion	292	150
✦	Self-Test	Answer Key	293	150

Unit 10 introduces the object pronouns, and provides practice in distinguishing them from subject pronouns. The text then provides a smooth transition into indirect objects, explaining the relationship between direct and indirect objects and providing practice distinguishing between them.

Indirect objects with *to* and *for* are taught and practiced before moving on to sentences that use indirect objects with certain verbs, such as *buy*, *get*, *make*, *explain*, *introduce*, and *repeat*. As with previous units, the correct forms of the sentence patterns are taught, the text explains how and when we use them, and it provides ample practice.

Possessive pronouns are taught and contrasted with possessive adjectives. Exercises incorporate practice of both. Finally, the indefinite pronouns are presented. The text explains how and when we use them, and it provides ample practice.

10A Object Pronouns

STUDENT BOOK P. 268

Notes on the Photo and Warm-up Activities

This is a photo of a young girl and boy. Because their arms are around each other and they are smiling, they appear to get along well—at least they did for this photograph!

Discuss Personality Differences

Have students work in small groups or pairs and present them with the following situation:

> The girl and boy in this photo are brother and sister. They are smiling and seem to be friends. Sometimes, however, they don't get along well. Discuss why they might not always get along. What does each person like and dislike? What does he do that bothers her? What does she do that bothers him? Share your ideas with the class.

Write a Description

Present students with this prompt:

> Do you have a brother or sister, or a friend who is like a brother or sister to you? Write a short description of this person. Describe what this person looks like. Do you get along well? Why or why not? Explain what things you like to do together, or what you don't like to do. Write at least six sentences about your relationship.

1 Practice

A.
1. We study English at the same school.
2. He is our teacher.
3. He teaches us English grammar.
4. He uses it to teach grammar.
5. The students like him.
6. They ask John Blackie questions.
7. He answers them.
8. Linda is a student in our class. She always asks questions.
9. We don't like to listen to her, but Mr. Blackie is very patient.
10. He always answers her questions.

 CD5/2, 3 B. Play tracks 2 and 3 so students can check their answers. Then play track 3 again so they can listen and repeat the sentences.

2 Practice

A. A 1. It   2. me   3. they   4. us   5. We   6. it   7. me
    B 1. her   2. she   3. me   4. her   5. He   6. him
    C 1. it   2. me   3. you   4. me   5. you 6. them

140 Unit 10

CD5/4, 5   **B.** Play tracks 4 and 5 so students can check their answers. Then play track 5 again so they can listen and repeat the sentences in A and the conversations in B and C.

3 Pair Up and Talk

B. Conversations will vary. Sample conversation:
  A: Do you like Madonna?
  B: Yes, I like her because she's a good singer and dancer.

C. Paragraphs will vary. Sample paragraph:
My favorite food is pizza. I like it best with cheese and pepperoni. My mother makes delicious homemade pizza. She got the recipe from her mother. Pizza is fun to eat with friends. It is healthy and almost everyone likes it!

Substitution Activity

✦ Write the list of object pronouns on the board.
✦ To practice the object pronouns, ask the students to think of nouns, or names of persons, places, or things. They can be proper nouns (*Mr. Jones, Rome, Toyota*) or common nouns (*teacher, city, cars*).
✦ Go down the list as individual students say a noun and the corresponding pronoun. For example:
teacher = me, student = you, Marcelo = him, Graciela = her, truck = it, Will and me = us, Grace and you = you, the Yankees = them.

10B Indirect Objects

STUDENT BOOK P. 272

Notes on the Photo and Warm-up Activity

This man is giving a bouquet of roses to a friend. The flowers probably have come from a florist's shop. It's more traditional for men to give women flowers, but women give flowers to men sometimes, too.

Role-play
Put students in pairs to role-play a conversation between the man and the woman he is giving the flowers to. Before the role-play, they must decide who these people are, what their relationship is, and why the man is giving the woman flowers. They must also decide how she feels about these flowers and how she will react.

Objects and Pronouns   **141**

4 Practice

1. The teacher handed <u>the paper</u> to (me).
2. He sends <u>newspapers</u> to (my parents).
3. She showed <u>the photos</u> to (us).
4. My grandfather told <u>stories</u> to (us).
5. I write <u>letters</u> to (my brother).
6. John passed <u>the book</u> to (Maria).
7. We lent <u>ten dollars</u> to (Kim).
8. My father gave <u>a watch</u> to (me).
9. His parents gave <u>an old computer</u> to (him).
10. Her brother gave <u>the message</u> to (her).

5 Practice

A.
1. The teacher handed me the paper.
2. He sends my parents newspapers.
3. She showed us the photos.
4. My grandfather told us stories.
5. I write my brother letters.
6. John passed Maria the book.
7. We lent Kim ten dollars.
8. My father gave me a watch.
9. His parents gave him an old computer.
10. Her brother gave her the message.

CD5/6, 7 B. Play tracks 6 and 7 so students can check their answers. Then play track 7 again so they can listen and repeat the sentences.

6 Practice

A.
1. the house, I gave it to my mother.
2. my car, I sold it to Mr. Black.
3. the television, I offered it to my neighbor.
4. an email, I sent it to my friends.
5. the news, I told it to my boss.
6. the photos, I showed them to my friends.
7. a birthday gift, I gave it to my roommate.
8. a theater ticket, I handed it to my sister.

CD5/8, 9 B. Play tracks 8 and 9 so students can check their answers. Then play track 9 again so they can listen and repeat the conversations.

142   Unit 10

Repetition Activity

To continue practicing pronouns, repeat **Practice 4** and **6**, changing all the nouns to pronouns. You may do this as a class or assign it to the students to do individually or in pairs. For example:

Practice 4
1. The teacher handed the paper to me.
   She/He handed it to me.

Practice 6
1. JIM: I gave my mother the house.
   TOM: Who did you give it to?
   JIM: I gave it to her.

10c Indirect Objects with *For*

STUDENT BOOK P. 275

Notes on the Photo and Warm-up Activities

The man in this photo is opening the door of his home to welcome two visitors. The visitors seem happy to be there, but we can't see the man's face to know how he feels. The visitors may have stopped by unexpectedly to say hello; the man at the door might be surprised. People from different cultures have different customs or expectations about visiting someone in their home. In some cultures, it is important to bring a small gift to someone's house. In others, a gift is not so important. It's not polite in all cultures for people to stop by someone's home without an invitation; yet, in some cultures it is acceptable and even common.

Discuss Visiting

Introduce these terms to students: *visitor* (someone who visits someone else's home, usually for a short time); *guest* (a visitor in someone's home, staying for any length of time); *houseguest* (a person who stays for one or more nights); and *host* (a person who invites or has guests in his or her home). Have students discuss these questions in small groups or as a class:

In your home culture, what do people usually do when they visit other people in their homes?
Is it necessary to be invited or is it acceptable to arrive unexpectedly, or "to drop in"?
Do visitors or guests usually bring gifts for their hosts? How do hosts prepare for their visitors?
When you are a host, what do you like to do for your visitors?
When you are a houseguest, what do you like to do for your host?

Write Tips for Hosts and Guests

Present this situation to students:

What do good hosts do for their houseguests? What do good houseguests do for their host? Write a short guide to being either a host or a houseguest in a particular country. List at least six points in six separate sentences.

7 Practice

A. 1. for   2. to   3. for   4. to   5. for   6. to   7. for   8. to

 CD5/10, 11

B. Play tracks 10 and 11 so students can check their answers. Then play track 11 again so they can listen and repeat the sentences.

8 Pair Up and Talk

Conversations will vary. Sample conversation:
- A: What do you do for your best friend on his/her birthday?
- B: I send a card to him/her. I buy a gift for him/her, too.

9 Practice

Answers will vary. Sample answers:

We/I will give him/her presents.
We/I will send him/her a card.

We/I will wish him/her a happy birthday.
We/I will sing him/her a song.

Notes on Usage: *to* vs *for*

✦ Students may ask about the difference in meaning between the prepositions *to* and *for* when used with indirect objects. One difference is that:

to indicates the "actual recipient," e.g., I gave a doll **to** my niece.

for indicates the "intended recipient," e.g., I bought a doll **for** my niece.

In the first sentence, we know that the doll was given to the niece. In the second case, we are not sure if the doll was given to the niece, although it was intended for her.

✦ Another difference in meaning is that *for* indicates "in place of."

She picked up the package **for** him because he was sick.

They took the photo **for** me because I forgot my camera.

In the first sentence, he couldn't pick up the package, so she did it in his place. In the second sentence, I couldn't take the photo, so they did it in my place.

10D Indirect Objects with Certain Verbs

Student Book p. 277

Note: See page 265 of this Teacher's Manual for a supplementary Internet Activity Procedure and reproducible Worksheet for this section.

Notes on the Photo and Warm-up Activities

In this photo, there are a couple of wrapped gifts. Although many people wrap their own presents, stores will often gift-wrap packages for their customers. Stores may also have gift registries where people who are getting married or having a baby can list the gifts they would like.

Discuss Gifts

Ask students to discuss these questions in small groups or as a class:

    For what occasions do you usually give and receive gifts?
    Where do you usually get gifts for people?
    Do you prefer to make or buy gifts? What do you usually buy? What do you usually make?
    How important is attractive wrapping on a gift?

Write about Gifts

✦ Have students brainstorm a list of gifts that they have bought or made and gifts that they have received. They can write their ideas in a two-column chart.

Gifts I Bought or Made	Gifts I Received

✦ Tell students to choose three favorite gifts from each column, and write a paragraph of at least six sentences about the best gifts they gave and received. Encourage them to use each of the verbs *buy*, *get*, and *make* at least once.

10 Practice

1. She bought a tie for her father. She bought her father/him a tie.
2. She got a blouse for her mother. She got her mother/her a blouse.
3. She made a sweater for her brother. She made her brother/him a sweater.
4. She bought a toy for her niece. She bought her niece/her a toy.
5. She got books for her sister. She got her sister/her books.
6. She made a cake for her neighbors. She made her neighbors/them a cake.
7. She bought a wallet for Brian. She bought Brian/him a wallet.
8. She got a plant for her boss. She got her boss/him/her a plant.

11 Practice

A.
1. The teacher explained the answer to us.
2. The teacher introduced indirect objects to us.
3. The teacher repeated the questions for us.
4. The teacher explained the meaning of the word to me.
5. The student repeated the sentence for her.
6. The teacher introduced the new student to us.
7. The student explained her problem to the teacher.
8. The teacher introduced the speaker to the class.

 CD5/12, 13

B. Play tracks 12 and 13 so students can check their answers. Then play track 13 again so they can listen and repeat the sentences.

12 Practice

1. Tim bought a gift for his wife. OR Tim bought his wife a gift.
2. He fixed the car for her.
3. He made dinner for her. OR He made her dinner.
4. He got flowers for her. OR He got her flowers.
5. He opened the door for her.
6. He showed a letter to her. OR He showed her a letter.
7. His wife told her ideas to him. OR His wife told him her ideas.
8. She gave advice to him. OR She gave him advice.

Notes on Vocabulary: verbs with *to* and *for*

✦ Students may ask for a list of verbs that take the prepositions *to* and *for*. Here is a partial list:

TO: deliver, give, hand, mail, present, say, send, show, tell, write
FOR: answer, buy, cash, fix, get, make, open, pick up, prepare, pronounce
TO and FOR: explain, introduce, repeat

✦ The last three verbs may be used with either *to* or *for*, with slight differences in meaning. For example, *to* indicates "actual recipient" and *for* indicates "in place of" in the following sentences:

The speaker explained her point **to** the audience.

The moderator explained the speaker's point **for** her.

10E Possessive Pronouns

Student Book p. 280

Notes on the Photo and Warm-up Activity

This woman has a pen that she may have borrowed. Students often borrow small things from classmates, especially if they know them well. Lending and borrowing habits may vary from culture to culture.

Discuss Lending and Borrowing

✦ Put students in pairs or small groups to talk about what they would be likely to borrow from or lend to the following people: a family member, a friend, a classmate, an acquaintance.

✦ Elicit examples from students (for example, *I lend my sister money*). Have students say their examples at least one other way (for example, *I lend money to my sister*).

13 Practice

1. These are the teacher's books. These are his books. These are his.
2. This is the nurse's thermometer. This is her thermometer. This is hers.
3. These are the travelers' suitcases. These are their suitcases. These are theirs.
4. This is the taxi driver's taxi. This is his taxi. This is his.
5. These are the children's toys. These are their toys. These are theirs.

Identifying Objects Activity

✦ Collect objects from students in the class.
✦ Elicit three sentences about each object (for example, *That is Hugo's watch. That is his watch. That is his*).

14 Practice

1. Yes, they're his. OR Yes, they are his.
2. No, it's not his. OR No, it isn't his.
3. Yes, they're theirs. OR Yes, they are theirs.
4. No, it's not his. OR No, it isn't his.
5. No, they're not hers. OR No, they aren't hers.
6. Yes, they're theirs. OR Yes, they are theirs.

15 Practice

A.
1. your, Mine
2. their, Theirs
3. my, my, mine
4. my, My, ours, Our
5. their, Theirs, hers
6. your, my, mine, yours, my
7. your, mine, yours
8. Our, her, ours

 CD5/14, 15

B. Play tracks 14 and 15 so students can check their answers. Then play track 15 again so they can listen and repeat the conversations.

16 Practice

1. It's   2. its   3. It's   4. its   5. It's   6. its   7. It's   8. its

Chant Activity

✦ Write the personal pronouns/adjectives on the board in four columns:

Subject Pronouns	Object Pronouns	Possessive Adjectives	Possessive Pronouns
<u>I</u>	<u>me</u>	<u>my</u>	<u>mine</u>
you	you	your	yours
<u>he</u>	<u>him</u>	<u>his</u>	<u>his</u>
she	her	her	hers
<u>it</u>	<u>it</u>	<u>its</u>	<u>its</u>
we	us	our	ours
<u>you</u>	<u>you</u>	<u>your</u>	<u>yours</u>
they	them	their	theirs

✦ Tell the students they are going to practice the pronouns in a chant, stressing the underlined words.
✦ Using a pointer or ruler to tap, chant the words, then have groups of students chant them.

17 Your Turn

Answers will vary. Sample answers:
My eyes are brown. Yours are blue. My shoes are old. Yours are new.

18 Pair Up and Talk

Conversations will vary. Sample conversation:
A: What are you going to do tonight?
B: I'm going to bring these books to my sister. They're hers.

148   Unit 10

10F Indefinite Pronouns

STUDENT BOOK P. 286

Notes on the Photo and Warm-up Activity

This photo shows people eating at an outdoor café on the Champs Elysees in Paris. The Arc de Triomphe is in the background. There are many outdoor cafés on this street, and many in the city of Paris.

Discuss Pros and Cons

Put students in pairs to list the pros (positive things) and cons (negative things) of eating outdoors vs indoors. Elicit ideas from the class and write them on the board.

19 Practice

1. someone, nobody, something
2. something, anything
3. something, nothing, anything
4. anything/something, nothing, something
5. something, anything
6. Something, anyone/anybody, anything
7. something/anything, anything, anything
8. anything, Nothing, something
9. anything, nothing, something
10. anything/something, anything, someone, anybody/anyone

20 Read

Possible answers:
1. The beggar found a leather purse.
2. He gave the purse back to the merchant.
3. He asked him for the reward.
4. The judge believed both of them.
5. He gave it to the beggar.

Guessing Game Activities

✦ Think of a famous person. Elicit *yes/no* questions from the class until they can guess who it is. Then call students to the front of the room to think of someone famous and elicit questions and guesses.

✦ Tell students that they are going to continue the guessing game using things in the classroom. After a few rounds, you can change categories to things in your dormitory/apartment, things outside, and so forth.

Listening Puzzle

STUDENT BOOK P. 289

A. CD5, 16

Answer: B. Thomas Edison

B. Students might discuss the following:

Albert Einstein was a scientist. Henry Ford invented/made the first automobile.

C. CD5, 17

Reading Challenge: Alexander Graham Bell

STUDENT BOOK P. 290

A. Answers will vary. Possible answers:
   1. telephone, television, computer, cell phone   2. I used a landline phone.

C. **Paragraph 1:** sound, his family, deaf people, a school, the deaf; **Paragraph 2:** Mabel Hubbard, her; **Paragraph 3:** an idea, an invention, electricity, the human voice, this idea, rooms, words, each other, the words, you, the memorable words; **Paragraph 4:** telephones, the first call

D. 1. B   2. A
E. 3. D   4. B   5. C
F. 6. D
G. 7. B
H. 8. C

Writing: Write an Expository Paragraph

STUDENT BOOK P. 292

Writing Expansion

On a piece of paper, have the students write the name of a major holiday in their country and the cards or gifts they give. On a bulletin board or large piece of cardboard, arrange the papers so that students can see them and compare customs.

Self-Test

STUDENT BOOK P. 293

A. 1. D   2. B   3. C   4. D   5. A   6. D   7. D   8. A   9. C   10. B
B. 1. B   2. B   3. B   4. B   5. C   6. A   7. B   8. D   9. C   10. B

Unit 11
Modals

Unit Sections	Notes/Activities	SB page	TM page
11A *Can*	Animal Activity	296	152
11B Questions with *Can*	Notes on Pronunciation: *can, can't, could*	298	154
11C *Could*: Past of *Can*	Chant Activity	300	155
11D *Be Able To*	Notes on Grammar: more on *can, could, be able to*	303	157
11E *Should*	Internet Activity; Advice Activity	307	159
11F *Must*	Rules and Regulations Activity	310	161
11G *Have To*	Notes on Usage: *don't have to* vs *mustn't;* Notes on Grammar: more on *should, must, have to*	312	162
11H *May I, Can I,* and *Could I*	Notes on Culture	317	164
✦ Listening Puzzle: Animals		321	166
✦ Reading Challenge: Tornado		322	167
✦ Writing: Write a Letter of Advice	Writing Expansion	324	167
✦ Self-Test	Answer Key	325	167

Unit 11 first introduces the modals of ability, *can, could,* and *be able to*. The unit teaches the modals' correct position in sentences, explains how and when we use them, and provides ample practice.

Next, the modals of necessity, *should, must,* and *have to,* are introduced. The text teaches the modals' correct position in sentences, explains the differences among them, and provides practice.

Finally, the modals to express polite requests and permission, *may I, can I,* and *could I,* are presented. Again, the text teaches their correct position in sentences, explains how and when we use them, and provides ample practice.

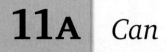 Can

STUDENT BOOK P. 296

Notes on the Photo and Warm-up Activity

This is a photo of a North American black bear. Black bears live in forests from northern Mexico to Canada. Black bears eat nuts, fruits, insects, and greens, and they don't eat much meat. Sometimes people see them when they go camping. Black bears rarely attack humans.

Talk about Bears

- Ask students these questions:

  Has anyone seen a bear in the wild or in the zoo?

  Has anyone seen bears in movies or cartoons?

  Does anyone know of any famous bear characters? (Smokey the Bear, Winnie the Pooh)

  Does anyone collect teddy bears?

  Does anyone come from a culture that has stories about bears?

  Are bears frightening or cute?

- Next, place students in small groups. Ask them to think of sentences about bears. Have one person write down the group's ideas. They can write about different kinds of bears, even teddy bears. Allow 10 minutes. Each sentence must use the word *can*, *can't*, or *cannot*. For example:

  Bears can run very fast for short distances.

  Bears can sleep for many months during the winter.

  Bears can scare humans.

  Teddy bears can make children happy.

- To make the activity competitive, award one point for each sentence that correctly uses one of these words with a verb. The group with the most points wins.

1 Practice

Answers will vary. Possible answers:

Affirmative
1. Elephants can swim.
2. Birds can sing.
3. Chickens can fly.
4. Bees can make honey.
5. Horses can run.
6. Penguins can swim.
7. Monkeys can climb trees.
8. Dogs can lie down.

Negative
1. Elephants can't fly.
2. Birds can't swim.
3. Chickens can't make honey.
4. Bees can't run.
5. Horses can't sing.
6. Penguins can't fly.
7. Monkeys can't sing.
8. Dogs can't climb trees.

2 Your Turn

Answers will vary. Possible answers:
I can play the violin. I can't play the piano.

Animal Activity

✦ Here is a more complete list of animals. You can write them on the board and ask students to go to the board and write sentences about the animals. Or students can stay in their seats and simply say sentences about the animals. Examples are provided.

Animals with Wings
Put a check (✓) beside the animals that can fly. Put an X beside the animals that can't fly.
bats ✓ chickens ✓ eagles ✓ penguins X turkeys ✓
Bats have wings, and they **can** fly.
Penguins have wings, but they **can't** fly.

Animals on Land
Put a check (✓) beside animals that can walk on two legs. Put an X beside the animals that must walk on four legs.
apes ✓ chimpanzees ✓ deer X giraffes X lions X
Apes **can** walk on two legs.
Deer **can't** walk on two legs. They **can** walk on four legs.

Insects
Put a check (✓) beside insects that bite or sting people. Put an X beside insects that don't bite or sting people.
bees ✓ flies X ladybugs X mosquitoes ✓ wasps ✓
Bees **can** bite or sting people.
Flies **can't** bite or sting people.

Modals

11B Questions with *Can*

STUDENT BOOK P. 298

Notes on the Photo and Warm-up Activity

This photo shows two boys peeking out from under a blanket. They may be playing hide-and-seek, or they might be using their imagination and playacting.

Use Your Imagination

- Have students work in pairs. Provide them with this prompt: *Imagine that these two boys are playacting. What are they pretending? Think of a situation, for example, maybe they are exploring a jungle. Make a list of their questions and answers using* can, *and the question words* where, when, *and* what. *Here are some examples:* Can we eat this fruit? No, we can't. It's too sour. Where can we stop and rest? We can rest under that tree.

- Invite students to share their ideas with the class as a role play.

3 Practice

B.
1. How old are you?
2. Can you drive?
3. Can you cook meals?
4. Can you read music?
5. Can you swim?
6. Can you tell stories?
7. Do you have a lot of energy?
8. What other things can you do?

4 Pair Up and Talk

Questions will vary. Partner's answers will be *Yes, I can* or *No, I can't*.

Notes on Pronunciation: *can, can't, could*

- Students often pronounce *can* and *can't* in a similar way, simply adding /t/ to the negative. However, native speakers pronounce the vowel differently—/ɪ/ for *can* vs /æ/ for *can't*. They also stress the negative form, but not the affirmative or question forms. For example:

Can you lend me a dollar?	C'n ya <u>lend</u> me a <u>dollar</u>?
I can lend you five if you want.	I c'n <u>lend</u> ya <u>five</u> if ya <u>want</u>.
Can you lend me ten?	C'n ya <u>lend</u> me <u>ten</u>?
No, I can't. I only have five.	No, I <u>can't</u>. I <u>only</u> h'v <u>five</u>.

- In short answers, however, both *can* and *can't* are stressed, but the vowels are still pronounced differently. The vowel in *can* is more open and in *can't* is more closed and slightly nasalized.

Can you lend me a dollar?	C'n ya <u>lend</u> me a <u>dol</u>lar?
Yes, I can./No, I can't.	<u>Yes</u>, I <u>can</u>./<u>No</u>, I căn't.

♦ In a similar way, the vowel sound in *could* is stressed and slightly longer in the negative than in the affirmative and question forms. For example:

Could he call you back?	C'd 'e <u>call</u> ya <u>back</u>?
No, he couldn't call back today.	No, 'e <u>couldn't</u> call <u>back</u> to<u>day</u>.
But he could call by tomorrow.	But 'e c'd <u>call</u> by to<u>mor</u>row.

♦ You can write these sentences on the board and explain them to the students. Then have them repeat the examples. For further practice, they can repeat the sentences in **Practice 1** and in **Your Turn 2**.

11C *Could*: Past of *Can*

STUDENT BOOK P. 300

Notes on the Photo and Warm-up Activities

The man in this photo has been badly injured. He is walking on crutches and has a cast on one leg and a broken toe. He has a bandage (or splint) around one wrist, a bandage around his head, and a neck brace. The neck brace suggests that he might have whiplash from a car accident. He is wearing a hospital gown, so he's probably still in the hospital.

Discuss the Photo

♦ Have students work with a partner or in groups of three. Ask them to imagine that they know the person in this photo and that the accident happened six months ago. They should decide how the man got hurt and how they know him. Are they his doctors? Family members/friends/classmates/neighbors?

♦ Have students discuss the man's abilities in both the past and the present. Each group should discuss what the man *could* or *couldn't* do before and after the accident. They should try to think of 10 things to say about him. Ask groups to report their ideas to the class. Encourage the class to ask each group follow-up questions about the man's current condition.

Write a Letter or Email

Present students with this prompt:

Imagine that you are the man in this photo. Six months ago, you were injured in an accident. Write a letter or an email to your friends and family. Tell them how you are doing. Explain what you could or couldn't do right after the accident and what you can or cannot do now.

Modals 155

5 Practice

A.
1. She couldn't ride a bicycle.
2. She couldn't run fast.
3. She couldn't drive a car.
4. She couldn't ski.
5. She couldn't take tests.
6. She couldn't work.
7. She couldn't write a letter.
8. She couldn't read a book.

 CD5/18, 19 B. Play tracks 18 and 19 so students can check their answers. Then play track 19 again so they can listen and repeat the sentences.

6 Your Turn

Answers will vary. Sample answers:
1. When I was younger, I couldn't use a computer, but I can use a computer well now.
2. Five years ago, I couldn't speak English, but I can speak English well now.
3. When I was a child, I couldn't live by myself, but I can live by myself now.
4. When I was ten, I couldn't drive, but I can drive now.

7 Practice

A.
1. He couldn't go to school.
2. He couldn't drive.
3. He couldn't play tennis.
4. He could read magazines.
5. He couldn't swim.
6. He couldn't visit friends.
7. He could watch TV.
8. He could work online.

 CD5/20, 21 B. Play tracks 20 and 21 so students can check their answers. Then play track 21 again so they can listen and repeat the sentences.

8 Pair Up and Talk

Questions will vary. Partner's answers will be *Yes, I could* or *No, I couldn't*. Students can be encouraged to use other appropriate answers using *could* and *couldn't*.

Chant Activity

✦ To practice pronunciation, stress, and rhythm, write this chant on the board for the students. Tap or clap the rhythm and invite them to do the same.

Can you <u>lend</u> me a <u>doll</u>ar?	I can <u>lend</u> you a <u>dime</u>.
Can you <u>come</u> out and <u>holl</u>er?	I can <u>shout</u> just <u>fine</u>.
Can you <u>find</u> me a <u>penn</u>y?	I can <u>find</u> a whole <u>bunch</u>.
Can you <u>give</u> me a <u>sand</u>wich?	I can <u>take</u> you to <u>lunch</u>.
Could you <u>come</u> to my <u>house</u>?	I could <u>come</u> right <u>now</u>.
Could you <u>catch</u> the <u>mouse</u>?	I could <u>catch</u> the <u>cow</u>.
Could you <u>find</u> my <u>ring</u>?	I could <u>find</u> all <u>ten</u>.
Could you <u>make</u> me <u>sing</u>?	<u>Again</u> and <u>again</u>.

✦ For variety, you can say the left part, and have students respond with the right part. Then one side of the room could say the left part and the other side the right part, or males and females, and so on.

11D *Be Able To*

STUDENT BOOK P. 303

Notes on the Photo and Warm-up Activities

The man in the photo is a weight lifter. He is wearing a special uniform for weight lifters or wrestlers. The name *Hercules* is significant. Hercules was a Greek hero known for his uncommon strength. In ancient Greek mythology, he was famous for carrying out 12 difficult physical tasks, including killing various beasts.

Discuss the Photo
Introduce the terms *weight lifting* and *wrestling*. Ask students to discuss these questions in groups or as a class:
  Have you ever watched or participated in weight lifting or wrestling?
  Do you like these sports? Why or why not?
  Are these popular sports in your country?
  Do you think that both men and women enjoy these sports? Why or why not?

Make a Report
✦ Place students in pairs and present them with the following situation:
  Imagine that you are sports reporters for a radio or TV program. You will report on Hercules Lewis, a great weight lifter (or wrestler). Talk about his abilities using *be able to* in the present, the past, and the future.
✦ Ask students to record or perform their commentary for the class. Remind the other students to listen specifically for what Lewis *is able to do* and *is not able to do*.

Modals

9 Practice

B.
1. At age three, he was able to play the piano.
2. After he heard a piece of music one time, Mozart was able to play it.
3. People were not able to believe it.
4. At age five, he was able to write music for the piano.
5. Soon his father wasn't able to teach him because little Mozart knew everything.
6. At 12, he was famous and was able to make money for his family.
7. Mozart worked long hours and was able to work very fast.
8. He was able to write an opera in just a few weeks.
9. He was able to work better at night because it was quiet.
10. He was able to write all kinds of music, even music for clocks.
11. We are still not able to understand why he died.
12. We are able to buy his music on tapes or CDs.

 CD5/22, 23

C. Play tracks 22 and 23 so students can check their answers. Then play track 23 again so they can listen and repeat the sentences.

10 Practice

Answers will vary. Possible answers:

1. When he was a baby, he could smile/he was able to smile.
2. Now, he can use a computer/he is able to use a computer.
3. When he is 16, he will be able to dance.
4. When he was a baby, he could sleep/he was able to sleep.
5. Now, he can ride a bicycle/he is able to ride a bicycle.
6. When he is 16, he will be able to drive a car.
7. When he was a baby, he could cry/he was able to cry.
8. Now, he can run/he is able to run.
9. When he is 16, he will be able to get a part-time job.
10. When he was a baby, he could eat/he was able to eat.
11. Now, he can play football/he is able to play football.
12. When he is 16, he will be able to sing in a group.

11 Pair Up and Talk

Conversations will vary. Sample conversation:
A: What will you be able to do in the future?
B: I will be able to read newspapers and watch movies in English.

2 Your Turn

Answers will vary. Possible answers:
I can play the violin. I can't play the piano.

Animal Activity

✦ Here is a more complete list of animals. You can write them on the board and ask students to go to the board and write sentences about the animals. Or students can stay in their seats and simply say sentences about the animals. Examples are provided.

Animals with Wings
Put a check (✓) beside the animals that can fly. Put an X beside the animals that can't fly.
bats ✓   chickens ✓   eagles ✓   penguins X   turkeys ✓
Bats have wings, and they **can** fly.
Penguins have wings, but they **can't** fly.

Animals on Land
Put a check (✓) beside animals that can walk on two legs. Put an X beside the animals that must walk on four legs.
apes ✓   chimpanzees ✓   deer X   giraffes X   lions X
Apes **can** walk on two legs.
Deer **can't** walk on two legs. They **can** walk on four legs.

Insects
Put a check (✓) beside insects that bite or sting people. Put an X beside insects that don't bite or sting people.
bees ✓   flies X   ladybugs X   mosquitoes ✓   wasps ✓
Bees **can** bite or sting people.
Flies **can't** bite or sting people.

11B Questions with *Can*

STUDENT BOOK P. 298

Notes on the Photo and Warm-up Activity

This photo shows two boys peeking out from under a blanket. They may be playing hide-and-seek, or they might be using their imagination and playacting.

Use Your Imagination

♦ Have students work in pairs. Provide them with this prompt: *Imagine that these two boys are playacting. What are they pretending? Think of a situation, for example, maybe they are exploring a jungle. Make a list of their questions and answers using* can, *and the question words* where, when, *and* what. *Here are some examples:* Can we eat this fruit? No, we can't. It's too sour. Where can we stop and rest? We can rest under that tree.

♦ Invite students to share their ideas with the class as a role play.

3 Practice

B.
1. How old are you?
2. Can you drive?
3. Can you cook meals?
4. Can you read music?
5. Can you swim?
6. Can you tell stories?
7. Do you have a lot of energy?
8. What other things can you do?

4 Pair Up and Talk

Questions will vary. Partner's answers will be *Yes, I can* or *No, I can't*.

Notes on Pronunciation: *can, can't, could*

♦ Students often pronounce *can* and *can't* in a similar way, simply adding /t/ to the negative. However, native speakers pronounce the vowel differently—/ɪ/ for *can* vs /æ/ for *can't*. They also stress the negative form, but not the affirmative or question forms. For example:

Can you lend me a dollar?	C'n ya <u>lend</u> me a <u>dollar</u>?
I can lend you five if you want.	I c'n <u>lend</u> ya <u>five</u> if ya <u>want</u>.
Can you lend me ten?	C'n ya <u>lend</u> me <u>ten</u>?
No, I can't. I only have five.	No, I <u>can't</u>. I <u>only</u> h'v <u>five</u>.

♦ In short answers, however, both *can* and *can't* are stressed, but the vowels are still pronounced differently. The vowel in *can* is more open and in *can't* is more closed and slightly nasalized.

Notes on Grammar: more on *can*, *could*, *be able to*

✦ Although students will probably not ask many questions about the differences between *can*, *could*, or *be able to* beyond those explained in the book, it is helpful for teachers to be aware of them.

✦ *Can* denotes ability, which includes being able to, being capable of, and knowing how to do something. Later in section **11H**, *can*, along with *may* and *could*, is used to denote permission, that is, being allowed or permitted to do something.

✦ *Could* denotes past ability, present or future permission, and present possibility.

11E Should

STUDENT BOOK P. 307

Note: See page 267 of this Teacher's Manual for a supplementary Internet Activity Procedure and reproducible Worksheet for this section.

Notes on the Photo and Warm-up Activity

This photo shows a cross-cultural encounter between Eastern and Western businessmen. The men are bowing as they greet each other. It is a custom in parts of Asia and some other parts of the world to bow when you greet someone. It is a Western custom to shake hands when you greet someone. Often, both types of greetings occur, especially when the participants are from different cultures.

Talk about the Photo

✦ Ask the class to explain what is going on in the picture. Have them discuss these questions in groups or as a class:

How do you think these two businessmen feel? Why?

In your own culture, how do people usually greet a businessperson? A friend?

What should (or shouldn't) the men do in this situation? What advice would you give them?

✦ If students do not know much about the customs of either culture, they should still try to think of advice. (For example, *He should read books about Asian culture. He should talk to people who have done business in North America.*) Call on groups to report back to the class.

12 Practice

1. shouldn't
2. should
3. shouldn't
4. should
5. should
6. shouldn't
7. should
8. shouldn't

13 Practice

A.
1. He shouldn't skip school.
2. He shouldn't come home late.
3. He should do his homework.
4. He should listen to his parents.
5. He should listen in class.
6. He should clean up his room.
7. He shouldn't always ask his parents for money.
8. He should be nice to his brother and sister.

 CD5/24, 25 B. Play tracks 24 and 25 so students can check their answers. Then play track 25 again so they can listen and repeat the sentences.

14 Practice

Answers will vary. Possible answers.
1. He should go to bed. He should take some aspirin. He shouldn't stay at work.
2. We should study for the test tomorrow. We shouldn't watch a long movie.
3. Tina should go to bed early. She shouldn't get up late. She should be on time for work.
4. Joe should wear a jacket. He shouldn't go outside in a T-shirt.
5. You should look for the waiter. You shouldn't drink the cold coffee.
6. Ken shouldn't drive so much. He should walk more. He should lose some weight. He shouldn't smoke cigarettes.

Advice Activity

✦ Write the following situation on the board. Ask the students to come to the board in pairs and write five sentences giving advice to their friend using *should* and *shouldn't*.

Your friend wants to come to the United States to study English. Tell your friend how to do the following things:

how to apply to the language center

how to get a passport

how to buy a plane ticket

how to find a place to live

how to adjust to life in the United States

how to learn English as quickly as possible

how to get a high TOEFL® iBT score

how to apply to an American university

✦ When the students finish, ask them to read their advice to the class.

11F *Must*

STUDENT BOOK P. 310

Notes on the Photo and Warm-up Activities

In this photo, a student is talking to another student while a teacher writes on the board. There are occasions when talking in class might be acceptable. For example, the girl speaking may be working with another student or a small group on a class project. She might be participating in a group discussion. Or she may be waiting for class to begin. If she is talking while the teacher is giving a lecture, however, then talking is not appropriate.

Discuss the Photo
Ask students to discuss these questions in small groups or as a class:

What do you think the teacher is writing on the board? What class is this?

Is the girl in the photo being rude by talking in class? Why or why not?

What do you think she is talking about?

Is it OK for her to wear a hat in class? Why or why not?

What are some rules for classrooms that you know of?

Write Rules
Imagine that the girl in the photo is a North American student. She is going to be an exchange student for one year in your home country or in some other country. Pretend that you are a teacher or a student at the school she will be going to. Tell her about the rules. Explain at least six things that she *must* or *must not* do. Also try to include information about what a student *should* do or *should not* do, *can* do or *cannot* do, and *could* do or *could not* do.

15 Practice

A.
1. You must
2. You must
3. You must
4. You must not
5. You must not
6. You must
7. You must not
8. You must
9. You must
10. You must
11. You must not
12. You must not

CD5/26, 27 B. Play tracks 26 and 27 so students can check their answers. Then play track 27 again so they can listen and repeat the sentences.

CD5/28 C. Answers: She wrote a note to Anita. She ate potato chips. She couldn't stay awake.

Modals   161

Rules and Regulations Activity

- When in another country, people must be aware of the rules and regulations. Ask students to think about the following situations, and talk about any differences in customs or rules between this country and their own:

    getting a driver's license and driving safely
    behaving properly in public
    behaving properly in an academic setting
    dressing properly for different occasions

- Divide the students into diverse groups of three or four and ask them to think of some rules and regulations. Have them write them down and compare them.
- After 10 minutes of discussion, have them share their views with the class.

11G Have To

STUDENT BOOK P. 312

Notes on the Photos and Warm-up Activities

- The photo on the left is of **a man in a garden**. Gardening may be his hobby, and he may spend a lot of time maintaining his home garden. Even though it is hard work, many people find gardening very relaxing. He could be a gardener or a landscaper working in someone else's garden or yard. Gardeners and landscapers plan, design, and/or maintain yards and outdoor spaces for both private homeowners and businesses.

- In the photo on the right, **a businessman** is walking down the street, carrying a briefcase. He is smiling, looks confident, and is wearing formal business attire—a suit and a tie. Different countries often have varying ideas about what is acceptable to wear to an office or a place of business. Acceptable business clothing may differ for men and for women in different cultures. Many North American businesses have become increasingly informal in what they permit employees to wear. Many allow casual clothing, such as khaki pants or even jeans, any day of the week. Friday, in particular, is often referred to as *dress-down Friday* or *casual Friday*.

Discuss the Photos

Ask students to discuss these sets of questions in small groups or as a class:
   Imagine that the man on the left is a landscaper. What does he have to do at his job?
   What doesn't he have to do?
   Do you want this job? Why or why not?
   What job do you think this businessman might have? What does he have to do at his job? What doesn't he have to do? Do you want this job? Why or why not? What kind of job do you want?

Discuss Ideal Jobs

Place students in pairs. The partners should take turns describing things that they would or would not have to do in their ideal jobs. Ask partners to think of the perfect jobs for each other. Invite each person to explain the ideal job for his or her partner and the reasons for the choice to the class using *have to*, *don't have to*, *had to*, and *didn't have to*.

Notes on Usage: *don't have to* vs *mustn't*

Make sure students understand the difference between *don't have to* and *mustn't*. We use *don't have to* to talk about things that are not required. We use *mustn't* to talk about things that we are not allowed to do.

16 Practice

Answers will vary. Possible answers:

1. We have to	4. We have to	7. We have to	10. We don't have to
2. We have to	5. We don't have to	8. We have to	
3. We have to	6. We don't have to	9. We don't have to	

17 Pair Up and Talk

Sample questions and answers:

Does a TV journalist have to have a degree?	No, he/she doesn't.
Does a TV journalist have to be a good speaker?	Yes, he/she does.
Does a TV journalist have to be attractive?	No, he/she doesn't.
Does a TV journalist have to be scientific?	No, he/she doesn't.

18 Practice

1. don't have to	3. don't have to	5. must not	7. must not
2. must not	4. must not	6. don't have to	8. don't have to

19 Practice

A.

1. had to	3. didn't have to	5. didn't have to	7. had to
2. didn't have to	4. had to	6. had to	8. had to

Modals 163

B. Answers will vary. Possible answers:
   1. She had to sign autographs.
   2. She didn't have to go shopping for food.
   3. She had to eat in restaurants.
   4. She had to smile a lot.

20   Pair Up and Talk

   A. Answers will vary. Sample answers:
   I had to hold my mother's hand.
   I didn't have to make my bed.

   B. Answers will vary.

Notes on Grammar: more on *should, must, have to*

- Students will probably not ask many questions about the differences between *should*, *must*, or *have to* beyond those explained in the book. However, it is helpful for teachers to be aware of them.
- *Should* is used to give advice or state that something is a good idea. *Shouldn't* is used to give advice or state that something is a bad idea.
- *Must* is used to show that something is important, necessary, or obligatory. *Must not* is used to show that something isn't right because it is against the rules or illegal.
- *Have to* is used to show that something is necessary. *Doesn't/don't have to* is used to show that something is not necessary, that there is a choice. *Had to* and *didn't have to* are used as the past of *must* and *have to*.

11H   *May I, Can I,* and *Could I*

STUDENT BOOK P. 317

Notes on the Photos and Warm-up Activities

- The photo on page 317 shows a **common interaction** with service personnel. The woman might be at a bank, in line at an airport, or at some other place of business. She is presenting her identification card. Common forms of identification include driver's licenses, social security cards, passports, and work or student ID cards.
- The photo on page 318 shows another common interaction—that between hotel personnel and a hotel guest. The man in this photo is a hotel **desk clerk**. Both his words and his friendly expression show that he has good manners.

Discuss When We Use IDs

Ask students to discuss these questions in small groups or as a class:

Where and when do people usually have to show identification?

What kinds of identification do they usually show?

What do people usually say when they ask for identification?

Is it important to carry identification with you at all times? Why or why not?

Role-play

+ Place students with a partner to discuss what they think is happening in the photo on page 317. Ask them to think about these questions:

    Where does this scene take place? Why is this woman presenting her identification? What kinds of requests or offers are being made?

+ Next, have students role-play a conversation as two people from this scene. They should use *may I*, *can I*, and *could I* to make permission requests and to offer help. In their responses, they should use both affirmative and negative short answers.

+ Call on students to perform their role-plays for the class.

21 Practice

Answers will vary. Possible answers:

1. May I
2. Could I/Can I
3. Can I
4. Could I/May I
5. May I
6. May I/Could I/Can I

22 Pair Up and Talk

Questions and answers may vary. Possible questions:

1. May I see your ticket, please?
2. Could I have a fork, please?
3. May I speak to you for a moment, please?
4. Could I carry those books for you?
5. Can I help fix your computer?
6. Could I go to the clinic next Monday?
7. Can I watch a movie tonight at 9:00?
8. May I sit at this table?
9. Could I help you carry some bags?
10. May I see your passport and ticket, please?
11. Can I take your order?
12. May I see the manager, please?

Notes on Culture

✦ Unlike speakers of many other languages, English speakers generally do not use the imperative when speaking with strangers. For example, in Europe and South America, it's often acceptable to use the imperative when asking a server in a restaurant for something. However, in North America, English speakers generally use *may I*, *could I*, or *can I* when requesting something.

✦ Of course, there are gender and age differences; men tend to be less deferential than women. Younger people are expected to be more deferential to older people, but because of changing manners, older people are sometimes more deferential than younger people.

23   Read

Possible answers:
1. The smuggler brought a donkey.
2. The official wasn't able to find anything.
3. He had to let the man cross the border.
4. The official wasn't able to find anything over ten years.
5. He wanted to know what the man was smuggling.
6. He was able to smuggle donkeys.

Listening Puzzle

STUDENT BOOK P. 321

A. CD5, 29

   Answer: A. kangaroo

B. Students might discuss the following:
   Koalas live in Australia, but they don't have long tails. Anteaters don't have pouches.

C. CD5, 30

Reading Challenge: Tornado

STUDENT BOOK P. 322

A. Answers will vary. Possible answers:
   1. hurricanes, tornadoes, blizzards, typhoons
   2. They destroy things.

C. **Paragraph 1:** <u>can</u> reach, <u>can</u> come; **Paragraph 2:** <u>Can</u> ... lift, it <u>can</u>, <u>can</u> suck up, <u>can</u> lift, <u>can</u> kill; **Paragraph 3:** <u>can</u> occur; **Paragraph 4:** <u>have to</u> be careful

Note: Some students may recognize that *'ll*, the contraction of *will*, in Paragraph 3 is also a modal.

D. 1. B 2. A
E. 3. C 4. C 5. C
F. 6. A
G. 7. D
H. 8. B

Writing: Write a Letter of Advice

STUDENT BOOK P. 324

Steps 1 and 2: Answers will vary. Sample answers:
1. You could bring flowers. You could bring a box of chocolates.
2. You should wear nice clean clothes.
3. You have to take your shoes off. You must take your coat off.
4. You should not be late, but you should not arrive too early.
5. You must not bring a friend.
6. You should say the food is good. You must not say the food is bad.

Writing Expansion

✦ Have a discussion with the students on what the proper behavior would be at a dinner with a public official. After the discussion, you can write a few sentences on the board about similarities and differences in various parts of the world.

✦ Have students write a letter in which they describe a problem they are having. Collect the letters and redistribute. Then have students write a letter in response that gives advice for the problem.

Self-Test

STUDENT BOOK P. 325

A. 1. A 2. B 3. D 4. B 5. C 6. A 7. C 8. B 9. D 10. B
B. 1. A 2. A 3. A 4. A 5. D 6. B 7. C 8. B 9. D 10. B

Modals

Unit 12

Special Expressions

Unit Sections	Notes/Activities	SB page	TM page
12A *Let's*	Notes on Usage: *let us*	328	169
12B *Would Like*	Contrast Activity	330	170
12C *Could You* and *Would You*	Store Activity	334	172
12D The Imperative	Internet Activity; Process Activity	336	174
✦ Listening Puzzle: Weather		339	175
✦ Reading Challenge: When Lightning Strikes		340	176
✦ Writing: Write about a Process	Writing Expansion	342	176
✦ Self-Test	Answer Key	343	176

Unit 12 presents and practices special expressions, beginning with *let's* and *would like*. The unit presents the polite forms used to make requests, *could you* and *would you*. Finally, the text introduces the imperative, both affirmative and negative. For each of these expressions, the text teaches their correct form and position in sentences, explains how and when we use them, and provides ample practice.

12A Let's

STUDENT BOOK P. 328

Notes on the Photo and Warm-up Activities

In this photo, a mother and son are walking together, perhaps outside a shopping mall or a shopping complex. Some parents find it challenging to shop with young children because they sometimes want things like candy or toys. Some grocery stores in North America are beginning to introduce *candy-free* checkout aisles so that children who shop with their parents will not see the candy.

Discuss Shopping

Ask students to discuss these questions in small groups or as a class:

Do you like shopping? Why or why not?

Do you like shopping malls? Why or why not?

What do you usually shop for? Where do you shop in your town?

Role-play

Place students in pairs or groups of three and present them with the following situation:

You are the parents or family members of the boy in the photo. You are shopping at a mall or a store in your town. Decide what you are shopping for. Imagine that the boy is difficult to shop with. He is tired and hungry. He also wants you to buy him things. Role-play a conversation. Make suggestions about what to do and where to go, or what not to do and where not to go. Use *let's* and *let's not*.

1 Practice

Answers may vary. Probable answers:

1. Let's not go to the beach.
2. Great, let's watch television.
3. Let's make sandwiches.
4. Let's open the window.
5. Then let's not turn on the stereo.
6. Quick! Let's clean up the apartment!

2 Pair Up and Talk

Conversations will vary. Sample conversation:

A: It's a beautiful day.

B: Let's go to the park.

Special Expressions 169

Notes on Usage: *let us*

✦ The construction *Let us ...* includes the speaker and those spoken to. The subject is in the objective case; in other words, instead of *we*, *us* is used because it comes after the verb (*let*). Here is another example: *Let him speak now or forever hold his peace*. *Him* (objective case) is used instead of *He*. This structure is used in more formal language.

✦ The imperative can be used from its strongest to mildest forms to give the following:
- commands or orders   Stop! Don't move!
- warnings or prohibitions   Do not enter. Keep out.
- instructions or directions Push the button. Turn left here.
- suggestions or advice   Do your best. Don't worry.
- polite requests   Please take off your shoes.

✦ The subject of an imperative sentence is *you*, although we don't write it.

12B Would Like

STUDENT BOOK P. 330

Notes on the Photo and Warm-up Activities

This photo shows a waiter at the table in a nice restaurant. He is offering cheese to the man and woman.

Discuss Restaurants

Instruct students to discuss some or all of these questions in small groups or as a class:

Do you think the restaurant in the photo is a nice one? Is it expensive? How can you tell?
Would you like to eat at a restaurant like this? Why or why not?
What are the differences between fast-food restaurants, family-style restaurants, and expensive restaurants?
In what kind of restaurant would you like to eat dinner?

Write an Email or Letter

✦ Present this prompt to students:

Who would you like to have dinner with? Think of a friend, a family member, a teacher, or even a famous person. Write an email or a letter to this person inviting them to have lunch or dinner with you. Explain why you would like to invite this person to eat with you. Explain when you would like to have a meal together, where you would like to go, and what you would like to eat. Write at least six sentences.

✦ Exchange letters or emails with a partner. Read the invitation. Imagine that you are the person who is invited to dinner. Decide if you will accept the invitation. Write a response and explain why you would or would not like to have dinner. Write at least six sentences.

3 Practice

A.
1. Would you like
2. Would you like, I would like
3. Would you like, I would like, would like
5. Would you like, would like
6. Would you like, would like
7. Would you like, would like

CD5/31, 32 B. Play tracks 31 and 32 so students can check their answers. Then play track 32 again so they can listen and repeat the conversations.

CD5/33 C. 1. False 2. False 3. False

4 Practice

Answers will vary. Possible answers:
1. Yes, I do./No, I don't.
2. Yes, I would./No, I wouldn't.
3. Yes, I do./No, I don't.
4. Yes, I would./No, I wouldn't.
5. Yes, I do./No, I don't.
6. Yes, I would./No, I wouldn't.
7. Yes, I do./No, I don't.
8. Yes, I would./No, I wouldn't.
9. Yes, I do./No, I don't.
10. Yes, I would./No, I wouldn't.

5 Pair Up and Talk

A. Answers will vary. Sample answers:
1. I'd/I would like to go to Tahiti.
2. I'd/I would like to be a movie actor.
3. I like to eat Japanese food.
4. I don't like to eat meat.
5. I'd/I would like to live in a peaceful country.
6. I wouldn't like to live in a country at war.
7. I'd/I would like to have an electric car.
8. I like to ride my bike by the river.
9. I'd/I would like to go to a movie.
10. I'd/I would like to meet the president.

B. Conversations will vary. Sample conversation:
A: What do you like to eat?
B: I like to eat sushi and other Japanese food.

Special Expressions   171

Contrast Activity

- To continue practicing the difference between *like* and *would like*, you can write these sentences on the board and have the students practice in pairs.

   I like green apples, and I'd like to eat one right now.
   I don't like flying, but I'd like to fly in a helicopter over the city.

- After a few minutes of practice, they can go to the board and write the sentences.

12c *Could You* and *Would You*

STUDENT BOOK P. 334

Notes on the Photos and Warm-up Activities

- The top photo shows **a woman and baby**. Her hands are very full. She is carrying a baby, a laundry basket, and a phone. This woman may be a housewife and stay-at-home mom. Or perhaps she has a job outside of the home or works from her home in addition to her other responsibilities. Many women and men struggle to keep the house clean, raise children, and work.
- The bottom photo shows **two colleagues**. They may work in an office or in a school. In many universities the lecturer has teaching assistants who help with many tasks. Sometimes the teaching assistant, or TA, grades tests and other assignments, but sometimes they actually teach a discussion section. The lecturer is responsible for managing the assistant.

Talk about Household Responsibilities

Ask students to discuss these questions in groups or as a class:

   Why do you think the woman in the photo is doing so many things at the same time?
   How do you think she feels?
   How much housework should women do?
   How much housework should men do?

Role-play

- Organize students into small groups or pairs and present them with the following situation:

   The woman in the photo is very busy. Unfortunately, her phone keeps ringing. At least five people call and interrupt her work. Who are they, and what do they want? Discuss possible callers and list your ideas, then share them with the class.

- Have students use their lists to role-play conversations between the woman and each phone caller. Each caller should ask her to do something. The woman should agree to some requests and refuse others.

Write a Letter or Email

Present students with this prompt:

> It's easy to feel stressed when we have many things to do. What things do you have to do? Who could you ask to help you? What things could you ask people to do for you? What things could you ask people not to do? Make a list of your ideas. Write letters or emails to two people you could go to for assistance. Ask for help with specific tasks.

6 Practice

A.
1. Could/Would you please carry my suitcase?
2. Could/Would you please open the car door?
3. Could/Would you please turn off the car radio?
4. Could/Would you please drive slowly?
5. Could/Would you please turn on the heat?
6. Could/Would you please speak louder? I can't hear you.
7. Could/Would you please repeat that? I didn't understand.
8. Could/Would you please close your window? There's too much noise.

B. Answers to the questions from **Part A** will vary. Possible answers:
1. Sure. Where do you want me to put it?
2. Of course.
3. Okay.
4. Okay. How slow?
5. Sure. It is a little cold in here.
6. Of course. Is this loud enough?
7. Sure.
8. Okay. It is noisy.

Store Activity

✦ Write the following words on slips of paper and give one slip to every three students. If there is an uneven number, there can be one salesperson and one customer.
- In a jewelry store: salesperson and two customers
- In a pet store: salesperson and two customers
- In an electronics store: salesperson and two customers
- In a music store: salesperson and two customers
- In a pharmacy: salesperson and two customers
- In a greengrocer's (fruit and vegetable store):   salesperson and two customers

✦ Tell the customers that they have to ask the salesperson for a specific item, look at it, and then ask for another. Finally, one buys an item, but the other one doesn't. They should use the structures *could you …, would you …, I'd like …, I wouldn't like …*

✦ They should plan and practice their role-plays and then present them to the class.

12D The Imperative

STUDENT BOOK P. 336

Note: See page 269 of this Teacher's Manual for a supplementary Internet Activity Procedure and a reproducible Worksheet for this section.

Notes on the Photo and Warm-up Activities

In this photo these workers are stretching. While this doesn't look like a yoga class, the stretch that the participants are doing looks like a yoga-influenced movement. Yoga began in India and has become increasingly popular throughout the world. There are various types of yoga, but all involve increasing strength and flexibility through learning different poses, or positions. Yoga also involves careful attention to breathing.

Discuss Yoga

Ask students to discuss these questions in small groups or as a class:

Do you do yoga? Did you ever try yoga in the past?

Would you like to try yoga? Why or why not?

What other activities or sports do you do for exercise or relaxation?

Give Directions

Organize students into groups to talk about activities they do for exercise or relaxation. Ask them to tell their group members why they should consider trying this activity. They should give advice and instructions using the imperative.

Write Directions for a Class or an Activity

Present students with one or both of these prompts:

Think of a class you take now or a class that you took in the past. It could be a yoga class, a dance class, an art class, or an academic class. Write advice and instructions for people who might take this class. What should they do before, during, and after this class? Imagine that your advice and instructions will be used on a website or in a brochure about this class.

Think of an activity you do now or an activity that you did in the past. It could be a group activity, such as belonging to a sports team or singing in a choir. It could also be an individual activity, such as running or sewing. Write advice and instructions for people who might try this activity. What should they do before, during, and after this activity?

7 Practice

A. 1. Lift the telephone receiver. Wait for the dial tone. Dial the number.
    2. Write the letter. Sign your name. Put the letter in the envelope. Address the envelope. Put a stamp on it. Mail it.
    3. Buy some fresh oranges. Cut the oranges in half. Squeeze the halves until all the juice is out. Throw away the seeds and pulp. Add a little sugar, if you wish. Drink.

B. Answers may vary. Possible answers:
1. Don't eat sweets like candy, cake, or cookies. Drink lots of water. Don't eat too much pasta, rice, or potatoes. Eat a lot of fruit and vegetables. Get 30 minutes of exercise a day.
2. Review each chapter of the book. Look at your notes from class. Make note cards of important facts. Get enough sleep so you're not tired the next day. Be on time and bring everything you need to the test.
3. Read about the company and prepare some questions. Wear nice clothes. Be on time for the interview. Answer the questions as well as you can. Ask the questions about the job. Call and thank the interviewer a few days later.

Process Activity

- Pair the students and tell them to think of a simple activity that has a few steps, like the ones in **Practice 7**.
- On a piece of paper, have them list the steps of the activity using the imperative. They can use the dictionary or ask a classmate or teacher. When they finish, have them check their work together.
- Then the students can go to the board and draw a simple diagram or put some phrases on the board. When everyone has finished, they should explain the process (the steps) to the class.

8 Read

Possible answers:
1. He asked for food.
2. He said, "Give me your best coat."
3. He said he would like a hat.
4. He went back to the farm.
5. He said, "Come in, sir. Eat all you want."
6. He said, "Eat all you want, beautiful clothes. The farmer likes you, not me."

Listening Puzzle

STUDENT BOOK P. 339

A. CD5, 34

Answer: C. tornado

B. Students might discuss the following points:
Blizzards are snowstorms. Hurricanes form over water.

C. CD5, 35

Special Expressions

Reading Challenge: When Lightning Strikes

STUDENT BOOK P. 340

A. Answers will vary. Possible answers:
1. that lightning will strike, start fires, kill people and animals
2. Don't use electricity, especially phones, and avoid high places.

C. **Paragraph 2:** do not use, avoid, Keep away, avoid, Do not go, Avoid, Do not go, Don't do, Find

D. 1. B   2. D
E. 3. B   4. C   5. A
F. 6. A
G. 7. C
H. 8. D

Writing: Write about a Process

STUDENT BOOK P. 342

Steps 1 and 2: How to Make Coffee—Answers:
1. Fill the kettle with water.
2. Boil the water.
3. Put some coffee in the coffee pot.
4. Fill the coffee pot with boiling water.
5. Leave it for a few minutes.
6. Pour the coffee into a cup.

Writing Expansion

After the students write their paragraph about how to make another drink in **Step 3**, they can illustrate it with a diagram for each step. The illustrated paragraphs can be put on a bulletin board or poster and hung in the classroom.

Self-Test

STUDENT BOOK P. 343

A. 1. D 2. C 3. B 4. B 5. B 6. B 7. C 8. A 9. C 10. A
B. 1. B 2. B 3. A 4. C 5. A 6. C 7. A 8. C 9. B 10. B

Unit 13

Adjectives and Adverbs

Unit Sections		Notes/Activities	SB page	TM page
13A	Adjectives and Nouns Used as Adjectives	Compound Noun Activity	346	178
13B	Word Order of Adjectives	Description Activity	350	180
13C	*The Same (As), Similar (To),* and *Different (From)*	Magazine Activity	353	182
13D	*Like* and *Alike*	Similes Activity	355	183
13E	Comparative Form of Adjectives: *-er* and *More*	Internet Activity; Comparative Adjectives Activity	357	184
13F	*As ... As, Not As ... As,* and *Less ... Than*	Comparison Activity	360	185
13G	Superlative Form of Adjectives: *-est* and *Most*	Superlative Adjectives Activity	366	188
13H	*One Of The* + Superlative + Plural Noun	Country Activity	370	190
13I	Adjectives and Adverbs	Description Activity	372	191
13J	Comparative and Superlative Forms of Adverbs	Jobs Activity	375	193
13K	*As ... As* with Adverbs	Comparison Activity	378	194
✦	Listening Puzzle: Living Things		381	195
✦	Reading Challenge: Hummingbirds		382	196
✦	Writing: Make a Comparison	Writing Expansion	384	196
✦	Self-Test	Answer Key	385	196

Unit 13 introduces adjectives and adverbs, beginning with the expressions *the same (as)*, *similar (to)*, *different (from)*, *like*, and *alike*. Then the comparatives with *-er* and *more*, as well as its other forms, are presented, followed by the superlatives with *-est* and *most*. Finally, comparative and superlative forms of adverbs, including *as ... as* are presented. For each, the unit teaches the correct form and position in sentences, explains how and when we use them, and provides ample practice.

13A Adjectives and Nouns Used as Adjectives

STUDENT BOOK P. 346

Notes on the Photos and Warm-up Activities

- Some **mountains**—like the ones depicted in the photo—get so much snow that the roads are closed during part or all of the winter. Many people like to go to mountains like these to enjoy winter activities such as skiing, snowboarding, snowshoeing, or just walking.
- The **woman** is at a café. She is drinking coffee and may be at a cyber, or Internet café. Internet cafés are popping up all over the world. They usually let people use computers at an hourly rate. These cafés are good places for people to go if they do not own a computer at home. They are also good places for travelers who want to send or check emails from the road.

Role-play

Place students in pairs and present them with the following situation:

Imagine that the two of you are in the mountains for the weekend. It is winter. One of you likes the cold and the snow. The other person does not. In fact, the person who doesn't like the cold and the snow wants to leave early. Each of you tells the other why you want to stay or go. Talk about your reasons using adjectives to describe the place and your feelings.

Design an Internet Café

- Organize students into groups or pairs to design an ideal Internet café. Ask them to decide the following things about the café:
  a. What is the name of the Internet café?
  b. Where is it located?
  c. What hours of the day is it open? How many days a week?
  d. What kind of people will use this café? (Whom will you advertise this café to?)
  e. What services will you offer at this café? Why should people go to this new café instead of the many other Internet cafés?
- Assign one person from each group to write down ideas. Encourage the use of adjectives for **steps d** and **e**.
- Call on students to present their ideal cafés to the class. They can either write a paragraph or present the café in the form of an advertisement. Encourage the class to discuss and vote on which Internet café seems to be the most likely to succeed.

1 Practice

1. good — adjective
2. university — noun
3. modern — adjective
4. favorite — adjective
5. doctor — noun
6. pretty — adjective
7. black — adjective
8. friends — noun

2 Pair Up and Talk

Conversations will vary. Possible conversation:
A: What does the boy look like?
B: He has short hair. It is thick. He is young, too.

3 Practice

A. <u>city</u> center, <u>town</u> hall, <u>office</u> buildings, <u>government</u> offices, <u>police</u> station, <u>bus</u> station, <u>coffee</u> shop, <u>movie</u> theater, <u>art</u> gallery, <u>flower</u> pots, <u>park</u> benches, <u>telephone</u> booth, <u>cardboard</u> box

B. Answers will vary. Sample answer:
The man was waiting for a telephone call. He was supposed to deliver the box to someone, but he didn't have the address.

4 Practice

Note: Some are two words, some are one. Encourage students to check with a dictionary.

1. notepad
2. lightbulb
3. key ring
4. coffeepot
5. tea cup
6. perfume bottle
7. sunglasses
8. paper clips
9. toothbrush

5 Practice

1. schoolteacher = a teacher at a school
   school entrance = an entrance of a school
   adult school = a school for adults
2. paper money = money made from paper
   money order = an order for money
   money box = a box to keep money in
3. piano music = music written for piano
   music concert = concert where music is performed
   music hall = a hall to listen to music in
4. housekeeper = a person who keeps (cleans) house
   housework = work done in a house
   country house = a house in the country
5. bank account = an account in a bank
   bank statement = a statement from the bank
   bank book = a book to keep bank transaction records in

Compound Noun Activity

✦ To give students more practice making compound nouns, write the lists that follow in columns on the board. **A** and **B** belong together to form **Things You Wear**, and **C** and **D** to form **Things for Sports**.

✦ Have the students go up to the board one by one, and draw a line between a pair of matching words. If they don't know any of the answers, they can "pass" and other students can continue answering.

✦ When the activity is finished, pronounce all the pairs and ask students to repeat as a class or individually.

A   ear   evening   hiking   neck   pant   rain   sports   sun   sweat   watch
B   band   boots   coat   gown   hat   jacket   lace   rings   shirt   suit
C   baseball   basketball   football   golf   hockey   ice   roller   ski   soccer   tennis
D   ball   blades   boots   clubs   glove   helmet   hoop   racket   skates   stick

Things You Wear: earrings, evening gown, hiking boots, necklace, pantsuit, raincoat, sports jacket, sun hat, sweatshirt, watchband; **Things for Sports:** baseball glove, basketball hoop, football helmet, golf clubs, hockey stick, ice skates, rollerblades, ski boots, soccer ball, tennis racket

13B Word Order of Adjectives

STUDENT BOOK P. 350

Notes on the Photo and Warm-up Activity

This young woman is posing as if for a formal photograph. Sometimes people have formal photographs taken for special times in their lives, such as their senior years of high school and college.

Write a Description of a Person

✦ Tell students to find a photograph of a person. It can be a favorite photo of themselves at a young age, a family member, a friend, or a famous person.

✦ Instruct students to write descriptions about the photo in the chart below. Use adjectives and nouns. For example: *kind face, short, elderly, white hair, wooden cane, silk kimono, Asian.*

Gender	Size	Age	Hair/Eye Color	Clothes	Other

✦ Have students write a one-paragraph description of this photograph, using ideas from the chart. They should describe the photograph as clearly as they can.

✦ Put students in groups of about 10 and display all of the portraits for each group to see. Have someone in each group read one of the paragraphs while the other students determine which portrait is being described. Continue with remaining photographs.

6 Practice

A.
1. a new gold credit card
2. an interesting diamond bracelet
3. a beautiful old Chinese plate
4. a small new Japanese computer
5. a beautiful black leather purse
6. an old gold Swiss watch
7. an expensive big blue ring
8. an old silk Persian carpet
9. a white pearl Japanese necklace
10. an antique silver English jewelry box

CD6/2, 3 B. Play tracks 2 and 3 so students can check their answers. Then play track 3 again so they can listen and repeat the sentences.

7 Practice

A.
1. quiet
2. red
3. wood
4. modern
5. rose
6. apple
7. leather
8. interesting
9. note
10. American

CD6/4, 5 B. Play tracks 4 and 5 so students can check their answers. Then play track 5 again so they can listen and repeat the sentences.

CD6/6 C. Answer: C

8 Your Turn

A. Answers will vary. Sample answers:
1. I'm wearing black high-heeled shoes.
2. I have a clean small apartment.
3. I bought an expensive digital camera.
4. I wear a new Japanese watch.
5. I have big brown eyes.
6. I have short black hair.

B. Paragraphs will vary. Sample paragraph:

Redusindo is a tall friendly Mexican man. He has very short black hair and a big smile. Today he's wearing dark pants and a clean white T-shirt. I think he came to class from work.

Description Activity

✦ To expand upon **Your Turn 8**, you can ask students to describe five things various classmates have or are wearing. They can do this orally or in writing.

Juan is wearing new white sneakers.   Elena and Sonia are wearing faded blue jeans.

Adjectives and Adverbs   **181**

13c The Same (As), Similar (To), and Different (From)

STUDENT BOOK P. 353

Notes on the Photos and Warm-up Activity

Sunflowers are popular in gardens in North America, Europe, and Asia. They can grow as tall as 9 feet (about 3 meters). In some places they are also grown for commercial purposes. Sunflower oil is a major crop produced in the United States. In addition, sunflower seeds can be harvested, dried, roasted, and eaten. The **tulip** in Photo Y is red, but tulips come in many different colors. Most tulips are grown in and exported from the Netherlands (Holland).

Memory Game

- Place students in small groups to create a memory match game.
- Give each group 16 index cards (or have them cut a piece of paper into 16 squares). Instruct them to create eight pairs of identical pictures. They can either find images on the Internet or in magazines, or they can draw the pictures themselves. Suggest that some pairs can be similar to, but not the same as, other pairs.
- To start the game students will place all the cards face down and shuffle them around on a table. They should then lay the cards out in rows and take turns turning two cards at a time face up. If the images on the cards are the same, the student must say they are the same and identify how they are the same. (*This picture is the same as that picture. They both have …*) They should then keep the matched pairs. If the pictures are not the same, the student must turn the cards back over after saying how the pictures are different. Each correct pair is worth one point, and the person with the most pairs wins.

9 Practice

1. the same
2. similar
3. the same as
4. similar to
5. different from
6. different

10 Practice

1. the same as
2. the same
3. different from
4. different from
5. different
6. the same
7. the same as
8. similar to

11 Your Turn

Answers will vary. Possible answers:
Mariko and I have the same backpack.

Sayed and I have similar glasses.

14 Practice

A.
1. older than
2. younger than
3. taller than
4. smaller than
5. thinner than
6. heavier than
7. friendlier than
8. quieter than

CD6/7, 8 B. Play tracks 7 and 8 so students can check their answers. Then play track 8 again so they can listen and repeat the sentences.

15 Practice

A.
1. older than
2. more crowded than
3. smaller than
4. taller than
5. more exciting than
6. more modern than
7. faster than
8. hotter than
9. rainier than
10. more interesting than
11. more expensive than
12. more polite than

CD6/9, 10 B. Play tracks 9 and 10 so students can check their answers. Then play track 10 again so they can listen and repeat the sentences.

C. Answers will vary. Sample answer:
I prefer New York because it's more exciting and less expensive.

Comparative Adjectives Activity

✦ Write some adjective pairs on the board, such as *tall/short, young/old, quiet/friendly, dark/light*. Have students walk around the room and observe their classmates.
✦ Then have students write sentences using the adjectives on the board.

13F *As ... As, Not As ... As, and Less ... Than*

STUDENT BOOK P. 360

Notes on the Photos and Warm-up Activity

The photo on the left shows **a man waiting at a train station**. He is talking on a cell phone. He is wearing casual, yet fashionable, clothes and nice sunglasses. The photo on the right is of **a man holding a laptop**. He is wearing glasses and a pocket protector. His pants are too short. He is not very fashionable.

Adjectives and Adverbs 185

> **Discuss the Photos**
>
> ✦ Put students in pairs to talk about the man in the photo on the left. Have students use their imagination to discuss these questions:
>
> How old do you think he is? Where is he going?
>
> What does he do for a living? What else can you tell about his life?
>
> ✦ Now have students compare the two photos. Have students discuss these questions:
>
> How are the lives of the two men different?
>
> What qualities do you think each man has?
>
> What does each man do for a living?

16 Practice

A. 1. as old as   3. as small as   5. as noisy as   7. as sporty as
    2. as clean as   4. as luxurious as 6. as trendy as   8. as powerful as

 CD6/11, 12   B. Play tracks 11 and 12 so students can check their answers. Then play track 12 again so they can listen and repeat the sentences.

17 Practice

A. 1. No change
    2. Joe's office is less luxurious than Mark's office.
    3. Joe's life is less complicated than Mark's life.
    4. No change
    5. Joe's clothes are less expensive than Mark's clothes.
    6. Joe's clothes are less fashionable than Mark's clothes.
    7. Joe's house is less sophisticated than Mark's house.
    8. Joe's house is less trendy than Mark's house.

B. Answers will vary. Sample answers:
    Joe's life is not as unconventional as Mark's life.
    Joe's life is not as unpredictable as Mark's life.

18 Practice

1. a bee   2. an ox   3. a bear   4. a picture   5. ice   6. a beet

19 Pair Up and Talk

Answers will vary. Sample answer:

In my language, we make comparisons with *tan … como* as in *El es tan feo como un oso* or "He is as ugly as a bear."

20 Practice

1. The room at the Victoria isn't as big as the room at the Hilton. OR
   The room at the Hilton isn't as small as the room at the Victoria.
2. The Victoria isn't as expensive as the Hilton. OR
   The Hilton isn't as cheap as the Victoria.
3. The bed in the Victoria isn't as comfortable as the bed in the Hilton. OR
   The bed in the Hilton isn't as uncomfortable as the bed in the Victoria.
4. The Hilton isn't as far from the city center as the Victoria. OR
   The Victoria isn't as close to the city center as the Hilton.
5. The hotel service at the Victoria isn't as good as at the Hilton. OR
   The hotel service at the Hilton isn't as bad as at the Victoria.
6. The Victoria isn't as crowded as the Hilton. OR
   The Hilton isn't as empty as the Victoria.
7. The coffee at the Hilton isn't as weak as the coffee at the Victoria. OR
   The coffee at the Victoria isn't as strong as the coffee at the Hilton.
8. The Victoria isn't as modern as the Hilton. OR
   The Hilton isn't as old-fashioned as the Victoria.
9. The furniture at the Hilton isn't as old as the furniture at the Victoria. OR
   The furniture at the Victoria isn't as new as the furniture at the Hilton.
10. The restaurant at the Victoria isn't as good as the restaurant at the Hilton. OR
    The restaurant at the Hilton isn't as bad as the restaurant at the Victoria.

21 Pair Up and Talk

Conversations will vary. Possible conversation:

A: Which hotel is more comfortable?
B: The Hilton Hotel is more comfortable than the Victoria Hotel. Which hotel is more expensive?
A: The Hilton Hotel is more expensive than the Victoria Hotel.

22   Pair Up and Talk

Conversations will vary. Possible conversation:
A: Monica's house is not as old as Olivia's house.
B: Olivia's house is less modern than Monica's house, too.

Comparison Activity

- Ask the students if they remember the similes from the **Similes Activity** in section **13D** (Teacher's Manual page 184). Say the beginning of a few of them to help students remember what they are. Then tell them that they are going to make up some comparisons as introduced in **Practice 18**.
- Write a few phrases on the board and ask students to fill in the subject.

    _____ ... is as cool as a cucumber.
    _____ ... is as big as a house.
    _____ ... is as wise as an owl.

- Then write a few more phrases on the board, asking students to complete them in pairs. If they can think of others, perhaps from their language, they can also write them.

    _____ ... is as playful as a puppy.
    _____ ... is as soft as a kitten.
    _____ ... is as fierce as a lion.

- When students have finished, have them read their comparisons to the class.

13G   Superlative Form of Adjectives: -est and Most

STUDENT BOOK P. 366

Notes on the Photo and Warm-up Activity

These three women appear to be friends. Perhaps they are college classmates or old friends from childhood.

Make a Detailed Comparison

- Tell students to imagine that they know these three women well. In small groups, have students think of as many sentences as they can that give information about the women. Encourage them to go beyond the more obvious physical characteristics. They can use humor, too, as long as the sentences make sense. Here are some examples: *Kara has the heaviest backpack. Beth has the loudest sneeze. Lorraine has the longest walk to school. Kara has the most difficult roommate. Lorraine has the squeakiest laugh.*

> - To personalize the activity, students could write similar sentences about the members of their small group as well.
> - Ask group members to share some of their favorite sentences with the class.

23 Practice

A.
1. the coldest
2. the hungriest
3. the wettest
4. the most useful
5. the most intelligent
6. the easiest
7. the best
8. the worst
9. the farthest/the furthest
10. the most boring
11. the most popular
12. the friendliest

 CD6/13, 14

B. Play tracks 13 and 14 so students can check their answers. Then play track 14 again so they can listen and repeat the phrases.

24 Practice

1. the smallest
2. the longest
3. the highest
4. the coldest
5. the biggest
6. the saltiest
7. the largest
8. the hottest

25 Practice

1. the tallest
2. the most famous
3. the most crowded
4. the farthest
5. the oldest
6. the busiest
7. the most important
8. the best

26 Practice

1. younger than/heavier than/taller than
2. the tallest/the heaviest
3. older than/taller than/heavier than
4. the oldest
5. taller than/heavier than/younger than
6. the heaviest/the tallest
7. shorter than/older than/thinner than
8. the youngest/the shortest/the thinnest
9. older than/taller than/heavier than
10. the shortest/the thinnest/the youngest
11. thinner than/shorter than/younger than
12. the thinnest/the shortest/the youngest

27 Pair Up and Talk

Questions all begin with *What is …* Answers will vary.

Adjectives and Adverbs

Superlative Adjectives Activity

✦ Tell the students to look at the superlative adjectives they wrote in **Practice 23** on Student Book page 367. They should think of a sentence about a classmate or the language school using one of the adjectives.

✦ Assign the words and have them go up to the board and write a sentence using that word.

✦ When they are finished, they can read their sentences to the class.

13H *One Of The* + Superlative + Plural Noun

STUDENT BOOK P. 370

Notes on the Photo and Warm-up Activity

This is a picture of the Mona Lisa, one of the most famous paintings in the world. Leonardo da Vinci painted Mona Lisa in the sixteenth century. People are fascinated by Mona Lisa's smile because they are not quite sure what she is smiling about. The Mona Lisa is displayed in the Louvre Museum in Paris.

Discuss the Mona Lisa

Have an unstructured, spontaneous class conversation about the painting. Encourage students to voice their opinions about this painting and the kinds of art they like.

28 Practice

1. The Taj Mahal is one of the most beautiful buildings in the world.
2. The Beatles are one of the most successful rock bands in the world.
3. Siberia is one of the coldest places in the world.
4. California is one of the largest states in the United States.
5. Egypt is one of the most interesting countries to visit.
6. The computer is one of the greatest inventions of our time.
7. New York is one of the most important cities in the United States.
8. Mont Blanc is one of the highest mountains in the world.
9. The Sears Tower in Chicago is one of the tallest buildings in the world.
10. Tokyo is one of the most crowded cities in the world.
11. A racehorse is one of the fastest animals in the world.
12. Boxing is one of the most dangerous sports in the world.

29 Pair Up and Talk

Questions and answers will vary. Possible questions and answers:
A: What is one of the most popular foods in the United States?
B: Pizza is one of the most popular foods in the United States.

Country Activity

- Ask the students to think of three things in their country that they can describe in the superlative.
- Put them in groups of three or four, and have them take turns describing the things in their country; for example, *Tokyo is one of the most crowded cities in the world.*
- Tell the other students to ask questions; for example, *How many people are there in Tokyo? How large is the Tokyo metropolitan area?* and so on.

13I Adjectives and Adverbs

STUDENT BOOK P. 372

Notes on the Photo and Warm-up Activities

This is a photo of a ballerina, a female ballet dancer. She is wearing a tutu and pointe shoes. Dancers must be in excellent physical shape because ballet requires a great deal of strength and flexibility. In fact, some professional athletes, such as baseball players and ice skaters, practice ballet as part of their training. There are many famous ballet dancers who are men.

Discuss Performers
Organize students into groups to discuss their favorite performers—actors, musicians, or dancers. Have each student explain what he or she likes about a performer. Encourage them to use adjectives and adverbs.

Write about a Performance
Present students with this prompt:

If possible, go to a dance performance, a play, or a concert in your area. Many communities have free or inexpensive artistic performances. There are sometimes free performances in public places, like city parks. If you cannot attend a performance, watch one on TV or think of a performance you attended in the past. Did you like the performance? Why or why not? Use adjectives and adverbs in your review. Write at least six sentences.

30 Practice

Adjective: noisy, dangerous, funny, good **Adjective or Adverb:** early, fast, hard, late
Adverb: carefully, easily, quietly, slowly

31 Practice

A. **Adverbs:** perfectly, hard, carefully, fast, badly
1. She does everything perfectly.
2. Yes, she works hard.
3. She drives her car to work.
4. She usually drives carefully.
5. She drove badly yesterday evening.
6. She almost had an accident.

B. Answers will vary. Sample answer:
Janet was tired because she worked hard all day.

32 Practice

A.
1. well
2. polite
3. easily
4. hard
5. good
6. fast
7. careful
8. clean
9. late
10. generously

 CD6/15, 16   B. Play tracks 15 and 16 so students can check their answers. Then play track 16 again so they can listen and repeat the sentences.

33 Practice

1. good
2. fluently
3. quickly
4. well
5. excellent
6. perfectly
7. correctly
8. easily
9. completely
10. fast

Description Activity

Write these words in columns on the board. Ask the students to match the subjects, verbs, and adverbs and say the sentence. You can draw lines between the correct words.

babies	dance	carefully
ballet dancers	design	fast
engineers	play	gracefully
football players	talk	hard
secretaries	type	loudly
students	walk	roughly
teenagers	work	slowly

13J Comparative and Superlative Forms of Adverbs

STUDENT BOOK P. 375

Notes on the Photo and Warm-up Activity

Snails are related to oysters, clams, and other shellfish. They have external shells for protection. Snails can live on land or sea, depending on the type of snail. They usually live 5 to 10 years, and some can grow as big as 15 inches (37.5 centimeters). **Tortoises** also have a shell for protection. They live even longer than snails—as long as or longer than people. Some tortoises live for 150 years.

Discuss Animals
Put students in pairs to list as many animals as they can in three minutes. Then have students make statements using superlatives about the animals in their lists (for example, *An elephant is the largest of these animals*).

34 Practice

1. more easily
2. more fashionably
3. faster
4. harder
5. more quickly
6. more fluently
7. better
8. more carefully

35 Practice

A. Answers will vary. Possible answers:
1. Sue is the most careful.
2. Lydia works harder than Gina.
3. Gina gets to work the latest.
4. Sue works the fastest.
5. Lydia gets to work the earliest.
6. Gina works more slowly than Sue and Lydia.
7. Sue is friendlier than Lydia.
8. Gina is the youngest person in the office.

B. Answers will vary. Possible answer:
Lydia will be the new manager because she has the most experience, gets to work the earliest, and works the longest number of hours each day.

36 Pair Up and Talk

Descriptions will vary, but students should make sure to use superlative adjectives.

Jobs Activity

Write the jobs listed below on the board and ask students to make sentences using different adverbs (such as *fast*, *better*, *slowly*, *quickly*, *easily*, and *carefully*) to compare the two jobs. For example: *A cook makes meals faster than a cashier.*

cook/makes meals	cashier/counts money
architect/designs buildings	street cleaner/cleans streets
plumber/fixes sinks	race car driver/drives race cars
teacher/teaches English	computer programmer/writes programs
pianist/plays music	doctor/performs operations

13K As ... As with Adverbs

STUDENT BOOK P. 378

Notes on the Photo and Warm-up Activity

This photo shows two men wearing ties. One is much more neatly dressed than the other. Many workplaces have dress codes that describe not only the type of clothing employees must wear, but also the style. For example, dress codes may specify that employees look neat, or that their clothing is clean and not torn.

Compare Workplaces
Put students in pairs or groups to compare different places where they have worked. Remind students to use comparatives in their discussion.

37 Practice

A. 1. as, does   3. as, does   5. as, do   7. as, do
    2. as, does   4. as, does   6. as, do   8. as, does

CD6/17, 18   B. Play tracks 17 and 18 so students can check their answers. Then play track 18 again so they can listen and repeat the sentences.

CD6/19   C. A. Alex   B. Mike   C. Mike   D. Alex

194   Unit 13

38 Practice

1. Get up as early as you can.
2. Study as hard as you can.
3. Come to school as early as you can.
4. Be as relaxed as you can.
5. Read the instructions as carefully as you can.
6. Answer the questions as completely as you can.
7. Write as fast as you can.
8. Write as neatly as you can.
9. Take as much time as you can.
10. Check your work as carefully as you can.

Comparison Activity

✦ Ask the students to think of a roommate, friend, or sibling and write six sentences (three affirmative and three negative) comparing themselves to this person. For example: *Yusef works as hard as I do. He doesn't get up as early as I do.*

✦ When they finish, they can read their sentences to a partner.

39 Read

Possible answers:
1. He wanted to be strong.
2. He wanted to talk to the sun because the sun is the strongest thing in the world.
3. It wanted to be strong like the sun.
4. The sun said it wasn't so strong. The cloud was stronger.
5. The wall can stop the wind.
6. The mouse can eat holes in the wall.

Listening Puzzle

Student Book p. 381

A. CD6, 20

Answer: B. insects

B. Students might discuss the following:
There are not 30 million kinds of mammals or fish in the world.

C. CD6, 21

Adjectives and Adverbs 195

Reading Challenge: Hummingbirds

STUDENT BOOK P. 382

A. **1.** nectar **2.** North, Central, and South America

C. **Paragraph 1:** (the) smallest, North, Central, South; **Paragraph 2:** fast, mid; **Paragraph 3:** sweet, long, narrow; **Paragraph 4:** special, swordbill, (the) deepest, bee, (the) smallest, ruby-throated

D. **1.** A **2.** A
E. **3.** D **4.** B **5.** D
F. **6.** A
G. **7.** A
H. **8.** A

Writing: Make a Comparison

STUDENT BOOK P. 384

Writing Expansion

In groups of three or four, ask the students to compare your language center to two other language centers in the area. Tell them to write about the age of the center, the price, the location, and number of students in each class. If they are not sure about this information, they can use the Internet to find out about them. Then they can make a chart on the board or on a poster comparing the centers.

Self-Test

STUDENT BOOK P. 385

A. **1.** C **2.** B **3.** C **4.** C **5.** B **6.** D **7.** A **8.** D **9.** C **10.** C
B. **1.** C **2.** B **3.** B **4.** C **5.** C **6.** B **7.** B **8.** D **9.** C **10.** A

Unit 14

The Present Perfect

Unit Sections		Notes/Activities	SB page	TM page
14A	The Present Perfect of *Be*: *For* and *Since*	Contrast Activity; Guessing Activity	388	198
14B	The Present Perfect: Regular and Irregular Verbs	Irregular Verb Activity	393	200
14C	The Present Perfect: Negative Statements and Questions	Internet Activity; Notes on Usage: contractions; Chant Activity	397	203
14D	The Present Perfect: *Ever* and *Never*	Vacation Activity	400	204
✦	Listening Puzzle: Vegetables		403	207
✦	Reading Challenge: Everest and Hillary		404	207
✦	Writing: Describe Experiences	Writing Expansion	406	207
✦	Self-Test	Answer Key	407	207

Unit 14 first introduces and practices the present perfect of the verb *be* with the prepositions *for* and *since* in time phrases. Then it presents the past participles of regular and irregular verbs with intriguing exercises that call for speculation from students. Negative statements, *yes/no* questions, and *wh-* questions are followed by the use of *ever* in questions and *never* in answers. For each of these sections, the unit teaches the correct form and position in sentences, explains how and when we use them, and provides ample practice.

14A The Present Perfect of *Be*: *For* and *Since*

STUDENT BOOK P. 388

Notes on the Photos and Warm-up Activities

- The photo on page 388 shows **a waiter** in a restaurant that is probably formal. The waiter is wearing a tuxedo and bow tie, which are extremely formal attire for men. It is worth mentioning to students that the terms *waiter* and *waitress* are increasingly being replaced by the gender-neutral term *server*. It might also be useful to identify other positions, such as *owner, manager, chef, line cook, host/hostess, dishwasher*.
- In the photo on page 389 are **two female friends**. Some people make friends more easily than others. Some people like to have many friends, while others prefer to have just a few close friends. As people grow older they sometimes find it more difficult to make new friends, especially if they move to a new place.

Discuss Jobs

Ask students to discuss some or all of these questions in small groups or pairs:

Have you ever worked in a restaurant? Have you been a waiter, a cook, a host, a dishwasher, or something else in a restaurant? Do you know someone who has?

Do you want to work in a restaurant? Why or why not?

What other jobs have you worked as? Which jobs have you liked the most? Which jobs have you liked the least?

Write about Skills

- Present students with the following prompt:

    Imagine that you are preparing to meet with a career counselor. This person will help you find the job that you want. The career counselor already has a résumé with your work experience listed. Now she would like to know about all of your skills (things you are good at) and your personal or professional interests. Write a list of your skills and interests. Explain how long you have had these skills, how you acquired them, and how long you have had these interests. Use *for* and *since*.

- Have students exchange lists with a partner and read each other's skills and interests. Instruct students to imagine that they are career counselors. Students should ask follow-up questions about items on the list. Have students suggest jobs that fit their partners' skills and interests.

Discuss Friends

Ask students to discuss these questions in small groups or pairs:

Do you make new friends easily? Why or why not?

Do you prefer to have a lot of friends or a smaller number of very close friends? Why?

Do you have a best friend or a very good friend?

How long have you and this person been friends? Where and how did you meet?

What kinds of things do you do together?

What kind of work does this friend do now?

1 Practice

A. 1. have been   3. have been   5. has been
    2. has been   4. has been   6. have been

CD6/22, 23 B. Play tracks 22 and 23 so students can check their answers. Then play track 23 again so they can listen and repeat the sentences.

CD6/24 C. 1. False   2. False   3. True

2 Practice

A. 1. for   3. since   5. since   7. since   9. since   11. for
    2. since 4. for   6. since   8. since   10. since   12. for

CD6/25, 26 B. Play tracks 25 and 26 so students can check their answers. Then play track 26 again so they can listen and repeat the sentences.

CD6/27 C. Answer: B

3 Practice

Answers will vary. Sample answers:

A. 1. September 2002   2. August   3. two years

B. 1. Kitano   3. June   5. September
    2. September 2004   4. 11 months   6. eight months

C. I have been in this school since 2002. My partner has been in the school for only eight months. She came to this city in June, last year. I moved here six years ago.

The Present Perfect 199

Contrast Activity

✦ To demonstrate how the present perfect differs from the past, write the following chart on the board and elicit sentences from the students. You can add to the list.

Last Year	This Year (so far)
Last year, I read __10__ books.	This year, I've read __2__ books.
Last year, I saw _____ movies.	This year, I've seen _____ movies.
bought _____ CDs.	bought _____ CDs.
took _____ courses.	taken _____ courses.
made _____ phone calls.	made _____ phone calls.
visited _____ cities.	visited _____ cities.

✦ Students can work in pairs saying the sentences to each other.

Guessing Activity

✦ Have students write four or five sentences about their partners in **Practice 3C**. Instruct students to write *my partner* rather than the name.

✦ Collect the papers and redistribute. Call on students to read the paper they received. Elicit guesses from the class as to who it is.

14B The Present Perfect: Regular and Irregular Verbs

STUDENT BOOK P. 393

Notes on the Photo and Warm-up Activities

This girl is holding a grammar book. She is probably a current student. She may be studying English or some other language as a first or second—or even third—language. Students often study the grammatical structures of their home language. In elementary and middle schools in the United States, the basics of English grammar and composition are taught in classes called "Language Arts." In high school, such classes are often referred to simply as "English" class.

Discuss School Experiences

✦ Begin by asking students how long they have studied English grammar. Talk about yourself first as an example: *I have studied English grammar since first grade. I have studied English grammar for 25 years!* If you'd like, you can take a class survey, charting students' responses on the board.

✦ Expand the discussion to include other classes in a typical curriculum (math, science, history, social studies, English literature, Spanish, etc.).

Make Sentences

✦ Ask each student to write the base form of a verb (for example, *run, own, play, know, study*) on a small piece of paper. Gather the slips of paper and place them in a small container.

✦ Have students take turns choosing a paper and then making a sentence using that verb in the present perfect with or without *for* or *since* (for example, *I have known Yumi since September. I have seen an eclipse*).

Note: You can play a variation of this activity later to reinforce *never* in section **14D** by adding a true/false element. Students can make sentences and then ask the class, "True or False?" For example:

A: I have ridden in a hot-air balloon. True or False?

B: False. You have never ridden in a hot-air balloon.

A: Yes, I have! I rode in one last year on my vacation.

OR

B: True. You rode in a hot-air balloon last year on your vacation.

A: That's right.

4 Practice

A.
1. has lived
2. has been
3. have known
4. has studied
5. has owned
6. has worked
7. has seen
8. has disappeared
9. has been
10. has had

CD6/28, 29

B. Play tracks 28 and 29 so students can check their answers. Then play track 29 again so they can listen and repeat the sentences.

C. He has disappeared.
Sample explanation: Brad has gone hiking. The battery in his truck is dead. He can't get back home. He is hoping that someone will come and look for him.

5 Practice

B.
1. Bob has lived on the farm all his life.
2. Bob and Brenda have been married for 55 years.
3. Bob and Brenda have been happy.
4. Bob has had a good life.
5. Jim has had an interesting life.
6. Jim and his children have not spoken for many years.
7. Jim has visited many countries.
8. Jim has made a lot of money.
9. Jim has lived alone for ten years.
10. Bob has written to Jim every Thanksgiving.
11. Bob has sent pictures of his family to Jim.
12. Bob has not seen Jim for a long time.

Irregular Verb Activity

✦ To introduce other irregular verbs, write this chart on the board. It will help the students see similarities and differences among verbs, and remember how the past and past participle are formed.

Present	Past	Past Participle
be/am/is/are	was/were	been
begin	began	begun
come	came	come
do	did	done
drink	drank	drunk
drive	drove	driven
eat	ate	eaten
find	found	found
get	got	gotten (Am.) got (Br.)
go	went	gone
have	had	had
know	knew	known
make	made	made
meet	met	met
pay	paid	paid
read	read	read
see	saw	seen
send	sent	sent
sleep	slept	slept
speak	spoke	spoken
stand	stood	stood
swim	swam	swum
take	took	taken
wear	wore	worn
write	wrote	written

✦ Say each set of verbs and have students repeat as a class. One set is one row, and it includes the present, the past, and the past participle forms of the verb. Then have individual students say each set of verbs.

✦ Erase the first column and have individual students say each set again. Erase the second column and have individual students say each set once more. After students have practiced several times, they should know most of the verbs. However, continual practice for at least a week is necessary for students to remember them.

14c The Present Perfect: Negative Statements and Questions

Student Book p. 397

Note: See page 273 of this Teacher's Manual for a supplementary Internet Activity Procedure and reproducible Worksheet for this section.

Notes on the Photo and Warm-up Activities

In this photo, a man and woman are talking. They might be businesspeople, or possibly students in a professional program. It might be useful at this point to introduce the term *small talk* as a type of light conversation used in social or business situations. People who don't know each other well usually make small talk. You may want to elicit examples of polite questions to ask to make small talk (for example, *What do you do? How long have you lived here? What kinds of things have you seen/done since you moved here?*).

Role-play
Organize students into small groups or pairs and present them with the following situation:
> The people in this photo, Sam and Laura, work together at the same company or attend the same university program, but they have just met. Decide where they work or attend school. What kinds of jobs do they have? What do they study? Role-play their conversation as they make small talk and try to get to know each other. Decide what each of them has and has not done in the past.

Write about a Dream Job
Present students with this prompt:
> What is your dream job? What job would you love to have? How long have you known that you wanted to work at this kind of job? Have you done anything to prepare for this job? Write a paragraph about your dream job.

Notes on Usage: contractions

- Point out that we often use contractions with the present perfect in the third person singular (*he's, she's, it's*).
- Suggest students listen for the past participle form to distinguish between the contractions with *has* and the contractions with *is*.

6 Practice

A. A 1. have   3. Have   5. have made
       2. been   4. made   6. has not improved

    B 1. have   3. Have   5. haven't
       2. had   4. had

The Present Perfect 203

C 1. have   6. have   11. have
   2. worked   7. have worked   12. lived
   3. have been   8. Have   13. hasn't been
   4. Have   9. lived   14. has been
   5. worked   10. have

 CD6/30, 31 B. Play tracks 30 and 31 so students can check their answers. Then play track 31 again so they can listen and repeat the conversations.

Chant Activity

✦ To help students practice the present perfect, write this chant on the board. The underlined words or syllables are stressed, so you can tap or clap on them and encourage students to do the same.

✦ Notice that the number of syllables between beats differs so students have to say some syllables faster and some slower to fit them in between beats.

✦ As with other chants, say each line and have students repeat. Then let the students say it by themselves. Then have them alternate lines, dividing the class into left and right sides, males and females, and so on.

Have you ever danced with someone under the stars?
Have you ever traveled in a spaceship to Mars?
Have you ever been in love and gazed at the moon?
Have you ever been lonely on a night in June?

Yes, I've danced with someone under the stars.
No, I've never traveled in a spaceship to Mars.
Yes, I've been in love and gazed at the moon.
No, I've never been lonely on a night in June.

I hope you keep dancing under the stars.
I hope you travel in a spaceship to Mars.
I hope you're in love and gaze at the moon.
I hope you're not lonely on a night in June!

14D The Present Perfect: Ever and Never

STUDENT BOOK P. 400

Notes on the Photo and Warm-up Activities

This young man and woman are talking. Their body language tells us a lot. Both are smiling and relaxed. Their body language shows that they are happy in each other's company. They may or may not know each other well, but they are both interested in the other person. The young man's shoulders are slightly raised, indicating that he may be slightly nervous, shy, or excited. Students from different cultures may have different opinions about the male/female body language in this photo.

Discuss the Photo

Ask students to discuss these questions in pairs:

> Who are the people in this photo? What is their relationship? How do they know each other? How long have they known each other? Do they enjoy each other's company? How can you tell?

Find Someone Who

- Organize students into pairs or groups to write a list of 10 questions they might ask someone whom they don't know very well. Give them topics (work, school, travel, and hobbies or personal interests) to help them write their questions. Each question should use the present perfect with *ever*.
- Have each group member copy the questions so that every student has his or her own list. Ask everyone to write at the top of their list: *Find Someone Who …*
- Direct students to go around the class and ask and answer questions until they find classmates who have done the things on the list. Students must ask and answer questions in complete sentences and the present perfect. Negative answers should use *never*. If a classmate answers in the affirmative, the student may write their classmate's name by that question. They should ask questions until they have someone's name by every question, or by as many as possible.

Play a Game

- This activity is a variation of the preceding *Find Someone Who* activity.
- Have students write three to five questions that begin with *Have you ever …?* Suggest students write questions to which most of the class can answer *yes* (for example, *Have you ever flown in a plane?*).
- Arrange the chairs in a circle. There should be enough chairs so that everyone who plays has a chair except one person. If you don't have separate chairs, put pieces of paper on the floor to mark each spot.
- Stand in the middle and have every student stand on a spot. Ask a question beginning with *Have you ever*. If students can answer *yes*, they must leave their spots and find a new one. You should also take a student's spot. The student without a spot must stand in the middle of the circle and ask a question.

7 Practice

B. *Note*: As in the example on Student Book page 401, the form of the answers may vary. Students may use the contraction *hasn't* in a short or long answer and either *never* or *not ever*.

1. A: Has Bob ever taken a plane?   B: No, he has never taken a plane.
2. A: Has Bob ever visited New York?   B: No, he has never visited New York.
3. A: Has Bob ever eaten sushi?   B: No, he has never eaten sushi.
4. A: Has Bob ever worn expensive clothes?   B: No, he has never worn expensive clothes.
5. A: Has Bob ever drunk champagne?   B: No, he has never drunk champagne.

6. A: Has Bob ever driven expensive cars?   B: No, he has never driven expensive cars.
7. A: Has Bob ever wanted to be a millionaire?   B: No, he has never wanted to be a millionaire.
8. A: Has Bob ever worked in the city?   B: No, he has never worked in the city.

C. Answers will vary. Sample questions and answers:

1. Has Bob ever gone outside of his small town?   No, he has never gone outside of his small town.
2. Has Bob ever been away from his family?   No, he has never been away from his family.

Vacation Activity

- Ask students to think about the vacations they have taken or the activities they've done that are unusual.
- Tell them to write three questions about these activities as you circulate and check the questions. Then allow them to write their questions on the board, taking care to omit questions that are the same.
- Depending upon how many questions there are, have the students go to the board and write the answers to two or three of them (not their own). For example:

    Have you ever ridden a camel?   *No, I haven't, but I've ridden an elephant.*
    Have you ever climbed a mountain?   *Yes, I have. I climbed one in the Alps last year.*
    Have you ever met a president?   *Yes, I have. I met President Fox of Mexico in 2004.*

- Note that answers can be in the present perfect or simple past, depending upon whether students say a specific past time reference.

8 Read

Possible answers:

1. He could survive one night on an icy mountain with nothing to warm him.
2. He took only a candle and a book. He did not win the bet.
3. He invited his friends for dinner.
4. They saw a huge pot of water over a candle.
5. The pot has been over the candle since yesterday.
6. No, it hasn't.

Listening Puzzle

STUDENT BOOK P. 403

A. CD6, 32

Answer: C. potatoes

B. Students might discuss the following reasons:
The favorite menu item at McDonald's must be French fries.

C. CD6, 33

Reading Challenge: Everest and Hillary

STUDENT BOOK P. 404

A. **1.** in the Himalayas (in Asia)   **2.** about 3,000

C. **Paragraph 1:** was, worked, liked, climbed, climbed, wanted; **Paragraph 2:** joined, set off, got, were, went, set off, reached, took, did not know, were; **Paragraph 3:** returned, became, continued, went, was, became, have been

D. **1.** A   **2.** D
E. **3.** A   **4.** A   **5.** C
F. **6.** A
G. **7.** C
H. **8.** D

Writing: Describe Experiences

STUDENT BOOK P. 406

Writing Expansion

You can ask students to write a similar paragraph describing their experiences since they came to this country. They can tell how long they've been here, where they've lived, what they've done, and how many friends they've made. They can share their paragraphs with a partner or the class.

Self-Test

STUDENT BOOK P. 407

A. **1.** A   **2.** A   **3.** C   **4.** D   **5.** B   **6.** D   **7.** A   **8.** C   **9.** C   **10.** C
B. **1.** B   **2.** B   **3.** B   **4.** A   **5.** B   **6.** A   **7.** B   **8.** A   **9.** B   **10.** B

Grammar Form and Function 1

Unit 1 Test

Name: _____ Date: _____

A. Choose the best answer, A, B, C, or D, to complete the sentence. Darken the oval with the same letter.

1. I _____ a doctor.
   - A. is
   - B. am
   - C. be
   - D. aren't

   Ⓐ Ⓑ Ⓒ Ⓓ

2. Marcelo is heavy. He's not _____.
   - A. old
   - B. short
   - C. married
   - D. thin

   Ⓐ Ⓑ Ⓒ Ⓓ

3. _____ Japanese.
   - A. Am not
   - B. We's
   - C. He
   - D. We're

   Ⓐ Ⓑ Ⓒ Ⓓ

4. He _____ a student.
   - A. are
   - B. aren't
   - C. is
   - D. am

   Ⓐ Ⓑ Ⓒ Ⓓ

5. The babies aren't sad. They're _____.
   - A. heavy
   - B. happy
   - C. short
   - D. old

   Ⓐ Ⓑ Ⓒ Ⓓ

6. They _____ from Indonesia.
   - A. is
   - B. are
   - C. be
   - D. is not

   Ⓐ Ⓑ Ⓒ Ⓓ

7. _____ beautiful.
   - A. You
   - B. isn't
   - C. is
   - D. You're

   Ⓐ Ⓑ Ⓒ Ⓓ

8. The monkey is young. He's not _____.
   - A. old
   - B. sad
   - C. tall
   - D. thin

   Ⓐ Ⓑ Ⓒ Ⓓ

9. Maria _____ in Australia.
   - A. isn't
   - B. are
   - C. aren't
   - D. am

   Ⓐ Ⓑ Ⓒ Ⓓ

10. The boys _____ teachers.
    - A. is
    - B. I'm
    - C. aren't
    - D. am

    Ⓐ Ⓑ Ⓒ Ⓓ

11. Mei isn't tall. She's _____.
    - A. single
    - B. thin
    - C. short
    - D. happy

    Ⓐ Ⓑ Ⓒ Ⓓ

12. _____ from Venezuela.
    - A. Me
    - B. Are
    - C. I'm
    - D. They

    Ⓐ Ⓑ Ⓒ Ⓓ

Grammar Form and Function 1 Unit 1 Test

13. Masa and Hiro _____ Turkish.

  A. aren't
  B. isn't
  C. is
  D. am

14. The teachers aren't married. They're _____ .

  A. tall
  B. happy
  C. single
  D. thin

15. _____ on the desk.

  A. She are
  B. Book
  C. The mouse is
  D. Am

(4 points each) _____ / 60

B. Write the plural of the following words.

Singular	Plural	Singular	Plural
1. girl		6. foot	
2. child		7. sandwich	
3. fish		8. mouse	
4. lady		9. man	
5. key		10. shelf	

(2 points each) _____ / 20

C. Write questions for the answers. Use *who*, *what*, and *where*.

1. _____ ?

    My name is Sylvia.

2. _____ ?

    Paulo is at school.

3. _____ ?

    They are from Canada.

4. _____ ?

    Those are giraffes.

5. _____ ?

    She's my sister.

(4 points each) _____ / 20

Score _____ / 100

Grammar Form and Function 1 Unit 1 Test

Grammar Form and Function 1 — Unit 2 Test

Name: _____   Date: _____

A. Choose the best answer, A, B, C, or D, to complete the sentence. Darken the oval with the same letter.

1. I am up _____ 8 o'clock.
   - A. on
   - B. at
   - C. in
   - D. to

2. It's hot _____ sunny in Houston.
   - A. or
   - B. in
   - C. but
   - D. and

3. How many clocks _____ in the apartment?
   - A. there aren't
   - B. is
   - C. are there
   - D. is there

4. Class is _____ 9:30 _____ 11:30.
   - A. at
   - B. on
   - C. in
   - D. from … to

5. _____ a teacher in the classroom.
   - A. There are
   - B. Is there
   - C. Is
   - D. There's

6. _____ any desks in the classroom?
   - A. There's
   - B. Are there
   - C. Was
   - D. There aren't

7. I have class _____ the morning.
   - A. is
   - B. on
   - C. from … to
   - D. in

8. It was good, _____ it was spicy.
   - A. but
   - B. there
   - C. isn't
   - D. or

9. Toshi was born _____ 1980.
   - A. from … to
   - B. am
   - C. in
   - D. on

10. _____ any dishes in my backpack.
    - A. There's
    - B. There are
    - C. There aren't
    - D. Is there

Grammar Form and Function 1 Unit 2 Test

11. Is your class in the afternoon _____ in the evening?

    A. at
    B. it's
    C. but
    D. or

12. _____ a holiday on Saturday.

    A. There was
    B. Is there
    C. There were
    D. Aren't

13. Was the food in the cafeteria good _____ bad?

    A. and
    B. or
    C. from
    D. but

14. It is _____ July 21st.

    A. on
    B. from
    C. at
    D. in

15. Our teacher is nice, _____ she gives us a lot of homework!

    A. there is
    B. and
    C. but
    D. or

(4 points each) _____ / 60

B. Answer the questions about the weather today and last Tuesday. Use forms of *be* and *there + be*.

Today		Last Tuesday	
City	Weather	City	Weather
Boston	rainy	Boston	cloudy
Chicago	windy	Chicago	cloudy
Denver	cloudy	Denver	sunny
Houston	sunny	Houston	cloudy
Los Angeles	sunny	Los Angeles	sunny
Miami	cloudy	Miami	sunny
New York	rainy	New York	sunny
San Francisco	windy	San Francisco	foggy

1. What's the weather like in Denver today?
   _____

2. What was the weather like in Boston last Tuesday?
   _____

3. Was it cold in Miami last Tuesday?
   _____

4. Is there rain in San Francisco today?
   _____

5. Are there sunny skies in Los Angeles and Houston today?
   _____

(4 points each) _____ / 20

C. Write questions for the answers. Use the simple past of *be* and *there* + *be*.

1. _____ ?

   Yes, the cats were asleep on my desk.

2. _____ ?

   No, Leonardo da Vinci was not an Italian president.

3. _____ ?

   Yes, there were cookies left at the end of the party.

4. _____ ?

   No, there wasn't a class this morning.

5. _____ ?

   No, there weren't any apples on the table.

(4 points each) _____ / 20

Score _____ / 100

Grammar Form and Function 1 Unit 2 Test

Grammar Form and Function 1 — Unit 3 Test

Name: _____   Date: _____

A. Choose the best answer, A, B, C, or D, to complete the sentence. Darken the oval with the same letter.

1. Our teacher _____ to the market every morning.
   - A. don't go
   - B. has go
   - C. goes
   - D. go

2. Do you _____ your hair every night?
   - A. brushes
   - B. brush
   - C. are brush
   - D. brushing

3. I _____ my parents every day.
   - A. am call
   - B. isn't call
   - C. don't call
   - D. doesn't call

4. _____ the students turn in their homework at the beginning of class?
   - A. Are
   - B. Do
   - C. Doesn't
   - D. Does

5. Pandas _____ rice.
   - A. don't eat
   - B. isn't eat
   - C. eats
   - D. don't eats

6. Her students _____ for the bus at 8:00.
   - A. are wait
   - B. waits
   - C. doesn't wait
   - D. wait

7. He _____ his homework at the kitchen table every day after school.
   - A. do
   - B. does
   - C. is do
   - D. don't do

8. Where _____ Frank live?
   - A. is
   - B. do
   - C. does
   - D. don't

9. At noon, I _____ a sandwich in the cafeteria.
   - A. has
   - B. am have
   - C. have
   - D. doesn't have

10. We _____ English well.
    - A. are not speak
    - B. don't speak
    - C. doesn't speak
    - D. speaks

Grammar Form and Function 1 Unit 3 Test

11. Does Heather _____ at parties?

   A. dances
   B. is dance
   C. dance
   D. goes dance

12. _____ MacGyver fly to California once a month?

   A. Do
   B. Is
   C. Does
   D. Don't

13. Our teacher _____ lunch in the teachers' room.

   A. haves
   B. is have
   C. has
   D. have

14. Ling _____ cold weather.

   A. don't like
   B. like
   C. is not like
   D. doesn't like

15. When _____ they usually get home from school?

   A. does
   B. do
   C. are
   D. are do

(4 points each) _____ / 60

B. Add the adverbs of frequency to the sentences.

1. (usually) I drink a cup of coffee for breakfast.
   _____

2. (often) He takes a taxi to work.
   _____

3. (never) It is snowy in Los Angeles.
   _____

4. (always) They read magazines in the evening.
   _____

5. (rarely) We are at home on weekends.
   _____

(4 points each) _____ / 20

Grammar Form and Function 1 Unit 3 Test

C. Write questions for the answers about giraffes. Use the underlined words to help you choose the correct question word.

1. _____ ?

   Yes, a giraffe runs very fast.

2. _____ ?

   No, a giraffe doesn't have a short neck.

3. _____ ?

   Giraffes live in Africa.

4. _____ ?

   Giraffes eat leaves from trees.

5. _____ ?

   Female giraffes have babies when they are three years old.

(4 points each) _____ / 20

Score _____ / 100

Grammar Form and Function 1 Unit 3 Test

Grammar Form and Function 1

Unit 4 Test

Name: _____ Date: _____

A. Choose the best answer, A, B, C, or D, to complete the sentence. Darken the oval with the same letter.

1. The artist _____ a picture in the park right now.
   - A. is paint
   - B. paints
   - C. is painting
   - D. aren't painting

2. I _____ out the window now.
   - A. is looking
   - B. am look
   - C. am not looking
   - D. aren't looking

3. I _____ the first day of class.
   - A. am remembering
   - B. don't remembering
   - C. don't remember
   - D. not remember

4. Manuel and Takeshi _____ their bicycles to class.
   - A. riding
   - B. rides
   - C. is riding
   - D. are riding

5. Listen! The baby _____ in the bedroom.
   - A. is cry
   - B. cries
   - C. does crying
   - D. is crying

6. _____ the student opening the door for his teacher?
   - A. Doesn't
   - B. Does
   - C. Is
   - D. Aren't

7. The groom _____ the bride.
   - A. love
   - B. isn't loving
   - C. loves
   - D. doesn't loving

8. Are the children _____ soccer in the street?
   - A. play
   - B. playing
   - C. plays
   - D. is play

9. It _____ in New York.
   - A. isn't raining
   - B. is not rain
   - C. doesn't raining
   - D. hasn't rain

10. We _____ to take a break now.
    - A. want
    - B. doesn't want
    - C. don't wanting
    - D. are wanting

11. The women _____ in the cafeteria
   A. doesn't working
   B. don't working
   C. aren't work
   D. aren't working

12. Ice cream _____ good.
   A. is tasting
   B. doesn't tasting
   C. tastes
   D. does tasting

13. Tanya _____ all her books.
   A. doesn't holding
   B. isn't holding
   C. isn't hold
   D. hold

14. The students _____ Japanese in class.
   A. are speaking
   B. doesn't speaking
   C. don't speaking
   D. aren't speak

15. _____ the children hear the music outside?
   A. Are
   B. Doesn't
   C. Don't
   D. Is

(4 points each) _____ / 60

B. Use the present progressive in the sentences if possible. Use the simple present if the present progressive is not possible.

1. (have) The beach _____ soft, white sand.
2. (run) The children _____ on the beach.
3. (feel) The wind _____ cool and fresh.
4. (stand) The parents _____ in the water.
5. (like) They _____ family vacations.
6. (sit) Isabella _____ on the porch.
7. (smell) She _____ fresh bread baking.
8. (work) She _____ on a big assignment.
9. (prefer) She _____ to work outside.
10. (believe) She _____ that the fresh air helps her concentrate.

(2 points each) _____ / 20

C. Write questions for the answers. Use the underlined words to help you choose the correct question word.

1. _____ ?

    I'm eating <u>a sandwich</u> for lunch.

2. _____ ?

    She's <u>not feeling well</u>. She has a cold.

3. _____ ?

    The students are going <u>to New York</u> for the weekend.

4. _____ ?

    The plane is leaving <u>at 7:00 this evening</u>.

5. _____ ?

    We're studying <u>because we have an exam tomorrow</u>.

(4 points each) _____ / 20

Score _____ / 100

Grammar Form and Function 1 Unit 4 Test

Grammar Form and Function 1 — Unit 5 Test

Name: _____ Date: _____

A. Choose the best answer, A, B, C, or D, to complete the sentence. Darken the oval with the same letter.

1. Lorena eats _____ cookies, and she drinks _____ milk every night.
   - A. much / a little
   - B. many / many
   - C. a few / a little
   - D. much / some

2. I need to buy _____ umbrella in _____ college bookstore.
   - A. an / an
   - B. the / some
   - C. a / the
   - D. an / the

3. How _____ time do you have to study on Wednesday?
   - A. many
   - B. much
   - C. few
   - D. lot of

4. Marco doesn't eat _____ toast or _____ eggs for breakfast.
   - A. a few / any
   - B. much / many
   - C. a lot of / much
   - D. many / many

5. At birthday parties, I always eat a _____ of cake.
   - A. head
   - B. slice
   - C. jar
   - D. can

6. The cook puts _____ tomatoes and _____ salt in the salad.
   - A. a few / a little
   - B. a little / a few
   - C. many / any
   - D. much / a lot of

7. _____ present on _____ teacher's desk is from Mikako.
   - A. A / a
   - B. The / the
   - C. Some / the
   - D. An / a

8. How _____ pounds of onions do you need?
   - A. much
   - B. little
   - C. many
   - D. some

9. Miguel wants to go to _____ university in _____ United States.
   - A. a / the
   - B. an / the
   - C. an / an
   - D. a / some

10. How _____ coffee do you drink in the morning?
    - A. bars of
    - B. many
    - C. any
    - D. much

Grammar Form and Function 1 Unit 5 Test

11. Students don't spend _____ time or _____ money on lunch.

    A. a lot of / many
    B. some / any
    C. many / much
    D. much / much

    Ⓐ Ⓑ Ⓒ Ⓓ

12. He eats a _____ of soup for lunch every Monday.

    A. roll
    B. piece
    C. bottle
    D. bowl

    Ⓐ Ⓑ Ⓒ Ⓓ

13. Tanya likes _____ chocolate and _____ nuts on her ice cream.

    A. many / many
    B. many / much
    C. a little / a few
    D. any / a lot of

    Ⓐ Ⓑ Ⓒ Ⓓ

14. The students eat _____ big pizza in _____ cafeteria every day for lunch.

    A. the / a
    B. some / some
    C. a / the
    D. a / a

    Ⓐ Ⓑ Ⓒ Ⓓ

15. How many _____ of water do you drink a day?

    A. boxes
    B. glasses
    C. loaves
    D. tubes

    Ⓐ Ⓑ Ⓒ Ⓓ

(4 points each) _____ / 60

B. Write the answers to the questions. Use *some* or *any* in your answers.

1. Are there any books in your backpack?
   _____

2. Is there any money in your pocket?
   _____

3. Are there any people in the hall?
   _____

4. Is there any candy in your room?
   _____

5. Are there any animals in your house?
   _____

(4 points each) _____ / 20

Grammar Form and Function 1 Unit 5 Test

C. **Write answers to the questions. Use ' (apostrophe) or 's to show possession.**

1. Whose motorcycle is this? (Leona)
   _____

2. Whose shoes are these? (children)
   _____

3. Whose house is this? (parents)
   _____

4. Whose books are those? (friends)
   _____

5. Whose coffee is that? (teacher)
   _____

(4 points each) _____ / 20

Score _____ / 100

Grammar Form and Function 1 Unit 5 Test

Grammar Form and Function 1 — Unit 6 Test

Name: _____ Date: _____

A. Choose the best answer, A, B, C, or D, to complete the sentence. Darken the oval with the same letter.

1. Pamela _____ Meg four times yesterday.
   A. called
   B. was call
   C. calls
   D. is calling

2. Meg and a friend _____ to New York last week.
   A. flies
   B. is fly
   C. does fly
   D. flew

3. They _____ there for a week.
   A. do stay
   B. is staying
   C. stay
   D. stayed

4. This morning, Mary Jane _____ that she's getting married.
   A. did said
   B. is saying
   C. said
   D. say

5. I _____ surprised to hear about Tony Bradson.
   A. am being
   B. was
   C. is
   D. are

6. Did he _____ out with Meg last year?
   A. did goes
   B. went
   C. is went
   D. go

7. He also _____ Meg to marry him last year.
   A. asked
   B. asking
   C. is asking
   D. asks

8. Did Pamela _____ to hear more of Meg's story?
   A. wanted
   B. wants
   C. want
   D. is wanting

9. When did Meg _____ you all about Tony?
   A. told
   B. tell
   C. did tell
   D. tells

10. After I thought about it, I _____ to talk to Mary Jane.
    A. was decided
    B. did decided
    C. decided
    D. am decide

11. Aliana got up _____ she ate breakfast.

   A. was before
   B. after
   C. is after
   D. before

12. _____ she took a shower, she put on her clothes.

   A. Before
   B. After
   C. After she is
   D. When after

13. She paid the bus driver _____ she found her money.

   A. before
   B. when before
   C. after
   D. is after

14. _____ she went into the classroom, she opened the door.

   A. When before
   B. Before
   C. Is before
   D. After

15. She took the homework out of her bag _____ she gave it to the teacher.

   A. before
   B. after
   C. was before
   D. is after

(4 points each) _____ / 60

B. Write short answers to the questions.

1. Was Jane Goodall born in England?

   Yes, _____ .

2. Did she travel to Africa after she finished school?

   Yes, _____ .

3. Did she study elephants in Africa?

   No, _____ .

4. Was she in Africa for 60 years?

   No, _____ .

5. Did she discover many things about chimpanzees?

   Yes, _____ .

(4 points each) _____ / 20

Grammar Form and Function 1 Unit 6 Test

C. Write questions for the answers. Use the underlined words to help you choose the correct question word.

1. _____?

   <u>A farmer</u> had three sons.

2. _____?

   He told them about <u>the gold</u>.

3. _____?

   They looked for the gold <u>in the vineyard</u>.

4. _____?

   They worked <u>hard</u> every day.

5. _____?

   They were happy <u>because many grapes grew</u>.

(4 points each) _____ / 20

Score _____ / 100

Grammar Form and Function 1 Unit 6 Test

Grammar Form and Function 1 — Unit 7 Test

Name: _____ Date: _____

A. Choose the best answer, A, B, C, or D, to complete the sentence. Darken the oval with the same letter.

1. The dog _____ on the sofa this morning.
   - A. was sleeping
   - B. sleeps
   - C. were sleeping
   - D. sleeped

2. While I _____ at the airport, I _____ an old friend.
   - A. waited / was seeing
   - B. wait / was seeing
   - C. was waiting / saw
   - D. did waiting / saw

3. We _____ dinner from 7:00 to 8:00 last night.
   - A. eated
   - B. were eating
   - C. was eating
   - D. were ate

4. He _____ toward me when he _____ down.
   - A. ran / was falling
   - B. was running / fell
   - C. is running / fall
   - D. runs / is falling

5. The teacher _____ on the computer before the exam.
   - A. working
   - B. is working
   - C. was working
   - D. did worked

6. When I _____ to him, he _____ up.
   - A. was getting / was standing
   - B. got / is standing
   - C. was getting / did stood
   - D. got / was standing

7. The children _____ yesterday.
   - A. did played
   - B. were played
   - C. play
   - D. were playing

8. While we _____ , they _____ us to the airplane.
   - A. was talking / did called
   - B. were talking / called
   - C. talked / called
   - D. are talking / were calling

9. Sofia _____ on her cell phone during the break.
   - A. was talked
   - B. talking
   - C. was talking
   - D. did talked

10. We _____ on the same plane so we _____ in line together.
    - A. were being / were waiting
    - B. was / waited
    - C. are / were waiting
    - D. were / waited

Grammar Form and Function 1 Unit 7 Test

11. They _____ at our tickets while we _____ in line. Then we _____ on the plane.

   A. were looking / were stood / got
   B. looked / did stood / got
   C. looked / were standing / got
   D. looked / were standing / were getting

12. I was making coffee _____ the telephone rang.

   A. while
   B. when

13. _____ he was brushing his teeth, he heard his roommate get up.

   A. While
   B. When

14. _____ she turned on the radio, music was playing.

   A. When
   B. While

15. They left the classroom _____ the other students were looking.

   A. while
   B. when

(4 points each) _____ / 60

B. Write short answers to the questions.

1. Was the cat drinking his milk?

   Yes, _____ .

2. Were the boys playing basketball?

   Yes, _____ .

3. Was the radio playing classical music?

   No, _____ .

4. Were the cars going fast?

   No, _____ .

5. Was it raining yesterday morning?

   Yes, _____ .

(4 points each) _____ / 20

Grammar Form and Function 1 Unit 7 Test

C. Write questions about what was happening in a restaurant. Use the underlined words to help you choose the correct question word.

1. _____?

   A woman was ordering some food.

2. _____?

   Two men were asking for the bill.

3. _____?

   A baby was crying.

4. _____?

   The children were playing under the table.

5. _____?

   The waiters were rushing because there were many customers last night.

   (4 points each) _____ / 20

   Score _____ / 100

Grammar Form and Function 1 — Unit 8 Test

Name: _____ Date: _____

A. Choose the best answer, A, B, C, or D, to complete the sentence. Darken the oval with the same letter.

1. Next Friday is my mother's birthday. We _____ a big party for her.
   A. will have
   B. are going to have
   C. is going to have
   D. haves

2. A: I think it will be sunny tomorrow.
   B: Okay, then I _____ my umbrella to class.
   A. will take
   B. won't take
   C. am not going to take
   D. am taking

3. _____ I smoke in the classroom?
   A. Might
   B. May
   C. Am
   D. Both A and B

4. We _____ the food for the family cookout at the farmer's market.
   A. buys
   B. are going to buy
   C. was bought
   D. will buy

5. I _____ lunch with Elizabeth tomorrow at 1:00.
   A. eats
   B. will eat
   C. ate
   D. am eating

6. A: Will the baseball game be cancelled if it rains?
   B: If it only rains a little, the baseball game _____ cancelled.
   A. is going to be
   B. will be
   C. won't be
   D. are going to be

7. You look very nice! Who _____ you _____ dinner with?
   A. is / having
   B. may / having
   C. are / having
   D. are / have

8. If the weather is sunny tomorrow, we _____ in the park.
   A. skate
   B. will go skating
   C. go skating
   D. skates

9. After class, she _____ go swimming or jogging.
   A. might
   B. may
   C. is
   D. both A and B

Grammar Form and Function 1 Unit 8 Test

10. Jay's schedule is very busy next week. He _____ with a lot of new clients.

    A. is meeting
    B. meets
    C. will meet
    D. met

11. If I get a low score, I think _____ the test again.

    A. taking
    B. I am taking
    C. I took
    D. I'll take

12. He's going to come home _____ .

    A. in next week
    B. tomorrow night
    C. four days
    D. next week from today

13. Are you _____ attend the graduation ceremony next week?

    A. will
    B. are going
    C. going to
    D. won't

14. If she's really tired, she _____ be able to finish her homework.

    A. won't
    B. is going to
    C. are not going to
    D. isn't

15. Tom _____ eat in the cafeteria or the snack bar.

    A. might
    B. may
    C. is
    D. both A and B

(4 points each) _____ / 60

B. Complete the sentences. Pay attention to time clauses and future conditionals.

1. Before I (call) _____ my parents today, I (check) _____ my bank account.

2. Armando (apply) _____ to college when he (finish) _____ this course.

3. After they (do) _____ their homework, they (play) _____ video games.

4. We (visit) _____ the museum if it (be) _____ open on Sunday.

5. If Camila (get) _____ a scholarship, she (go) _____ to a university in Canada.

(2 points each) _____ / 10

Grammar Form and Function 1 Unit 8 Test

C. **Write short answers to these questions.**

1. Are you going to see your cousin today?

   Yes, _____ .

2. Will the teacher give back our exams tomorrow?

   Yes, _____ .

3. Are they going to take the TOEFL® iBT test next month?

   No, _____ .

4. Will it snow here in January?

   No, _____ .

5. Am I going to see you again?

   Yes, _____ .

(3 points each) _____ / 15

D. **Write questions for the answers. Use the underlined words to help you choose the correct question word.**

1. _____ ?

   My roommate and I <u>are going to paint our apartment</u> this weekend.

2. _____ ?

   We are watching *The X-Men* <u>from 8:00 to 10:00</u>.

3. _____ ?

   <u>Yes</u>, I predict that scientists will find a cure for the flu in my lifetime.

4. _____ ?

   Will's band is going to play <u>at the club near our apartment</u> on July 2.

5. _____ ?

   <u>Jenny</u> is playing the cello with the band at that show.

(3 points each) _____ / 15

Score _____ / 100

Grammar Form and Function 1 Unit 8 Test

Grammar Form and Function 1 — Unit 9 Test

Name: _____ Date: _____

A. Choose the best answer, A, B, C, or D, to complete the sentence. Darken the oval with the same letter.

1. There are 50 states in the United States. _____ the states are near the ocean.
   - A. All of
   - B. Most
   - C. Some of
   - D. Every

2. _____ the states are not near the ocean.
   - A. Every
   - B. Some
   - C. All of
   - D. Most of

3. _____ the states are in North America.
   - A. All of
   - B. Some of
   - C. Every
   - D. Most of

4. It is _____ hot in the summer.
   - A. too much
   - B. too many
   - C. every
   - D. very

5. It sometimes is _____ hot to study.
   - A. very
   - B. too much
   - C. too
   - D. too many

6. There is _____ on the table for our party.
   - A. very much food
   - B. too many food
   - C. enough food
   - D. too lot of food

7. I have _____ books. I should give some away.
   - A. too much
   - B. too many
   - C. too
   - D. very

8. I'm not cold. It's _____ in my apartment.
   - A. warm enough
   - B. too warm enough
   - C. enough warm
   - D. very warm enough

9. In Canada, there is _____ snow in the winter to walk to work.
   - A. too many
   - B. too much
   - C. very much
   - D. too

10. There are _____ in the classroom for all of the students.
    - A. too much chairs
    - B. very many chairs
    - C. chairs enough
    - D. enough chairs

11. There are ten provinces in Canada. _____ the provinces are large.

   A. Many
   B. Very much of
   C. Most of
   D. Every

   Ⓐ Ⓑ Ⓒ Ⓓ

12. _____ province has a capital.

   A. All of
   B. Every
   C. Some of
   D. Very many of

   Ⓐ Ⓑ Ⓒ Ⓓ

13. The earrings are expensive. They're not _____ to buy.

   A. enough cheap
   B. too cheap
   C. cheap enough
   D. very cheap

   Ⓐ Ⓑ Ⓒ Ⓓ

14. My bag is _____ heavy. There are a lot of books in it.

   A. too
   B. very
   C. too much
   D. very much

   Ⓐ Ⓑ Ⓒ Ⓓ

15. It's almost midnight. There isn't _____ to see a movie.

   A. time enough
   B. enough time
   C. too many time
   D. very many time

   Ⓐ Ⓑ Ⓒ Ⓓ

(4 points each) _____ / 60

B. **Complete the sentences with words from the list.**

carry   go   rainy   sleepy   study   drive   heavy   ride   small   tired

1. Today it's too _____ to _____ for a walk.
2. The suitcase is too _____ to _____ by myself.
3. The students are too _____ to _____ for the test.
4. The driver was too _____ to _____ the taxi.
5. The child was too _____ to _____ the bicycle.

(4 points each) _____ / 20

C. **Write short answers to the questions.**

1. Do you have enough money to take a taxi? Yes, _____.
2. Is it too cold in the classroom? No, _____.
3. Are there enough pencils for all of the students? No, _____.
4. Does every bus have a driver? Yes, _____.
5. Do all of the offices have a clock? No, _____.

(4 points each) _____ / 20

Score _____ / 100

Grammar Form and Function 1 Unit 9 Test

Grammar Form and Function 1   Unit 10 Test

Name: _____   Date: _____

A. Choose the best answer, A, B, C, or D, to complete the sentence or to replace the underlined words. Darken the oval with the same letter.

1. <u>My classmates and I</u> like to study English.
   - A. Us
   - B. We
   - C. They
   - D. Me

   Ⓐ Ⓑ Ⓒ Ⓓ

2. María made cookies _____ the class.
   - A. to
   - B. for
   - C. either A or B

   Ⓐ Ⓑ Ⓒ

3. Did you see _____ at the bus stop?
   - A. someone
   - B. nothing
   - C. no one
   - D. anyone

   Ⓐ Ⓑ Ⓒ Ⓓ

4. Yes, _____ was at the bus stop.
   - A. nothing
   - B. someone
   - C. anyone
   - D. no one

   Ⓐ Ⓑ Ⓒ Ⓓ

5. Our teacher makes <u>the class</u> interesting.
   - A. they
   - B. it
   - C. him
   - D. them

   Ⓐ Ⓑ Ⓒ Ⓓ

6. The students send email _____ their friends every day.
   - A. to
   - B. for
   - C. either A or B

   Ⓐ Ⓑ Ⓒ

7. I don't see _____ .
   - A. something
   - B. anything
   - C. nothing
   - D. no one

   Ⓐ Ⓑ Ⓒ Ⓓ

8. The teacher gives <u>the students</u> a test every week.
   - A. him
   - B. he
   - C. they
   - D. them

   Ⓐ Ⓑ Ⓒ Ⓓ

9. Juan sometimes fixes computers _____ his classmates.
   - A. to
   - B. for
   - C. either A or B

   Ⓐ Ⓑ Ⓒ

10. I rang the doorbell, but nobody answered. There's _____ at home.
    - A. something
    - B. someone
    - C. no one
    - D. anyone

    Ⓐ Ⓑ Ⓒ Ⓓ

11. The tests are difficult to finish for <u>my friends and me</u>.
    - A. they
    - B. them
    - C. us
    - D. we

    Ⓐ Ⓑ Ⓒ Ⓓ

12. Is there _____ new at the mall?

    A. anything
    B. something
    C. anyone
    D. nothing

13. No, there's _____ new.

    A. anything
    B. something
    C. nothing
    D. anyone

14. The tutor helps <u>the girl</u> learn English.

    A. us
    B. him
    C. her
    D. them

15. She read the directions _____ us.

    A. to
    B. for
    C. either A or B

(4 points each) _____ / 60

B. Write short answers to the questions using possessive pronouns.

1. Is this your umbrella? Yes, _____.
2. Is that Michael's car? No, _____.
3. Was your mother's coat red? Yes, _____.
4. Is our food on the table? No, _____.
5. Are those books the students'? Yes, _____.

(4 points each) _____ / 20

C. First underline the direct objects and circle the indirect objects. Then write answers to the questions using object pronouns.

1. Did you give the books to your classmate?

   Yes, _____.

2. Do your parents send money to you?

   Yes, _____.

3. Does the teacher give an exam to the students?

   No, _____.

4. Did the school send letters to people?

   Yes, _____.

5. Do your grandparents write email to you?

   No, _____.

(4 points each) _____ / 20

Score _____ / 100

Grammar Form and Function 1 Unit 10 Test

Grammar Form and Function 1 — Unit 11 Test

Name: _____ Date: _____

A. Choose the best answer, A, B, C, or D, to complete the sentence. Darken the oval with the same letter.

1. Amanda _____ run very fast when she was a child.
   - A. can
   - B. must not
   - C. could
   - D. needs to

   Ⓐ Ⓑ Ⓒ Ⓓ

2. I _____ clean the apartment before the party.
   - A. has to
   - B. must to
   - C. could to
   - D. have to

   Ⓐ Ⓑ Ⓒ Ⓓ

3. What _____ you do when you meet people for the first time?
   - A. could to
   - B. should
   - C. can
   - D. didn't

   Ⓐ Ⓑ Ⓒ Ⓓ

4. Last week, Christopher _____ do any journal writing. He had broken a finger!
   - A. didn't has to
   - B. must not
   - C. couldn't to
   - D. couldn't

   Ⓐ Ⓑ Ⓒ Ⓓ

5. When Joe drives, he _____ obey the traffic laws.
   - A. must
   - B. can
   - C. can't
   - D. could

   Ⓐ Ⓑ Ⓒ Ⓓ

6. Allison _____ put away her toys when she is finished.
   - A. haves to
   - B. has to
   - C. could to
   - D. must to

   Ⓐ Ⓑ Ⓒ Ⓓ

7. You _____ go out if you are sick.
   - A. can
   - B. has to
   - C. shouldn't
   - D. couldn't

   Ⓐ Ⓑ Ⓒ Ⓓ

8. We _____ work. It was a holiday.
   - A. could
   - B. can't
   - C. shouldn't to
   - D. didn't have to

   Ⓐ Ⓑ Ⓒ Ⓓ

9. Michelle _____ sing extremely well. It is her profession.
   - A. could
   - B. can
   - C. shouldn't
   - D. must to

   Ⓐ Ⓑ Ⓒ Ⓓ

10. Carlo _____ get plenty of sleep before the race last weekend.
    - A. has to
    - B. could to
    - C. had to
    - D. should

    Ⓐ Ⓑ Ⓒ Ⓓ

(4 points each) _____/40

B. Write short answers to the questions using *can* or *can't*.

1. Can birds sing? _____
2. Can a horse lay eggs? _____
3. Can a monkey climb trees? _____
4. Can dogs make honey? _____
5. Can a chicken swim? _____

(4 points each) _____ / 20

C. Change the forms of *can* or *could* to *be able to*.

1. When I came to this country, I (couldn't) _____ live alone.
2. Now I (can) _____ do many things by myself.
3. I (can) _____ study and work here.
4. I (could) _____ drive in my country.
5. I (can) _____ drive here, but I still (can't) _____ buy a car.

(4 points each) _____ / 20

D. Write questions for the answers. Use *may*, *can*, or *could*. More than one answer may be correct.

1. _____ ?

   No, you may not smoke in the classroom.

2. _____ ?

   Yes, you may smoke outside.

3. _____ ?

   You can't eat, but you can drink in the office.

4. _____ ?

   Certainly, I'll open the window.

5. _____ ?

   Of course, I'll be glad to sign it for you.

(4 points each) _____ / 20

Score _____ / 100

Grammar Form and Function 1 Unit 11 Test

Grammar Form and Function 1 — Unit 12 Test

Name: _____   Date: _____

A. Choose the best answer, A, B, C, or D, to complete the sentence. Darken the oval with the same letter.

1. _____ go to a baseball game tomorrow afternoon.
   - A. Would
   - B. Let's
   - C. Let
   - D. Would like

2. _____ your homework after midnight.
   - A. Wouldn't like
   - B. Could do
   - C. Don't do
   - D. Would do

3. Cheryl is very hungry. She _____ to have dinner now.
   - A. wouldn't like
   - B. could do
   - C. don't do
   - D. would like

4. _____ please hold the door for me? My hands are full.
   - A. Would like you
   - B. Let's
   - C. Could you
   - D. You

5. Where would _____ to go today?
   - A. like you
   - B. you like
   - C. could you
   - D. you

6. _____ the teacher questions if you don't understand.
   - A. Ask
   - B. Could ask
   - C. Do ask
   - D. Let ask

7. Could you please _____ the cats?
   - A. fed
   - B. to feed
   - C. feeding
   - D. feed

8. I _____ to study all weekend.
   - A. let's
   - B. would
   - C. could
   - D. wouldn't like

9. A: It looks like rain.
   B: _____
   - A. Couldn't forget our umbrellas.
   - B. Don't let's forget our umbrellas.
   - C. Let's not forget our umbrellas.
   - D. Would like to not forget our umbrellas.

10. _____ like to go to the movies with us?
    - A. Would he to
    - B. Would he
    - C. Could you
    - D. Would

11. Midge could _____ the plants while I am away.

   A. to water
   B. watering
   C. watered
   D. water

   Ⓐ Ⓑ Ⓒ Ⓓ

12. A: Would they like to come to the museum with us?
    B: _____

   A. Yes, they wouldn't.
   B. Yes, let's.
   C. No, they wouldn't.
   D. Yes, they do.

   Ⓐ Ⓑ Ⓒ Ⓓ

13. A: My roommate wants to come to the game.
    B: _____ invite him to go with us.

   A. Let's
   B. Let
   C. Could
   D. Would like

   Ⓐ Ⓑ Ⓒ Ⓓ

14. _____ Martha work in the garden today?

   A. Could
   B. Let's
   C. Would like
   D. Could like

   Ⓐ Ⓑ Ⓒ Ⓓ

15. _____ Martha _____ work in the garden today?

   A. Could / like
   B. Wouldn't / to
   C. Couldn't / to
   D. Would / like to

   Ⓐ Ⓑ Ⓒ Ⓓ

(4 points each) _____ / 60

B. **Write short answers to the questions.**

1. Do you like chocolate milk?

   Yes, _____ .

2. Would you like an espresso?

   No, _____ .

3. Does the teacher like cats?

   No, _____ .

4. Would she like your cat in class?

   No, _____ .

5. Would you like to have your cat in class?

   Yes, _____ .

(4 points each) _____ / 20

Grammar Form and Function 1 Unit 12 Test

C. Write polite requests with *could you* or *would you*.

1. I'm cold.

    (close the window) _____?

2. I can't hear you.

    (turn down the radio) _____?

3. I don't have any money.

    (lend me a dollar) _____?

4. I forgot my book.

    (give me yours) _____?

5. I don't have my watch.

    (tell me the time) _____?

(4 points each) _____ / 20

Score _____ / 100

Grammar Form and Function 1 — Unit 13 Test

Name: _____ Date: _____

A. Choose the best answer, A, B, C, or D, to complete the sentence. Darken the oval with the same letter.

1. I'm going to bring my _____ umbrella.
   A. red new interesting
   B. interesting new red
   C. new interesting
   D. new red interesting

2. Professor Smith is (intelligent) _____ the other professors.
   A. intelligenter than
   B. the more intelligent than
   C. most intelligent than
   D. more intelligent than

3. Roberto learns English fast, but Lina learns it _____ .
   A. more fast
   B. more faster
   C. faster
   D. the fastest

4. This coat _____ that coat. It is half the price.
   A. is as expensive as
   B. isn't as expensive as
   C. is not more expensive as
   D. the less expensive than

5. _____ student in our class is Pablo.
   A. The most happy
   B. The happier
   C. Happiest
   D. The happiest

6. Ronald just bought a(n) _____ sports car.
   A. Italian small
   B. small Italian blue
   C. small blue Italian
   D. blue small

7. The painting hangs in _____ museums in the world.
   A. one of the large
   B. one of the largest
   C. the largest
   D. the larger

8. Sima writes carefully, but Lorenzo writes _____ .
   A. more carefully
   B. most carefully
   C. the more careful
   D. carefuller

9. The necklace _____ the bracelet. They both have a lovely design.
   A. is as more beautiful as
   B. isn't as beautiful as
   C. is as beautiful as
   D. the most expensive than

10. My dorm room is _____ my friend's dorm room.
    A. the bigger than
    B. bigger than
    C. more big than
    D. the most bigger than

11. Ella's going to a(n) _____ university.
   A. large old English
   B. old large
   C. English large
   D. large English old

12. Leo is _____ Adam. He is very outgoing, and Adam is very shy.
   A. more different than
   B. similar to
   C. different from
   D. the same as

13. Cristina writes _____ of all the students.
   A. more carefully than
   B. the most careful
   C. the most carefully
   D. the more careful

14. My two cats have the same kind of fur. Their fur is _____ .
   A. like
   B. similar
   C. most similar
   D. alike

15. The restaurant near here has _____ food of all.
   A. the most delicious
   B. the more delicious
   C. more delicious than
   D. as delicious as

(4 points each) _____ / 60

Grammar Form and Function 1 Unit 13 Test

B. Complete the sentences with *the same as, similar to, different from, like,* or *alike.*

Mary has blond hair, blue eyes, and a white sweater and jeans.
Martha has blond hair, brown eyes, and a white shirt and jeans.

1. Mary's hair is _____ Martha's hair.
2. Mary's eyes are _____ Martha's eyes.
3. Mary's clothes are _____ Martha's clothes.

Jose has blue-gray glasses, short hair, and sandals.
Pedro has blue glasses, short hair, and sneakers.

4. Pedro's glasses are _____ Jose's glasses.
5. Pedro's shoes are _____ Jose's shoes.
6. Pedro's hair is _____ Jose's hair.

Sandra and her daughter have the same eyes, nose, and mouth.
Sandra and her daughter like to eat ice cream and cake.
Sandra likes to read and watch TV, but her daughter likes to dance and sing.

7. Sandra and her daughter look _____ .
8. Sandra's face is _____ her daughter's face.
9. Sandra's favorite desserts are _____ her daughter's.
10. Sandra's favorite activities are _____ her daughter's.

(2 points each) _____ / 20

C. Complete the sentences with *as ... as, not as ... as,* or *less ... than.*

The Park Plaza and Ritz Central are large new hotels. The Country Inn is a small old hotel.

1. (luxurious) The Park Plaza is _____ the Ritz Central.
2. (modern) The Country Inn is _____ the Park Plaza.
3. (cheap) Rooms in the Park Plaza are _____ rooms in the Country Inn.
4. (spacious) The Park Plaza is _____ the Ritz Central.
5. (new) The Country Inn is _____ the Ritz Central.

(4 points each) _____ / 20

Score _____ / 100

Grammar Form and Function 1 Unit 13 Test

Grammar Form and Function 1 — Unit 14 Test

Name: _____   Date: _____

A. Choose the best answer, A, B, C, or D, to complete the sentence. Darken the oval with the same letter.

1. She _____ Korean food only a few times in her life.
   - A. has ate
   - B. ate
   - C. has eaten
   - D. have eaten

2. I've lived in Boston _____ 1998.
   - A. since
   - B. ever for
   - C. for
   - D. been since

3. _____ you _____ a giant sea turtle in the ocean?
   - A. Did / ever see
   - B. Have / ever seen
   - C. Have / ever saw
   - D. Did / ever saw

4. Who _____ the marathon before?
   - A. has ran
   - B. has run
   - C. have run
   - D. ran

5. My roommate has been here _____ only a year.
   - A. since
   - B. since for
   - C. for
   - D. ever for

6. I _____ the Pyramids of Giza.
   - A. have never saw
   - B. never saw
   - C. have never seen
   - D. never seen

7. They _____ to a skateboard competition.
   - A. have never went
   - B. never went
   - C. never gone
   - D. have never gone

8. I've been studying physics _____ two years.
   - A. been for
   - B. for
   - C. since
   - D. been since

9. _____ they _____ any email since they got home?
   - A. Have / wrote
   - B. Did / write
   - C. Have / written
   - D. Has / writing

10. My roommate has studied chemistry _____ September.
    - A. since
    - B. for since
    - C. for
    - D. been since

11. Has Eric _____ to him yet?

   A. spoke
   B. speaked
   C. speaks
   D. spoken

12. How long _____ here?

   A. you were
   B. have you been
   C. has you been
   D. was you

13. She's had a cell phone _____ three months.

   A. since
   B. ever
   C. since for
   D. for

14. She _____ dinner for us in a long time.

   A. didn't make
   B. has made
   C. haven't made
   D. hasn't made

15. _____ she _____ about the test for very long?

   A. Did / know
   B. Did / knew
   C. Have / known
   D. Has / known

(4 points each) _____ / 60

B. Write questions using verbs in the present perfect.

1. (the teacher / live here long)
   _____

2. (you / study English for five years)
   _____

3. (Leilani / call her parents this month)
   _____

4. (the students / study hard this week)
   _____

5. (we / see a movie in class this semester)
   _____

(4 points each) _____ / 20

C. Write short answers to the questions from Part B.

1. _____   3. _____   5. _____
2. _____   4. _____

(4 points each) _____ / 20

Score _____ / 100

Grammar Form and Function 1 Unit 14 Test

Unit Test Answer Key

Unit 1
A. 1. B 2. D 3. D 4. C 5. B 6. B 7. D 8. A 9. A
   10. C 11. C 12. C 13. A 14. C 15. C
B. 1. girls 2. children 3. fish 4. ladies 5. keys
   6. feet 7. sandwiches 8. mice 9. men
   10. shelves
C. 1. What is your name?
   2. Where is Paulo?
   3. Where are they from?
   4. What are those animals?
   5. Who is she?

Unit 2
A. 1. B 2. D 3. C 4. D 5. D 6. B 7. D 8. A 9. C
   10. C 11. D 12. A 13. B 14. A 15. C
B. 1. It's cloudy. 2. It was cloudy. 3. No, it wasn't.
   4. No, there isn't. 5. Yes, there are.
C. 1. Were the cats asleep on your desk?
   2. Was Leonardo da Vinci an Italian president?
   3. Were there cookies left at the end of the party?
   4. Was there a class this morning?
   5. Were there any apples on the table?

Unit 3
A. 1. C 2. B 3. C 4. B 5. A 6. D 7. B 8. C 9. C
   10. B 11. C 12. C 13. C 14. D 15. B
B. 1. I usually drink a cup of coffee for breakfast.
   2. He often takes a taxi to work.
   3. It is never snowy in Los Angeles.
   4. They always read magazines in the evening.
   5. We are rarely at home on weekends.
C. 1. Does a giraffe run very fast?
   2. Does a giraffe have a short neck?
   3. Where do giraffes live?
   4. What do giraffes eat?
   5. When do female giraffes have babies?

Unit 4
A. 1. C 2. C 3. C 4. D 5. D 6. C 7. C 8. B 9. A
   10. A 11. D 12. C 13. B 14. A 15. C
B. 1. has 2. are running 3. feels 4. are standing
   5. like 6. is sitting 7. smells 8. is working
   9. prefers 10. believes
C. 1. What are you eating for lunch?
   2. How is she feeling?
   3. Where are the students going for the weekend?
   4. When is the plane leaving?
   5. Why are we studying?

Unit 5
A. 1. C 2. D 3. B 4. B 5. B 6. A 7. B 8. C 9. A
   10. D 11. D 12. D 13. C 14. C 15. B
B. 1. There are some books in my backpack. (OR) There aren't any books in my backpack.
   2. There is some money in my pocket. (OR) There isn't any money in my pocket.
   3. There are some people in the hall. (OR) There aren't any people in the hall.
   4. There is some candy in my room. (OR) There isn't any candy in my room.
   5. There are some animals in my house. (OR) There aren't any animals in my house.
C. 1. This/That is Leona's motorcycle.
   2. These/Those are the children's shoes.
   3. That/This is my parents' house.
   4. These/Those are my friends' books.
   5. This/That is the teacher's coffee.

Unit 6
A. 1. A 2. D 3. D 4. C 5. B 6. D 7. A 8. C 9. B
   10. C 11. D 12. B 13. C 14. B 15. A
B. 1. Yes, she was. 2. Yes, she did. 3. No, she didn't.
   4. No, she wasn't. 5. Yes, she did.
C. 1. Who had three sons?
   2. What did he tell them about?
   3. Where did they look for the gold?
   4. How did they work every day?
   5. Why were they happy?

Unit 7
A. 1. A 2. C 3. B 4. B 5. C 6. D 7. D 8. B 9. C
   10. D 11. C 12. B 13. A 14. A 15. A
B. 1. Yes, he was. 2. Yes, they were. 3. No, it wasn't.
   4. No, they weren't. 5. Yes, it was.
C. 1. Who was ordering some food?
   2. What were the two men asking for?
   3. What was the baby doing?
   4. Where were the children playing?
   5. Why were the waiters rushing?

Unit 8
A. 1. B 2. B 3. B 4. B 5. D 6. C 7. C 8. B 9. D
   10. A 11. D 12. B 13. C 14. A 15. D
B. 1. call, am going to check
   2. is going to apply, finishes
   3. do, are going to play
   4. are going to visit, is
   5. gets, is going to go

Unit Test Answer Key

C. 1. Yes, I am.
2. Yes, he/she will.
3. No, they aren't.
4. No, it won't.
5. Yes, you are.

D. 1. What are you going to do this weekend?
2. When are you watching *The X-Men*?
3. Will scientists find a cure for the flu in your lifetime?
4. Where is Will's band going to play on July 2?
5. Who is playing the cello with the band at that show?

Unit 9
A. 1. C 2. D 3. A 4. D 5. C 6. C 7. B 8. A 9. B 10. D 11. C 12. B 13. C 14. B 15. B

B. 1. rainy, go 2. heavy, carry 3. tired/sleepy, study 4. sleepy/tired, drive 5. small, ride

C. 1. Yes, I do.
2. No, it isn't.
3. No, there aren't.
4. Yes, it does.
5. No, they don't.

Unit 10
A. 1. B 2. B 3. D 4. B 5. B 6. A 7. B 8. D 9. B 10. C 11. C 12. A 13. C 14. C 15. C

B. 1. Yes, it's mine. 2. No, it's not his.
3. Yes, hers was red. 4. No, ours isn't on the table.
5. Yes, they're theirs.

C. 1. Did you give the books to your classmate?
Yes, I gave them to him/her.
2. Do your parents send money to you?
Yes, my parents send it to me.
3. Does the teacher give an exam to the students?
No, the teacher doesn't give it to them.
4. Did the school send letters to people?
Yes, the school sent them to them.
5. Do your grandparents write email to you?
No, my grandparents don't write it to me.

Unit 11
A. 1. C 2. D 3. B 4. D 5. A 6. B 7. C 8. D 9. B 10. C

B. 1. Yes, they can. 2. No, it can't. 3. Yes, it can. 4. No, they can't. 5. No, it can't.

C. 1. When I came to this country, I wasn't able to live alone.
2. Now I am able to do many things by myself.
3. I am able to study and work here.
4. I was able to drive in my country.
5. I am able to drive here, but I still am not able to buy a car.

D. 1. May I/we smoke in the classroom?
2. May I/we smoke outside?
3. Can I/we eat and drink in the office?
4. Can/Could you open the window?
5. Can/Could you sign this paper for me?

Unit 12
A. 1. B 2. C 3. D 4. C 5. B 6. A 7. D 8. D 9. C 10. B 11. D 12. C 13. A 14. A 15. D

B. 1. Yes, I do. 2. No, I wouldn't. 3. No, he/she doesn't. 4. No, she wouldn't. 5. Yes, I would.

C. 1. Could/Would you close the window?
2. Could/Would you turn down the radio?
3. Could/Would you lend me a dollar?
4. Could/Would you give me yours?
5. Could/Would you tell me the time?

Unit 13
A. 1. B 2. D 3. C 4. B 5. D 6. C 7. B 8. A 9. C 10. B 11. A 12. C 13. C 14. D 15. A

B. 1. the same as 2. different from 3. similar to/like 4. similar to/like 5. different from 6. the same as 7. alike 8. similar to/like 9. the same as 10. different from

C. 1. as luxurious as
2. less modern than/not as modern as
3. not as cheap as
4. as spacious as
5. not as new as

Unit 14
A. 1. C 2. A 3. B 4. B 5. C 6. C 7. D 8. B 9. C 10. A 11. D 12. B 13. D 14. D 15. D

B. 1. Has the teacher lived here long?
2. Have you studied English for five years?
3. Has Leilani called her parents this month?
4. Have the students studied hard this week?
5. Have we seen a movie in class this semester?

C. 1. Yes he/she has. (OR) No, he/she hasn't.
2. Yes, I have. (OR) No, I haven't.
3. Yes, she has. (OR) No, she hasn't.
4. Yes, they have. (OR) No, they haven't.
5. Yes, we have. (OR) No, we haven't.

Internet Activity Procedure: Countries around the World

Unit 1   The Present of *Be* ✦ 1ɪ   *Yes/No* Questions with *Be*, Student Book Page 21;
1ᴊ   Questions with *What*, *Where*, and *Who*, Student Book Page 24

Objectives and Overview

- Use the Internet to find facts about, and maps of, another country.
- Write *yes/no* questions with *be* and questions with *What*, *Where*, and *Who*.

Have students work individually, in pairs, or in groups to visit websites about other countries. They should use the reproducible Internet Activity Worksheet to prepare for and conduct research. They will then share information through a poster presentation.

Websites

http://www.factmonster.com/countries.html
http://www.infoplease.com/atlas

Prepare

1. **Have students discuss the photo on page 21.** Ask them what facts they know about India. For example, where is it located on a world map? (India borders Pakistan, China, Nepal, Bhutan, Bangladesh, Myanmar.) Is English spoken there? (Hindi and English are both official languages.) What is the capital? (New Delhi)

2. **Introduce the idea of research questions.** Help students formulate *yes/no* and *what*, *where*, and *who* questions about India. Explain that research questions are answered by doing research—looking up information in resources such as the library or the Internet.

3. **Ask students to choose a country to research and write down any facts they know or ideas they have.** They should use the Worksheet to prepare for their research.

4. **Instruct students to read the research questions in the chart.** Ask them to add two research questions of their own. They will not answer until they look at the websites.

Research and Writing

5. **Ask students to find two maps.** They should visit the website in Step 3. One map should show where the country is on a continent or in the world. The second should be a country map. If printing the maps is not possible, have them draw the maps.

6. **Have students use the Internet to find answers to the research questions in the chart.** They should visit the website in Step 5 for this task.

7. **Assign students to prepare a poster about their country.** The poster should include their maps. They will explain the maps, along with other facts, in their presentation. Students can add other images, such as the flag, photos, or drawings of the country, etc.

Wrap-Up

8. **Have students do a poster presentation.** Encourage the audience to ask *yes/no* and *wh-* questions to follow up each presentation. Ask students to imagine they are doing a larger research project on each country or are planning a trip there. Based on the presentation, what else do they want to know about? Brainstorm additional research questions.

Internet Activity Worksheet

Name: _____

Unit 1   The Present of *Be* ✦ 1ɪ *Yes/No* Questions with *Be*, Student Book Page 21;
1ᴊ   Questions with *What*, *Where*, and *Who*, Student Book Page 24

Countries around the World

Objectives
- Use the Internet to find information about a country that interests you.
- Write *yes/no* questions with *be* and questions with *What*, *Where*, and *Who*.

1. **Choose a country to research.** Country: _____

2. **What do you know about this country?** What ideas do you have about this country? (Where is it? What language do they speak? Is it big or small?) Write any facts or ideas you have about this country here:

   _____
   _____
   _____
   _____
   _____

3. **Find two maps.** Use the Internet to find a map of the continent the country is on, or a world map that shows where the country is. Then find a map of the country alone. Print or draw the maps. Visit this website: http://www.infoplease.com/atlas

4. **Read the research questions in the chart below.** Write two research questions of your own. Do not write answers until you get to Step 5.

Questions	Answers
Is it a small country or a large country?	
What is the population?	
Where is it (which continent)?	
What is the capital of this country?	
What is the official language? OR What are the official languages?	
Is there a president of this country? Who is the president or leader of this country?	
Your question:	
Your question:	

5. **Use the Internet to find answers to the questions.** Write your answers in the chart above. Visit this website to find answers: http://www.factmonster.com/countries.html

Grammar Form and Function 1 Unit 1 Internet Activity Worksheet

Internet Activity Procedure: Weather around the World

Unit 2 Be: It, There, and the Simple Past of Be ◆ 2A It to Talk about the Weather, Student Book Page 36

Objectives and Overview

- Use the Internet to find information about the weather in three cities.
- Use *it* to talk about the weather and temperatures.

Have students work individually, in pairs, or in groups and visit websites to learn about weather in different cities. They should use the reproducible Internet Activity Worksheet to prepare for and conduct research. They will then either present their information to the class in the form of a TV weather report or write their information as a newspaper weather report.

Website

http://www.cnn.com/WEATHER

Prepare

1. **Instruct students to choose three cities.** The cities can be from the same country or continent, or from different ones. You should make sure students research different cities. Tell students they are going to visit websites to learn about the weather in these three cities.

2. **Have students write what they think today's weather is like in the places they have chosen.** They should use the Worksheet to prepare for their research.

Research and Writing

3. **Have students use the Internet to find information.** They can visit one of the websites listed on their Worksheet. Alternatively, they can use an Internet search engine to find a website that gives a weather report for their region.

4. **Ask students to take notes.** They should use the Worksheet to write the names of major cities and current weather conditions or temperatures. If possible, they should print or draw a map of the region to use in their presentation.

Wrap-Up

5. **Have students share their information with the class.** They can give a weather report orally, as a TV news report, using a map of the region. Or they can write their information as a newspaper weather report and distribute it to the class. Alternatively, students can post their weather reports on a large world map.

6. **Discuss the weather reports.** Encourage students to ask follow-up questions about the weather. Ask students these questions: Do some cities in the world have very different kinds of weather at the same time? Which places do or don't you want to visit, based on the weather? Why?

Internet Activity Worksheet

Name: _____

Unit 2   *Be: It, There,* and the Simple Past of *Be* ✦ 2A   *It* to Talk about the Weather, Student Book Page 36

Weather around the World

Objectives
✦ Use the Internet to find information about the weather in three cities.
✦ Use *it* to talk about the weather and temperatures.

1. **Choose three cities to research.** Write the names of the cities and the countries they are in here:

   City 1: _____

   City 2: _____

   City 3: _____

2. **What do you think the weather is like today in these cities?** Write your ideas. For example: *I think it's hot and sunny in Honolulu.*

   City 1: _____

   City 2: _____

   City 3: _____

3. **Use the Internet to get information.** Visit the website below or search the Internet by typing the (*city name*) + *weather* in a search engine.
   http://www.cnn.com/WEATHER

4. **Read the website to find information.** Take notes about the temperature, weather, and any other weather-related information for today in each city.

City	Date	Temperature	Weather (*sunny, cloudy,* etc.)	Other Information about Weather in this City

Grammar Form and Function 1 Unit 2 Internet Activity Worksheet

Internet Activity Procedure: Unusual Animals

Unit 3   The Simple Present ✦ 3G   The Simple Present: *Wh-* Questions, Student Book Page 82

Objectives and Overview
- Use the Internet to find information about an unusual or interesting animal.
- Ask *wh-* questions in the simple present.

Have students work individually, in pairs, or in groups and visit websites to learn about unusual or interesting animals. They should use the reproducible Internet Activity Worksheet to prepare for and conduct research. They will write research questions using *wh-* questions and the simple present. They will then present their information to the class in the form of a poster presentation.

Websites
http://www.animaland.org/asp/encyclopedia/index.asp
http://www.animalomnibus.com
http://www.factmonster.com/spot/unusualanimals1.html

Prepare
1. **Write the word *zoo* on the board.** Ask how many students have visited a zoo. Ask these questions: What kinds of animals are at the zoo? Where can you find information about the animals at a zoo?
2. **Ask students to choose an animal to research.** It can be one they have seen or have never seen, from their country or from another country. Tell students they will visit websites to learn about this animal and then present their information as a poster. They will imagine that this animal is at a zoo, and the poster gives information about it to visitors.
3. **Have students write down ideas and questions about their animal.** They should use the Worksheet to prepare for their research.

Research and Writing
4. **Instruct students to use the Internet to find information.** They can visit one of the websites listed on their Worksheet. Alternatively, they can use an Internet search engine to find a website about the animal.
5. **Ask students to take notes.** They should use the Worksheet to write information about the animal. If possible, they should print or draw a picture of the animal to use in their presentation. They may also include a map of the place(s) where the animal is found.
6. **Have students create a poster with facts about and pictures of the animal.**

Wrap-Up
7. **Invite students to present their posters to the class.** Encourage the class to ask *wh-* questions to get more information about the animal.
8. **Discuss the animals that students presented.** Ask questions such as the following: Did you ever see or hear of any of these animals? Which ones? Would any of these animals make good pets? Why? Is it a good idea to have zoos? Is it important for people to see unusual animals from around the world in zoos? Why or why not?

Internet Activity Worksheet

Name: _____

Unit 3   The Simple Present ✦ 3G   The Simple Present: *Wh-* Questions, Student Book Page 82

Unusual Animals

Objectives

✦ Use the Internet to find information about an unusual or interesting animal.

✦ Ask *wh-* questions in the simple present.

1. **Choose an unusual or interesting animal to research.** Write the name of the animal here:
   _____

2. **What do you already know about this animal?** Write your ideas here:
   _____
   _____

3. **What do you want to know about this animal?** Write *wh-* questions below. Leave room for your answers.

   QUESTION: _____

   ANSWER: _____

   QUESTION: _____

   ANSWER: _____

   QUESTION: _____

   ANSWER: _____

   QUESTION: _____

   ANSWER: _____

4. **Use the Internet to get information.** Visit one of these websites:
   http://www.animaland.org/asp/encyclopedia/index.asp
   http://www.animalomnibus.com
   http://www.factmonster.com/spot/unusualanimals1.html

   You can also search the Internet using a search engine and the name of the animal. For example: *kangaroo, pelican, tapir, platypus, octopus.*

5. **Read the website to find answers to your questions.** Write the answers in Step 3, under your questions.

6. **Find a picture of the animal.** Print a picture from the Internet or draw a picture of the animal. You will use this picture for your presentation. You should also print or draw a map to show where the animal lives.

Grammar Form and Function 1 Unit 3 Internet Activity Worksheet

Internet Activity Procedure: Famous Landmarks

Unit 4   The Present Progressive ✦ 4F   Verbs Not Used in the Present Progressive, Student Book Page 109

Objectives and Overview

- Use the Internet to find information about a famous landmark.
- Write *wh-* questions.
- Use verbs not used in the present progressive, such as *see*, *hear*, and *smell*.

Have students work individually, in pairs, or in groups and visit websites to learn about a famous landmark. They should use the reproducible Internet Activity Worksheet to prepare for and conduct research. They will then present their information in the form of a TV travel show, or write their information in a passage for a travel guidebook.

Websites

http://library.thinkquest.org/J0113129/landmarks.html
http://greatbuildings.com/buildings.html

Prepare

1. **Have students list at least three landmarks that they've heard of in the chart.** The landmarks should be buildings, monuments, or other manmade structures.

2. **Instruct students to use the Internet and find landmarks that are new to them.** They should write at least three that interest them in the right-hand column of the chart.

3. **Ask students to choose a landmark they want to research.** From both lists in the chart, have them select one landmark that they want to research. This can be a landmark they have visited in person, one near where they live, or one in some other part of the world. Tell students they will visit the websites again to learn more about this landmark.

Research and Writing

4. **Instruct students to use the Internet to find information about their landmark.** They should use the Worksheet and write answers to the questions in Step 3.

5. **Tell students to write their feelings about this landmark.** Make sure they use the Worksheet and answer this question: How does the landmark make you feel?

6. **Ask students to print or draw a picture of the landmark.** They may also want to print or draw a map to show where the landmark is located.

Wrap-Up

7. **Invite students to share information with the class.** They can give an oral presentation, pretending that they are the host of a TV travel show, or they can write their information as a short report for a travel guidebook.

8. **Discuss the landmarks.** Encourage students to ask follow-up questions about them, for example: Which landmarks have students visited? Which landmarks would they like to visit? Why? Which landmarks would they not like to visit? Why not?

Internet Activity Worksheet

Name: _____

Unit 4   The Present Progressive ✦ 4F   Verbs Not Used in the Present Progressive, Student Book Page 109

Famous Landmarks

Objectives

- Use the Internet to find information about a famous landmark.
- Write *wh-* questions.
- Use verbs not used in the present progressive, such as *see*, *hear*, and *smell*.

1. **Use the Internet to find landmarks.** In the left column of the chart, write three landmarks that you know about. Then visit one of the websites below to find three landmarks that are new to you. Write them in the right column.
   http://library.thinkquest.org/J0113129/landmarks.html
   http://greatbuildings.com/buildings.html

Landmarks I Know About	Landmarks I Don't Know About

2. **Choose a landmark to research.** Circle that landmark in the chart.

3. **Read the website to find more information.** Answers these questions.
   (*Note*: You can use one of the websites or you can search the Internet by the landmark's name.)

   What is the name of the landmark? _____

   Where is the landmark? _____

   When was the landmark built? _____

   Who built it? _____

   What is the purpose of this landmark? _____

   What do people do at this landmark? _____

4. **How does this landmark make you feel?** Imagine that you are sitting at this landmark now. What do you see? Hear? Smell? Feel? Write at least three sentences.

   _____
   _____
   _____

5. **Print or draw a picture of the landmark.** Include this in your presentation or report. You might also want to print or draw a map to show where the landmark is located.

Grammar Form and Function 1 Unit 4 Internet Activity Worksheet

Internet Activity Procedure: Food from around the World

Unit 5   Nouns and Pronouns ✦ 5A   Count and Noncount Nouns, Student Book Page 124

Objectives and Overview

+ Use the Internet to find information about a special dish from a particular culture.
+ Use count and noncount nouns, articles, and *some* and *any* to describe food and recipes.

Have students work individually, in pairs, or in groups and visit websites to learn about a special dish from one culture. They should use the reproducible Internet Activity Worksheet to prepare for and conduct research. They will then present their information orally in the form of a cooking show, or in writing as a cookbook.

Note: This activity can be used after presenting section 5B (*A/An* and *Some*), 5C (*A/An* or *The*), 5E (*Some* and *Any*), and/or 5F (Measurement Words). Students could then practice using quantity words as well as count/noncount nouns.

Website

http://globalgourmet.com/destinations

Prepare

1. **Have students choose a country and one meal from that country.** They can research a meal from their own culture or another culture that interests them.
2. **Ask students to read the list of questions in Step 2.** Make sure they do not write answers to these questions until they go on the Internet.

Research and Writing

3. **Instruct students to use the Internet to find information and a recipe.** They can visit the website listed on their Worksheet and search for recipes by country. Alternatively, they can use an Internet search engine to find a recipe by typing in *food* and the name of the country they chose.
4. **Ask students to take notes.** They should use the Worksheet and write answers to the questions in Step 2. They should also print or draw a picture of the food. Have them write the recipe on the Worksheet or on a separate page.

Wrap-Up

5. **Ask students to share their information with the class.** They can give their report orally, demonstrating how to make the meal. If cooking supplies and food are not available, they can pantomime or use props. You might ask students to imagine they are on a cooking show (for example, a show on the Food Network). Alternatively, they can write their report for an international cookbook to be shared with everyone in the class.
6. **Discuss the food reports.** Ask students to discuss these questions in small groups or as a class: Which meals are easy to make? Which are difficult? Why?
7. **If possible, have a potluck dinner.** Have students try to make the meals they chose or bring in international food for the class to taste.

Internet Activity Worksheet

Name: _____

Unit 5   Nouns and Pronouns ✦ 5A   Count and Noncount Nouns, Student Book Page 124

Food from around the World

Objectives
- Use the Internet to find information about a special dish from a culture that interests you.
- Use count and noncount nouns, articles, and *some* and *any* to describe food and recipes.

1. **Choose a country and a dish to research and get the recipe for.**
   Country: _____   Dish: _____

2. **Read the following questions.** You will use the Internet to find answers to these questions. You can write the answers after you look at the websites.

   a. What does this food or meal look and taste like? (Print a picture of it from the website, or draw it on the back of this page.)

   _____
   _____

   b. When do people eat this food? (Is it for breakfast, lunch, dinner, or dessert? Do people eat it on holidays or special occasions?)

   _____
   _____

   c. What ingredients do you need to make this dish? List them here:

   _____   _____   _____

   _____   _____   _____

   _____   _____   _____

3. **Use the Internet to get information.** Visit this website:

   http://www.globalgourmet.com/destinations (Click on a country, then scroll down to read about that country's traditional food, meals, and recipes.)

   You can also search by typing into a search engine the name of the country (use the adjective form) and one of these words: *food, cooking, cuisine,* or *recipes*. For example: *Thai food, Mexican cuisine, French cooking*.

4. **Read the website to find information and a recipe.** Write answers to the questions in Step 2. Then write the recipe you chose on a separate piece of paper.

Grammar Form and Function 1 Unit 5 Internet Activity Worksheet

Internet Activity Procedure: Sports History

Unit 6   The Simple Past ✦ 6H   The Simple Past: *Wh-* Questions, Student Book Page 173

Objectives and Overview
✦ Use the Internet to find information about the history of a sport.
✦ Use *wh-* questions with the simple past.

Have students work individually, in pairs, or in groups and visit websites related to sports history. They should use the reproducible Internet Activity Worksheet to prepare for and conduct research. They will then share their information as a presentation on a TV sports channel or as a written report for a sports magazine. *Note*: This activity can be used with 6G (*yes/no* questions).

Websites
http://www.hickoksports.com/history/sprtindx.shtml
http://inventors.about.com/library/inventors/blsports.htm

Students may also search by typing *history of* and the name of the sport into a search engine. For example: *history of surfing*, *history of soccer*, *history of lacrosse*.

Prepare
1. **Brainstorm types of sports to research.** Have students brainstorm sports that would be interesting to research and discuss why.

2. **Have students choose a sport to research.** Remind them that they will be researching the history of this sport, not looking for information about the sport today or how it is played. Ask students to write their ideas and questions about this sport. They should use the Worksheet to prepare for their research and write *wh-* questions. If desired, you can instruct them to include *yes/no* questions to review the material from section 6G.

Research and Writing
3. **Ask students to use the Internet to find information.** They can visit one of the websites on their Worksheet. Alternatively, they can use an Internet search engine to find websites about the history of the sport.

4. **Ask students to take notes using the Worksheet.** They can also use the back of the Worksheet to note other interesting facts they find, or to generate new questions.

5. **Ask students to locate a picture.** The picture should show someone doing the sport in the past or the equipment used in the past. Ask them to print, copy, or draw it.

6. **Have students give an oral presentation or write a report.** Tell them to imagine they are appearing on a TV sports channel or writing a report for a sports magazine.

Wrap-Up
7. **Invite students to present their information to the class.** Encourage the class to ask follow-up *wh-* questions (and *yes/no* questions) about each sport.

8. **Discuss the sports that the students presented.** Ask these types of questions: Which sport changed the most from the past to the present? Which sport changed the least from the past to the present? Which sport looks like it was difficult to do in the past? Why?

Internet Activity Worksheet

Name: _____

Unit 6   The Simple Past ✦ 6H   The Simple Past: *Wh-* Questions, Student Book Page 173

Sports History

Objectives
- Use the Internet to find information about the history of a sport that interests you.
- Use *wh-* questions with the simple past.

1. **Choose a sport to research.** Write the name of it: _____

2. **What do you know about this sport?** Write your thoughts:

   _____

   _____

3. **What do you want to know about this sport?** Write at least four *wh-* questions.

   Question: _____

   Answer: _____

   Question: _____

   Answer: _____

   Question: _____

   Answer: _____

   Question: _____

   Answer: _____

4. **Use the Internet to get information.** Visit one of these websites:

   http://www.hickoksports.com/history/sprtindx.shtml

   http://inventors.about.com/library/inventors/blsports.htm

   You can also search by typing *history of* and the name of the sport into a search engine. For example: *history of surfing, history of soccer, history of lacrosse.*

5. **Read the website(s) to find answers to your questions.** Did you find other interesting information? Write it here or on the back of this Worksheet.

   _____

   _____

6. **Find a picture to go with your presentation or report.** Print or copy a picture of someone doing this sport in the past or of the equipment people used for this sport.

Grammar Form and Function 1 Unit 6 Internet Activity Worksheet

Internet Activity Procedure: Dream Interpretation

Unit 7 The Past Progressive ◆ 7A The Past Progressive, Student Book Page 190

Objectives and Overview

- Use the Internet to find information about dreams.
- Use the past progressive.

Have students work individually, in pairs, or in groups to visit websites related to dream interpretation. They should use the reproducible Internet Activity Worksheet to prepare for and conduct research. They will then share their information orally or in writing.

Website

http://hyperdictionary.com/dream

Prepare

1. **Ask students to write down a dream they have had.** Make sure they write their dream on the Worksheet. As a variation, they can interpret a partner's dream for this activity.

2. **Instruct students to underline important or interesting things in this dream.** They should pay attention to people, animals, objects, events, and colors.

3. **Have students choose three things from their dreams and write their ideas about each.** If they cannot think of what these things mean, they should write how they feel about them. Do these things make students feel happy? Sad? Worried? Confused? Angry? Something else?

Research and Writing

4. **Tell students to use the Internet to find ideas about their dreams.** Students should be advised that while there are many dream websites, some are not reliable. Strongly caution students never to give credit card or personal information. Also remind students that dream interpretation is just for fun. *Note*: Tell students they can search for a specific word on the website by clicking on the first letter of the word. For example, if they dreamed about a turtle, they click on *t* and look for the word *turtle*. They can also type the word they want to find in the *search dictionary*. First they will see definitions of the word. Tell them to scroll down to the *Dream Dictionary* definition at the end of the web page.

5. **Ask students to take notes.** They should use the Worksheet to write about the three things they thought were important in their dreams. Encourage them to compare the ideas from the Dream Dictionary with their ideas in Step 2.

Wrap-Up

6. **Call on students to present their information.** They can explain their dream as an oral presentation, or write their interpretation (including the dream) as a report. These dreams could then be collected and distributed to the class to read, or posted around the room.

7. **Discuss the dream interpretations.** Ask questions about the dreams: Did some people dream of similar things? Do you agree with the interpretations? If not, what do you think these things mean? Who had the strangest dream? The scariest dream? The happiest dream?

Internet Activity Worksheet

Name: _____

Unit 7   The Past Progressive ◆ 7A   The Past Progressive, Student Book Page 190

Dream Interpretation

Objectives
- Use the Internet to find information about your dreams.
- Use the past progressive.

1. **Think of a dream you had.** Write about the dream here:

   _____
   _____
   _____
   _____
   _____

2. **What things are important in this dream?** Underline people, animals, objects, events, and colors in your dream above. Then choose the three most important or interesting objects in your dream. Write them in the first column in the chart below.

3. **What are some possible meanings of these three objects?** Write your ideas about each object in the second column below. Or you can write about how these objects make you feel. Happy? Sad? Worried? Confused?

Object	Your Interpretation	Internet Interpretation

4. **Use the Internet to get more ideas about the *possible* meanings of your dreams.** Visit the website listed below. You can click on a letter and scroll through that section to find your word, or you can type the word into the *search dictionary* box.

   http://hyperdictionary.com/dream

5. **Write the meanings that you found on the Internet.** Write them in column three above.

Grammar Form and Function 1 Unit 7 Internet Activity Worksheet

Internet Activity Procedure: Job Interview Strategies

Unit 8　The Future ◆ 8F　Future Time Clauses with *Before, After,* and *When*
Student Book Page 227

Objectives and Overview
- Use the Internet to find out what to do before, during, and after a job interview.
- Use future time clauses with *before, after,* and *when*.

Have students work individually, in pairs, or in groups and visit websites related to job interviews. They should use the reproducible Internet Activity Worksheet to prepare for and conduct research. They will then share their information as an oral presentation for a student career center, or in writing as a guide to job interviews.

Websites
http://www.careerowlresources.ca/Interviews/Int_Frame.htm

http://www.dressforsuccess.org/interview_tips/dosanddonts.asp

Prepare
1. **Call on students to discuss their experiences with job interviews.** Ask them to discuss these questions: Did you ever go on a job interview? What happened before, during, and after the interview? How did you feel before, during, and after the interview? What did you wear? What kinds of questions did the interviewer ask? Did you get hired?

2. **Ask students to brainstorm ideas of what to do before, during, and after a job interview.** Write their ideas on the board in three columns while students take notes on their Worksheets. Ask if men and women should do anything differently in interviews.

Research and Writing
3. **Instruct students to use the Internet to find advice about job interviews.** Advise students that some websites only offer career services for a fee. Remind students not to give credit card or personal information over the Internet. Tell students, or let them discover on their own, that the site www.dressforsuccess.org is geared mainly toward women.

4. **Ask students to take notes using the Worksheet chart.** Because there is a lot of information on the sites, students must prioritize. Instruct them to note eight to ten things to do in each stage of the interview process. From that list, they will select what they think are the most important tips for each stage. They will then present those tips in their final report.

Wrap-Up
5. **Call on students to present their information.** Students can give an oral presentation for a career center workshop. This might include a mock interview as a demonstration (both good and bad interviews can be modeled). Alternatively, they will write a guide to job interviews. Guides should be exchanged and read in class; students might imagine that they are at a job workshop or career fair as they read them.

6. **Discuss the job interview advice.** Ask the following questions: What advice is useful? What information is surprising? What part of the job interview process seems difficult? Will men and women need to do anything differently before, during, or after an interview? Will you use some of this advice for your job interviews in the future?

Internet Activity Worksheet

Name: _____

Unit 8   The Future ✦ 8F   Future Time Clauses with *Before*, *After*, and *When*,
Student Book Page 227

Job Interview Strategies

Objectives

✦ Use the Internet to find out what do before, during, and after a job interview.
✦ Use future time clauses with *before*, *after*, and *when*.

1. **Imagine that you will go to a job interview soon.** What do you think will happen before, during, and after the interview? Write your ideas here:

   What will you do before the interview? (How will you prepare for it? What will you wear?)

   _____
   _____

   What will happen when you go to the interview?
   (What will the interviewer probably ask you? How will you feel?)

   _____
   _____

   What will happen after the interview? (What will the employer probably do? What will you do?)

   _____
   _____

2. **Use the Internet to get information and advice.** Visit one or both of the websites below. Write down eight to ten things to do for each stage of the job process in the chart. Does any of this information match your ideas above?
   http://www.careerowlresources.ca/Interviews/ Int_Frame.htm
   http://www.dressforsuccess.org/interview_tips/dosanddonts.asp

Before the Job Interview	During the Job Interview	After the Job Interview

3. **Select three to five important tips in each column.** Circle them in the chart above.

4. **Give a presentation on what to do before, during, and after a job interview.** Include the tips that you circled in your chart above. Explain this information to other students.

Grammar Form and Function 1 Unit 8 Internet Activity Worksheet

Internet Activity Procedure: Healthy Commuting: Bicycling

Unit 9   Quantity and Degree Words ✦ 9D   *Too Many* and *Too Much*, Student Book Page 252

Objectives and Overview
✦ Use the Internet to find information about one way to commute to school or work without a car—bicycling.
✦ Use *too many* and *too much* in a poster and an oral presentation.

Have the class visit websites about healthy commuting. The class will work in groups to research bicycling using the reproducible Internet Activity Worksheet. Each group will share their information as a community poster or flier on the benefits of bicycling. They will also give an oral presentation explaining the poster or flier.

Websites
http://www.bikeleague.org/programs/bikemonth.htm
http://www.sacramento-tma.org/Bicycling.htm

Prepare
1. **Discuss as a class how students currently commute to work or to school.** Do an informal class survey. How many people experience traffic jams on a regular basis? What other problems do they have with their usual form of transportation?

2. **Ask students to brainstorm both the possible benefits and problems of bicycling as an alternative form of commuting.** They should write their ideas on their Worksheets.

Research and Writing
3. **Instruct students to use the Internet to find information about alternative commuting.** Students should use the websites on their Worksheet.

4. **Ask students to take notes.** Have them read to find answers to the questions.

5. **Encourage students to print or copy images from these websites.** They can use these images to create their flier or poster.

6. **Have students create a flier or a poster promoting this form of alternative commuting.** Remind them that the purpose of the flier or poster is to get people in their own community interested in commuting without using their cars.

Wrap-Up
7. **Invite students to present their information.** They should display and explain their fliers or posters. Have students ask follow-up questions using *too much* or *too many*. (Example: There is too much traffic on Central. How can people ride their bikes there?)

8. **Discuss the presentations.** Ask students questions like these: Which form of alternative commuting, walking or bicycling, do you think is best? What form of alternative commuting might or might not work well where you live?

Internet Activity Worksheet

Name:_____

Unit 9   Quantity and Degree Words ✦ 9D   *Too Many* and *Too Much*, Student Book Page 252

Healthy Commuting: Bicycling

Objectives
- ✦ Use the Internet to find information about one way to commute to work or school without a car.
- ✦ Use *too many* and *too much* in a poster and a presentation.

1. **What do you think are some benefits of bicycling to work or to school?** Write your ideas here:
   _____

2. **What are some possible problems with bicycling to work or to school?** Write your ideas here:
   _____

3. **Use the Internet to get information.** Visit the websites below and answer the questions that follow.
   http://www.bikeleague.org/programs/bikemonth.htm
   http://www.sacramento–tma.org/Bicycling.htm

   a. When is National Bike Month?   _____

   b. When did National Bike Month begin?   _____

   c. When is Bike-to-Work Week?   _____

   d. What are some physical benefits of bicycling? _____

   e. What are some mental benefits of bicycling?   _____

   f. Why is it important for people to bicycle? The website lists many reasons. Write three of them here:
      _____

   g. What are some tips for people who want to try bicycling to work or school?
      _____
      _____

4. **What do you think is the most important reason for people to ride their bikes to work?** Write your reason here:
   _____

5. **Print or copy images from the website to use for your poster or flier.** Remember, you want to persuade people to bike to work.

Grammar Form and Function 1 Unit 9 Internet Activity Worksheet

Internet Activity Procedure: Gift-Giving Customs

Unit 10   Objects and Pronouns ✦ 10D   Indirect Objects with Certain Verbs, Student Book Page 277

Objectives and Overview

- Use the Internet to find information about gift-giving customs in other countries.
- Give advice about gift giving in other countries.
- Use indirect objects.

Have students work individually, in pairs, or in groups and visit websites on gift-giving customs around the world. They should use the reproducible Internet Activity Worksheet to prepare for and conduct research. They will then share their information either as a presentation for a TV travel show or as an article for a new website that offers advice about giving gifts.

Websites

http://wishlist.com.au/Info/CorporateGiftEtiquette.
    asp?type=international#asia
http://www.executiveplanet.com (Click on a country. Then scroll down and click on *gift giving*.)
Alternatively, type a country name and *gift giving* into a search engine (for example, *Brazil gift giving*).

Prepare

1. **Ask students to discuss giving and receiving gifts.** What kinds of gifts do they like to give and receive? Are gifts always physical objects, or are there other kinds of gifts? (For example, can you give someone a gift of your time? Services? Something else?)

2. **Have students brainstorm occasions when people give gifts.** They should write their ideas on the Worksheet.

3. **Instruct students to choose two countries to research.** Explain that they are going to research gift-giving customs in these countries on the Internet.

Research and Writing

4. **Have students use the Internet to find information about gift giving in a country that interests them.** Students should use the websites listed on their Worksheet.

5. **Ask students to take notes.** Their goal is to find answers to the two questions in the chart on the Worksheet. In addition, have them write and find answers to three of their own questions. If students have difficulty thinking of additional questions, here are some suggestions: What items don't people give as gifts? Why? What do people do or say when they receive gifts? How are gifts wrapped? Is gift giving formal or informal?

Wrap-Up

6. **Call on students to present their information to the class.** They should give an oral presentation, imagining they are on a TV show about travel, or write an article, as if it will be used for a website about gift-giving customs. Written reports can be distributed and read in class. Encourage students to ask each other follow-up questions.

7. **Discuss the reports on gift giving.** Ask students these questions: Which cultures have similar gift-giving customs? Different gift-giving customs? Think of the gifts you like to give or receive. Would they be good gifts to give in any of the cultures you learned about? Why or why not?

Internet Activity Worksheet

Name: _____

Unit 10   Objects and Pronouns ✦ 10D   Indirect Objects with Certain Verbs, Student Book Page 277

Gift-Giving Customs

Objectives
- ✦ Use the Internet to find information about gift-giving customs in other countries.
- ✦ Give advice about gift giving in other countries.
- ✦ Use indirect objects.

1. **What are some occasions when people usually give gifts?** Write your ideas here:

   _____

   _____

   _____

2. **Choose two countries to research.** You will learn about their gift-giving customs. Write the names of the countries here: _____ and _____

3. **What do you know or predict about gift-giving customs in these countries?** For example, is it important to wrap gifts? Do you open them immediately or wait?

   _____

   _____

   _____

4. **Use the Internet to get information.** Visit the websites below or type the country name and the words *gift giving* into a search engine (for example, *Brazil gift giving*).
   http://wishlist.com.au/Info/CorporateGiftEtiquette.asp?type=international#asia
   http://www.executiveplanet.com (Click on a country. Then scroll down and click on *gift giving*.)

5. **Read the website to get information.** Find answers to the questions below and take notes in the chart. Write and find answers to three questions of your own.

Questions	Country 1: _____	Country 2: _____
When (for what occasions) do people give gifts?		
What kinds of gifts do people usually give?		
Your question:		
Your question:		
Your question:		

Grammar Form and Function 1 Unit 10 Internet Activity Worksheet

Internet Activity Procedure: Cultural Customs

Unit 11   Modals ✦ 11E   *Should*, Student Book Page 307

Objectives and Overview

- Use the Internet to find information about a country's customs.
- Give advice to people visiting a country.
- Use *should* and *should not*. (Optional: Use *must, must not, have to, don't have to*.)

Students work individually or in pairs and visit websites to find information about cultural customs. They should use the reproducible Internet Activity Worksheet to prepare for and conduct research. They will write a guide to a country's customs, explaining things that people should or should not do. *Note*: This activity can be combined with 11F (*Must*) and 11G (*Have To*).

Websites

http://executiveplanet.com
http://www.e-thologies.com (Click on *English*; select a country; click on *Culture*.)
Alternatively, search by country name and customs using a search engine (for example, *Thai customs*).

Prepare

1. **Write the word *customs* on the board and brainstorm examples of cultural customs.** Ask students what *customs* means (expected social behaviors; traditions; etiquette). Ask if anyone has had problems or funny experiences in understanding a country's customs.

2. **Tell students that they will visit websites to find information about a country's customs.** They will use the information to write a guide for travelers and businesspeople.

3. **Ask students to choose a country to research.** They should not choose the country they are currently living in or the country they are originally from.

4. **Have students write ideas and questions about this country's customs.** They should use the Worksheet to prepare for their research.

Research and Writing

5. **Instruct students to use the Internet and find information.** Students can visit one of the websites listed on their Worksheet.

6. **Ask students to take notes.** They should write answers to the questions in the chart in Step 3. They should also write down any other interesting facts that they find on the back of the Worksheet.

7. **Have students use their notes to write their guide.** They will write eight tips using *should* or *should not*. (Students can also use *must, must not, have to, don't have to*).

Wrap-Up

8. **Call on students to share their guides with the class.** They can give an oral poster presentation, or write a visitor's guide, which can be exchanged or read aloud in class.

9. **Discuss the guides as a class.** Which countries' customs are the most similar? The most different? Which country would be the easiest to do business in? The most difficult?

Internet Activity Worksheet

Name: _____

Unit 11   Modals ✦ 11E   *Should*, Student Book Page 307

Cultural Customs

Objectives
- Use the Internet to find information about a country's customs.
- Give advice to people visiting a country.
- Use *should* and *should not*. (Optional: Use *must, must not, have to, don't have to*)

1. **Choose a country.** It shouldn't be your own country or the country where you live now. Write the name of the country here: _____

2. **Write your ideas.** Do you know any customs from this country? Write at least three ideas about this country here:
   _____
   _____

3. **Read the questions in the chart.** Write three questions about customs. (For example: *What should you bring to a dinner party? How should you greet businesspeople?*) Do not write answers until after you look at the websites.

Questions	Answers
What is the capital of this country?	
What size is the population of this country?	
What are the main languages in this country?	
Your question:	
Your question:	
Your question:	

4. **Use the Internet to get information.** Visit these websites:
   http://executiveplanet.com
   http://www.e-thologies.com (Click *English*; select a country; click *Culture*.)
   You can also search by country name and customs using a search engine (for example, *Thai customs*.)

5. **Read the website to find information.** Now complete the chart in Step 3. Also take notes on other interesting facts. Use the back of this Worksheet or a separate piece of paper.

6. **Write a guide for visitors.** Write eight tips for people visiting or doing business in the country you researched. Use *should* or *should not*.

Grammar Form and Function 1 Unit 11 Internet Activity Worksheet

Internet Activity Procedure: Exercise *Do's* and *Don'ts*

Unit 12   Special Expressions ✦ 12D   The Imperative,   Student Book Page 336

Objectives and Overview

- Use the Internet to find advice about exercise.
- Give advice about exercise using the imperative.

Have students work individually, in pairs, or in groups and visit websites related to exercise. They should use the reproducible Internet Activity Worksheet to prepare for and conduct research. They will then share their information as a poster presentation for a TV show about exercise and fitness, or in an article written for a website about exercise and fitness.

Websites

http://www.intelihealth.com (Go to the *Healthy Lifestyle* box and click on the word *Fitness*; scroll down and click on a link under *Take Action Now* or *Keep on Track*.)

http://www.sparkpeople.com/resource/fitness_article.asp

Prepare

1. **Ask students to discuss their exercise habits.** Do they exercise each day? Each week? What activities do they do? Which activities are sports? Classes? Day-to-day activities?

2. **Have students write down their ideas about exercise.** What advice have they heard about exercise? They should use the Worksheet to prepare for their research.

3. **Ask students to read and write questions about exercise.** They should read the questions in the chart on the Worksheet and add two questions. Encourage them to write a *yes/no* and a *wh-* question. Explain that they will go to websites to find answers.

Research and Writing

4. **Have students use the Internet to find information.** They should visit the websites listed on their Worksheet.

5. **Ask students to take notes.** They should write answers to the questions in the chart. In the last row, they can write any other interesting information or advice they find.

6. **Ask students to choose what they think is the most important advice.** Have them phrase the advice as affirmative and negative imperatives and write them in a two-column chart on the back of their Worksheet. Most of the advice they find may already be in the affirmative form, so they may need to rephrase some as negative imperatives.

7. **Instruct students to find pictures.** These can be printed or copied from websites.

Wrap-Up

8. **Call on students to present their information.** They can give a poster presentation for a TV show, or write a report for a website or brochure; these can be posted on a class website, or distributed and read in class. Encourage follow-up questions.

9. **Discuss the *do's* and *don'ts*.** Ask the following types of questions: Which exercise *do's* are the most important? Which exercise *don'ts* are the most important? Do you follow any of this advice in your own habits? Will you follow any of this advice in the future?

Internet Activity Worksheet

Name: _____

Unit 12   Special Expressions ✦ 12D   The Imperative, Student Book Page 336

Exercise *Do's* and *Don'ts*

Objectives

✦ Use the Internet to find advice about exercise.
✦ Give advice about exercise using the imperative.

1. **What advice do people sometimes give about exercise?** (For example: *Drink plenty of water when you exercise.*) Write your ideas here:

   _____

   _____

2. **Read these questions about exercise.** Write two more questions of your own in the chart. Do not write answers until after you visit the websites.

Question	Answer
What should you do when you start an exercise program?	
What should you do to stay on an exercise program?	
Your question:	
Your question:	
Other information:	

3. **Use the Internet to get information.** Visit these websites:
   http://www.intelihealth.com (Go to the *Healthy Lifestyle* box and click on *Fitness*; scroll down and click on a link under *Take Action Now* or *Keep on Track*.
   http://www.sparkpeople.com/resource/fitness_article.asp

4. **Read the website(s) to find answers to the questions in Step 2.** Write the answers. Take notes in the last row on any other interesting information or advice.

5. **Decide on the most important advice.** From your chart in Step 2, decide on the three most important things you should do when you exercise (*do's*) and three things you should not do (*don'ts*). Write them as affirmative and negative imperatives in a two-column chart on the back of this Worksheet or on a separate piece of paper. Use the heads *Exercise Do's* and *Exercise Don'ts* in your chart.

6. **Make a poster or chart showing your *do's* and *don'ts*.** Print, copy, or draw pictures to illustrate some of your do's and don'ts.

Grammar Form and Function 1 Unit 12 Internet Activity Worksheet

Internet Activity Procedure: Homes for Sale

Unit 13　Adjectives and Adverbs ✦ 13E　Comparative Form of Adjectives: *-er* and *More*, Student Book Page 357

Objectives and Overview

- Use images and text on the Internet to compare and/or contrast two homes.
- Use the comparative form of adjectives: *-er* and *more*.

Have students work individually, in pairs, or in groups and visit websites related to real estate. They should use the reproducible Internet Activity Worksheet to prepare for and conduct research. They will then share their information as an oral presentation, or as an advertisement for a real estate magazine. *Note*: This activity can be combined with 13A (Adjectives and Nouns Used as Adjectives), 13B (Word Order of Adjectives), 13C (*The Same [As]*, *Similar [To]*, and *Different [From]*) and/or 13D (*Like and Alike*).

Websites

http://www.RealEstate.com
http://www.realtor.com

Prepare

1. **Ask students to think of a city in which they want to find a house.** Explain that they will use the Internet to find ads for homes. Students can choose two cities/towns and find a home in each, or one city/town and compare two homes there.

Research and Writing

2. **Direct students to read the questions on the Worksheet.** They do not need to write answers at this time. Clarify any terminology.

3. **Have students use the Internet to find information.** To search, they should use Step 1 and type a desired number of bedrooms and bathrooms, and a price range.

4. **Ask students to choose two homes with photos to compare.** They can choose two homes from the same city, or one home each from different cities or countries. **Make sure they print or copy pictures of the two homes for their presentations or reports.**

5. **Have students take notes in the chart on the Worksheet.** They should be able to complete the chart by reading about the homes and by looking at the photos.

6. **Ask students to compare the two homes and choose the one they prefer.** They should circle information in their chart and emphasize these points in their presentation or ad.

Wrap-Up

7. **Have groups use their notes and pictures to compare or contrast houses.** Students can either give their presentations orally, explaining which home they want to buy, or they can write an advertisement for a real estate magazine and share it with the class.

8. **Lead the class in a discussion of the presentations or reports.** Which homes are the most similar? The most different? Which homes are the most expensive and least expensive? Which cities/towns are the most expensive and least expensive? Which homes do they think would be the most fun to live in?

Internet Activity Worksheet

Name: _____

Unit 13   Adjectives and Adverbs ✦ 13E   Comparative Form of Adjectives: *-er* and *More*, Student Book Page 357

Homes for Sale

Objectives

✦ Use images and text on the Internet to compare two homes for sale.
✦ Use the comparative form of adjectives: *-er* and *more*.

1. **Where do you want to look for a home?** Imagine that you just won the lottery. You can live anywhere you want.

   Where would it be? _____ and _____

   Do you want to look for houses, condos, or apartments? _____

   How many bedrooms do you want? _____

   How many bathrooms do you want? _____

   Do you know how much you want to pay for a home? _____

   What other things are important to you in a home? _____

2. **Look over the chart below.** Do not write in the chart until you visit the websites.

	Home A	Home B
a. location		
b. price		
c. number of bedrooms		
d. number of bathrooms		
e. size: How many square feet/meters? How many floors?		
f. Other features of the house		
g. Describe the house. Use at least three adjectives.		

3. **Use the Internet to get information.** Visit the websites below to find two homes that you like. Choose homes with photos. Complete the chart in Step 2.

   http://www.RealEstate.com
   http://www.realtor.com

4. **Print or copy a picture of each house.** You will use these pictures in your ad or presentation.

5. **Compare the two homes and decide which one you prefer.** Circle information in the chart that will help you explain your reasons. Write five or six reasons. Use the back of this Worksheet or a separate piece of paper.

Grammar Form and Function 1 Unit 13 Internet Activity Worksheet

Internet Activity Procedure: Small Talk

Unit 14   The Present Perfect ✦ 14c   The Present Perfect: Negative Statements and Questions, Student Book Page 397

Objective and Overview

✦ Use the Internet to find advice about how to make small talk with other people.

Have students work individually, in pairs, or in groups and visit websites related to making small talk. They should use the reproducible Internet Activity Worksheet to prepare for and conduct research. They will then share their information by demonstrating two people making small talk, followed by an explanation.

Websites

http://www.ehow.com/how_10812_make-small-talk.html

http://speaking.englishclub.com/small-talk_wh.htm

Be sure to encourage students to click on *Conversation Starters* at the bottom of the web page and *Practice Conversations* at the bottom of that page.

Prepare

1. **Introduce the term *small talk*.** Write it on the board and be sure that students understand that it means light conversation on topics that are not serious. Explain that small talk is usually employed by people who don't know each other, who are getting to know each other, or who are in a business situation but aren't ready to do business yet.

2. **Discuss small talk with the class.** Ask questions like these: When do people usually make small talk? Is it easy or difficult to make small talk in English? Is it easy or difficult to make small talk in your native language?

3. **Ask students to brainstorm good and bad topics for small talk.** They should take notes on the Worksheet. Remind students that ideas of good and bad topics may vary among different cultures and encourage them to notice any differences.

4. **Have students brainstorm ideas about how people can improve their small-talk skills.** They should write their ideas on the Worksheet.

Research and Writing

5. **Instruct students to use the Internet to find information.** They should visit both of the websites listed on their Worksheet.

6. **Ask students to take notes.** They should use the chart on the worksheet and circle what they think are the most interesting or important points in each column.

Wrap-Up

7. **Have groups use the information from their research to create a small-talk dialogue.** Call on groups to demonstrate their dialogue for the class and then explain what advice it follows. Ask each group to give their top five tips for improving small-talk skills.

8. **Ask the class to discuss what made the dialogues effective or not.** Ask these questions about each presentation: What were the small-talk topics? What else could the speakers have done to make small talk? What kind of body language did you see? How important is body language when people are making small talk in this kind of situation?

Internet Activity Worksheet

Name: _____

Unit 14 The Present Perfect ✦ 14c The Present Perfect: Negative Statements and Questions, Student Book Page 397

Small Talk

Objective

✦ Use the Internet to find advice about how to make small talk with other people.

1. **What are some good topics for small talk?** Write your ideas here:
   _____
   _____

2. **What are some bad topics for small talk?** Write your ideas here:
   _____
   _____

3. **What do you think people can do to improve their small-talk skills?** Write your ideas here:
   _____
   _____

4. **Use the Internet to get more information.** Visit both of these websites:
   http://www.ehow.com/how_10812_make-small-talk.html
   http://speaking.englishclub.com/small-talk_wh.htm (Be sure to click on *Conversation Starters* at the bottom of the web page and *Practice Conversations* at the bottom of that page.)

5. **Read the website(s) to find information.** Write your information in the chart.

Good Topics	Bad Topics	Good Places to Start Conversations	Good Ways to Start Conversations	Ways to Improve Small-Talk Skills

6. **Choose the three most interesting or important points in each column from the chart in Step 5.** Circle them. You will use these to write your small-talk dialogue and explanation.

Grammar Form and Function 1 Unit 14 Internet Activity Worksheet